AN ANTIDOTE TO THE EN~

THE AULD ALLIAN

For Simone and Daisy

An Antidote to the English

THE AULD ALLIANCE, 1295–1560

Norman Macdougall

TUCKWELL PRESS

First published in Great Britain in 2001 by
Tuckwell Press
The Mill House
Phantassie
East Linton
East Lothian EH40 3DG
Scotland

Copyright © Norman Macdougall 2001

ISBN 1 86232 145 0

The Publishers acknowledge subsidy from
the Scottish Arts Council towards the
publication of this volume

British Library Cataloguing in Publication Data
A catalogue record for this book is available on
request from the British Library

Typeset by Antony Gray
Printed and bound by Creative Print and Design
Ebbw Vale, Wales

CONTENTS

List of Plates, Maps and Tables   vi

Preface and Acknowledgements   vii

INTRODUCTION.   *'The Oldest Alliance in the World'*   3

CHAPTER 1.   *Uncertain Beginnings: 1295–1326*   9

CHAPTER 2.   *Two Theatres of War: The Fourteenth Century*   28

CHAPTER 3.   *'La Grande Armée Ecossaise': 1419–1429*   53

CHAPTER 4.   *Diplomacy and the Scottish Diaspora:*
    The Mid-Fifteenth Century   78

CHAPTER 5.   *Renewal: 1484–1517*   97

CHAPTER 6.   *Indian Summer: 1517–1560*   121

EPILOGUE.   *A Path not Taken*   143

Further Reading   147

Index   155

PLATES, MAPS AND TABLES

PLATE 1.   *The Treaty of Paris, 1295*

PLATE 2.   *John Balliol performs homage to Edward I of England.*

PLATE 3.   *Edward I performs homage to Philip the Fair of France*

PLATE 4.   *Silver groat of Robert II, founder of the Stewart dynasty*

PLATE 5.   *The siege of Orléans, 1428*

PLATE 6.   *Margaret of Scotland enters Tours, 1436*

PLATE 7.   *Charles VII attended by the* Garde Ecossaise

PLATE 8.   *Bérault Stewart, Lord of Aubigny*

PLATE 9.   *Remains of the Château of Concressault in Berry*

PLATE 10. *La Verrerie, built by Bérault Stewart and his successor Robert*

PLATE 11. *The chapel at La Verrerie*

PLATE 12. *The west front of the cathedral of Bourges*

PLATE 13. *James V and Mary of Guise*

PLATE 14. *Falkland Palace*

PLATE 15. *Mary, Queen of Scots, around the age of thirteen*

MAP 1.   *France's Second Front: Anglo-Scottish Warfare in the Fourteenth Century*   37

MAP 2.   *Late Medieval France*   52

MAP 3.   *1419–1424: Scottish Military Assistance to the Dauphin (Charles VII)*   61

MAP 4.   *War and Settlement: Scots in France (Fifteenth and Early Sixteenth Centuries)*   68

TABLE 1.   *The French Succession: Capetians, Valois, and Plantagenets*   29

TABLE 2.   *The Scottish Succession: Bruces and Stewarts*   47

TABLE 3.   *The House of Valois in the Fifteenth Century*   57

PREFACE AND ACKNOWLEDGEMENTS

This is a modest-sized book about a vast subject. Its aim is to provide the student and general reader with a straightforward account of the workings of the Franco-Scottish alliance from its inception at the end of the thirteenth century to its final abandonment in 1560. Thus this is a book about diplomacy and war. It is intended partly to fill a gap, for historical writing about the alliance, though extensive, is not always easily accessible; and partly also to provide a starting point for those seeking an introduction to the subject. If it succeeds in either or both of these objectives, I shall be well satisfied.

I should like to thank the Leverhulme Trust for the award of a fellowship during 1998-9 to study Scots in France in the fifteenth and early sixteenth centuries. This book, though not the direct outcome of research undertaken during the tenure of that fellowship, has, I hope, benefited from it, especially in Chapter 4; and following further research in France in the near future, I intend to write a more detailed study of Scots in France.

I should like to acknowledge the work of many pioneers in the field of Franco-Scottish relations; my debt to Philippe Contamine and Bernard Chevalier will be obvious. I should also like to thank M. Pascal Dubrisay, deputy mayor of Loches, and my friend Michel Duchein, who has done more than anyone else in the recent past to introduce French readers to Scottish history. Within Scotland, I should have been lost without the wit and wisdom – both written and oral, and delivered with passion and conviction – of that formidable septet of historians of medieval Scotland, Drs. Steve Boardman, Michael Brown, Jamie Cameron, Christine McGladdery, Michael Penman, Roland Tanner, and Fiona Watson. In chapter 3, I have drawn extensively on Malcolm Vale's penetrating study of Charles VII of France. I am also very grateful to Geoff Stell of the RCAHMS, especially for his well-judged advice that Aubigny and La Verrerie would yield much for political and architectural historians alike.

John and Val Tuckwell have, as ever, shown themselves to be model publishers throughout, considerate, enthusiastic, and accommodating. Mrs. Margaret Richards, with her customary patience and good humour, has turned my forest of frenzied scribbling into an elegant, user-friendly text. A special word of thanks must go to Simone, the other half of my own Auld Alliance, who has been a tower of strength on research visits to France, and has acted as picture editor for the book. To our labrador Daisy, whose principal aim in life is to distract me for as long as possible from the study of Scottish history, I owe an inestimable debt.

NORMAN MACDOUGALL
St Andrews, June 2001

'THE OLDEST ALLIANCE IN THE WORLD'

'The Oldest Alliance in the World'

'Truly', exclaimed Pope Martin V around Easter of 1421, 'the Scots are an antidote to the English!' The occasion of the pope's remark was the arrival of the news of a great Franco-Scottish victory at Baugé in Anjou, in which John Stewart, earl of Buchan, had decisively defeated the English and killed their commander, Thomas duke of Clarence, brother of Henry V of England. Walter Bower, who recorded the pope's remark some twenty years later, was not a man to rely on subtle inference when he could spell things out, and he went on to explain what Martin V had meant – that is, that the poison of the English infected those whom it touched, but that the Scots lessened the swelling which the English had caused. In their partisan way, the pope and the chronicler were extolling one of the major successes of the Franco-Scottish alliance, a battle which occurred almost exactly at the halfway point in the two-and-a-half centuries of an alliance which the French were already describing as 'ancien' in the fourteenth century and which the Scots subsequently dubbed the 'Auld Alliance'.

Closely defined, this alliance was a military one, made by successive French and Scottish governments, frequently renewed, and always directed against the English. Its theatres of war were northern England, southern Scotland, France, and the sea; it was fuelled by the Hundred Years' War (1337–1453) and its sixteenth-century renewals, but demonstrably came to an end in 1560. However, many Scots, and some French people, have sought a much wider definition of the Auld Alliance, and twentieth-century nostalgia has played its part in redefining the alliance to suit those whose primary interest is Franco-Scottish artistic intercourse, others with Jacobite leanings, still others with feelings of nostalgia for Franco-Scottish military camaraderie during the Second World War, and even those who seek to explain the popularity of the Tartan Army in Paris during the football World Cup of 1998. The alliance, it seems, must be all things to all men. Early in 2000 the department of Scottish History at St Andrews received a phone call from a journalist working for a tabloid newspaper, anxiously enquiring how the then current French ban on imports of Scottish beef would affect the Auld Alliance. In this case, at least the journalist concerned knew who the two contracting parties to the alliance were, or had been.

Rather more worrying was the case of the researcher who phoned up from the Foreign Office in 1994, assuming that the Auld Alliance was rather similar to the Entente Cordiale of 1904; on being informed that the alliance was an offensive and defensive Franco-Scottish union directed against England, she refused to believe it. The concept of civilised life on the planet before the existence of a unitary British state quite defeated her.

Yet the publicity accorded the Auld Alliance in the recent past, at both popular and scholarly levels, has been extensive. As early as June 1942, General Charles de Gaulle, opening the Scottish Free French House in Edinburgh, had declared that the alliance was 'the oldest alliance in the world'. He may have been primed by his Scottish hosts; but equally, he could have been drawing on the mid-sixteenth century French tradition that the friendship between Scotland and France stretched back eight centuries to the Emperor Charlemagne. The Scots, seeking to enhance the respectability of the alliance in the fifteenth century, also dated it back to Charlemagne, and specifically to a treaty made between the Emperor and the mythical Scottish King Achaius. Modern scholarly opinion has discounted the alliance's eighth-century beginnings; but its longevity was celebrated recently with two conferences, the first held in Paris in October 1995 to mark the 700th anniversary of the Franco-Scottish Treaty of Paris, the second in Edinburgh in February 1996 to commemorate the Scottish ratification, at Dunfermline in February 1296, of the original French treaty. The large and enthusiastic turnout for these events in both cities, and the subsequent publication of most of the papers given in Paris and Edinburgh, are evidence of a strong and enduring popular interest in the alliance in both Scotland and France. The existence for over a century of the Franco-Scottish Society and its French equivalent, the 'Association Franco-Écossaise', has helped to foster cultural links between the two countries; and the publication, over the last century-and-a-half, of works on the Franco-Scottish military connection and on a shared artistic and architectural heritage, has not only given the Auld Alliance a wider appeal, but also, to some extent, sanitised it to suit the needs of a modern audience. The bloody military encounters of the Hundred Years' War, together with their dramatic diplomatic shifts of allegiance, desertion, treachery, and betrayal, can somehow be redeemed through reference to a shared Franco-Scottish culture and heritage boasting a long and distinguished pedigree.

It is of course true that the Auld Alliance, though beginning life as the pragmatic response to a perceived military threat, gradually developed to become much more than a military and diplomatic relationship. Scots settled in France in large numbers in the late fourteenth and fifteenth centuries, especially in Berry, Touraine, and Anjou. Most of them arrived as mercenary soldiers, an astonishing 15,000 (at least) in the few years between 1419 and 1424. Those who survived the bloody wars against the English in the 1420s often did very well for themselves, and the existence of Scottish émigrés in France, close to French centres of power yet still conscious of, and sometimes keenly interested in, political events in Scotland, helped to stimulate the alliance during the 1460s and 1470s, when it appeared to be flagging. Some of these Franco-Scots were patrons of the arts; some, like the Stewarts of Aubigny-sur-Nère in Berry, were also builders, and the Stewart château of La Verrerie at Oizon near Aubigny is a remarkable combination of French and Italianate Renaissance styles. Following his French holiday and marriage (1536–7), James V of Scotland paid eloquent tribute to his allies by importing French masons to instruct their Scottish counterparts in the building of the palace of Stirling, and – even more strikingly – Falkland palace, aptly described as a French Renaissance château set down in Fife.

All this Franco-Scottish intercourse might seem well worth celebrating; but the Auld Alliance has not been without its detractors over the years. One of the most forceful advocates of a negative view has been John Prebble. Writing his obituary notice of the Auld Alliance in 1971, he remarked that:

> it had rarely been more than a union of convenience . . . to the French it was always a political counter in the interminable wars, and they might have agreed with Shakespeare's arrogant reference to the 'weasel Scot', raiding the nest when the eagle England was in prey . . . The Auld Alliance would be kept alive in Jacobite emotion, and four centuries after the surrender at Leith [1560] its ludicrous survival would be seen on the backs of automobiles.

The effectiveness of this splendid, high-flown dismissal of the alliance is rather spoiled by Mr Prebble's use of Shakespeare's *Henry V*, almost as historical evidence; for during Henry's reign, the 'weasel Scot' was fighting in his thousands, in sieges and pitched battles, against the English in France, often with great success, enjoying the rewards of assisting in the survival of King Charles VII. As to Mr Prebble's more serious point, it must be admitted that, on occasion, the French used the Scots to deflect the English war effort away from France. But his view of the Scots as French dupes, hopelessly out of their depth in European politics and rushing to act as cannon fodder for their cynical allies, does not convince. Certainly both parties to the Auld Alliance often acted in a pragmatic and self-interested way, but the same is surely true of diplomatic relationships in any age. And there are now significantly more 'Ecosse' stickers on the backs of 'automobiles' than there were when Prebble wrote in 1971.

What sustained the alliance for so long? Scotland was, after all, a remote and impoverished kingdom on the north-western fringe of Europe, while France was a great power at the heart of the Continent. Throughout the period of the alliance, the Scots' diplomatic focus was almost invariably France, but the same could not be said in reverse. Nevertheless the two-and-a-half centuries between 1295 and 1560 reveal that the alliance worked to the advantage of both kingdoms, not France alone. Thus the French provided sanctuary for one Scottish king, David II, in the 1330s, and sanctuary and a husband for Queen Mary in the 1540s and 1550s; Charles VII of France may have considered flight to Scotland in February 1429, and his younger contemporary, James II of Scotland, may have contemplated fleeing to France in the early 1450s. Charles VII acted as a marriage broker for James I's string of daughters in the 1440s, having first married his own son, the dauphin Louis, to the Scottish king's eldest daughter Margaret in 1436. The Scots' firm adherence to the alliance in the 1530s produced two French brides, Madeleine (1537) and Mary of Guise (1538) for James V; and after James's death his French queen played a major role in Scottish politics for almost two decades, ending her life as Queen Regent presiding over a largely French administration. Most important of all, in the military sphere the outbreak of the Anglo-French Hundred Years' War in 1337, the result of Edward III of England's claim to the throne of the Valois Philip VI, probably saved the Scottish kingdom, riven as it was with internal struggles, from dismemberment by the English king and his vassals.

The Franco-Scottish alliance operated at various different levels. Trade between the two countries existed before it and was enhanced by it; Scots scholars found their way regularly to France, to the Sorbonne in Paris, to Orléans, and to the new universities of the fifteenth century. At its formal level, however, the alliance consisted of a series of treaties between two allies of apparently equal standing and importance. As Françoise Autrand has pointed out, nothing in the vocabulary of the various Franco-Scottish treaties suggests any idea of subjection of the smaller kingdom to the greater. Furthermore, almost from its inception in 1295–6, the alliance was not simply an agreement between two kings, but between two kingdoms, with the ruler's subjects in both countries closely involved. And it may be significant that the author of the 'Chronique des quatre premiers Valois' (1327–1393), in referring to the year 1369, makes a distinction between kings and their peoples. Citing Edward III of England as 'one of the most powerful princes in the world', the chronicler remarks that the English king made a treaty with David II of Scotland 'and sent him great sums of money. But the Scots, especially those of the major burghs ('les bonnes villes'), had no desire to ally against the King of France or against the French.'

In the last analysis, however, the longevity of the Franco-Scottish alliance was firmly based on mutual necessity. It would be pleasant to believe, with Étienne de Conty in 1400, that the Scots had always loved the French, and the French, the Scots; but beyond that, both sides paid a high price for their long-standing special relationship. The French paid in providing a European outlet for so many Scots, in artists, masons and shipwrights, and in the huge sums of money which they poured into the Scottish war effort on land and sea. The Scots paid in manpower and blood.

I

Uncertain Beginnings: 1295–1326

In the early autumn of 1295, four Scottish commissioners, appointed in parliament the previous July, arrived in Paris to conclude an offensive and defensive alliance between their king, John Balliol, and the formidable ruler of France, Philip IV (the Fair). The Treaty of Paris which followed on 23 October 1295 has long been viewed as the beginning of the Auld Alliance directed against England by the French and Scots, though in fact the two countries had looked to each other for aid against England – on widely scattered occasions – since the late twelfth century; and two thirteenth-century Scottish kings had married French brides.

What is certain about the 1295 treaty is its initially disastrous consequences for the Scots, amounting to nothing less than comprehensive military defeat, the humiliating deposition of John as King of Scots, an imposed English government, and the extinction of the kingdom. Yet such an outcome was perhaps inevitable, given that for a decade the Scots had lurched from one political crisis to the next, and had presented to their predatory southern neighbour, Edward I of England, the spectacle of a kingdom divided within itself and ripe for external domination.

'The Nearest by Blood who must Inherit' (1280–1292)

The origins of the 1295 treaty and the subsequent Scottish débâcle may be traced back to the early 1280s, when the eighth Canmore king, Alexander III, a mature ruler in full command of his kingdom, appeared to have taken all steps possible to secure the continuance of his dynasty and the survival of an independent Scotland. An attempt in 1278 by Edward I and his counsellors to have Alexander perform homage to the English king for his kingdom of Scotland – rather than simply for those lands which Alexander held in England – had been skilfully parried; and the Scottish king had two sons and a daughter, so that it appeared that – for the first time since 1165 – the Canmore dynasty would witness a smooth transition from father to adult son without enduring the perils of a royal minority.

However, the apparent stability of the Scottish kingdom was shattered in the early 1280s. Alexander III's younger son David died at Stirling in the summer of 1281; his daughter Margaret, queen of Norway, died in April 1283, leaving a one-year-old daughter Margaret, 'Maid of

Norway'; and worst of all, the heir to the Scottish throne, Prince
Alexander, aged 20 and recently married to the daughter of the Count of
Flanders, died at the end of January 1284. In less than three years, King
Alexander's family had been wiped out, with the solitary and
unpromising exception of his infant Norwegian granddaughter; and the
Canmore dynasty was staring into the abyss.

Alexander III was still only in his early forties, and took immediate and
vigorous remedial steps to shore up his dynasty. First, within a week of his
heir's death, he assembled a council of his nobility at Scone; there, on 5
February 1284, he secured the support of some thirty-eight of them for an
entail which, failing issue of the king, named Alexander's granddaughter,
the 'Maid of Norway', as rightful heir to the king. There seems to have
been some reluctance amongst the Scottish magnates to accept the
possibility of the Maid's succession – not surprisingly, for the entail of
1284 ran contrary to Western European practice, in which the claim of a
female to inherit a kingdom was likely to be challenged; and in Scotland
itself, male primogeniture was the norm. Furthermore, if the Maid could
not be accepted as a queen reigning in her own right, the important issue
of her marriage raised the spectre of enormous political and diplomatic
problems.

For these reasons, Alexander III clearly hoped to avoid putting the
entail of 1284 to the test. Instead, he would remarry, restock the royal
house with heirs, and perhaps also seek to create a new Scottish foreign
policy. His chosen bride was Yolande of Dreux, who was Gascon; and in
Gascony Edward I of England ruled as duke, a vassal of the new French
king Philip the Fair (1285–1314). It may be that Alexander's marriage to
Yolande, which took place at Jedburgh in October 1285, was seen as a
threat to English influence in Scotland. After all, the king's first wife
Margaret, who had died in 1275, was English, Edward I's sister; and the
family which Alexander III had just lost in quick succession had been her
offspring. Alexander's marriage to the daughter of Robert, count of
Dreux, could have been seen in England as complementing his earlier
domestic policy of ensuring that important lands and offices within
Scotland did not go to those whose landed interests lay primarily in
England. However, no real evidence exists before 1286 for a specifically
anti-English policy on the part of Alexander III; indeed, such a policy
would have been unworkable in a Scotland in which twelve magnates
held land in Yorkshire, sixteen in Cumberland, and twenty-four in
Northumberland. The king's second marriage was surely motivated by
necessity; and if Edward I, as duke of Gascony, was a vassal of Philip the
Fair, the father of Yolande of Dreux was in his turn a vassal of Edward I.
Thus the Scottish king's aim in 1285 may have been to try to create a

balance between the rulers of England and France by choosing a bride acceptable to both.

In the event, Alexander III had very little time left. With benefit of hindsight, later chroniclers portrayed the last months of the reign as a doom-laden period, opening with the sinister figure who marred the wedding festivities at Jedburgh and ending with prophecies that 19 March 1286 would be the Day of Judgement. On the night of 18–19 March, Alexander III, hazarding himself during a violent storm against the advice of the Dalmeny ferryman and one of the bailies of Inverkeithing, attempted the journey from Edinburgh to the royal manor house at Kinghorn in Fife to visit Yolande of Dreux, who was apparently pregnant. In the morning he was found dead on the Kinghorn shore, his neck broken.

The king was buried at Dunfermline on 29 March, and about a month later the great men of the kingdom met at Scone to make provision for the government of the country. They faced the worst imaginable scenario – a baby Norwegian granddaughter as heiress to the kingdom, a newly pregnant queen who might – or might not – bear a son, and a predatory English king who had attempted to have Alexander III perform homage for Scotland as recently as eight years before. And as Professor Barrow reminds us, 'in 1286 the gravest threat to the peace of Scotland came from Scotsmen'.

These individuals showed their faces almost at once. From the outset the aged Robert Bruce, lord of Annandale, denied the right of any female to succeed to the kingdom and advanced his own claim. John Balliol, whose power bases included Barnard Castle in County Durham and extensive lands in Galloway, at once contested the Bruce claim, and there followed what has been described as a 'bitter pleading' by both men. Within weeks of Alexander III's death, therefore, the Bruce-Balliol battle lines had been drawn. Their struggle would achieve far greater prominence in the early 1290s; but in 1286 the infant Maid of Norway was alive and Queen Yolande was pregnant. So little could be done other than to appoint an interim government – six *custodes* or guardians drawn from the clergy and aristocracy – and to have those present take an oath, replacing that of 1284, to 'the nearest by blood who by right must inherit' the throne. The guardians charged with this difficult, if not impossible, task were William Fraser, bishop of St Andrews, Robert Wishart, bishop of Glasgow, Duncan, earl of Fife, Alexander Comyn, earl of Buchan, James the Steward, and John Comyn, lord of Badenoch – two bishops, two earls, and two barons.

In recent times, a strong case has been advanced for the appointment of the guardians as evidence of sophisticated constitutional thinking

amongst the Scottish 'community of the realm'. Perhaps so; but the
reality of the political situation was that the struggle for the succession to
Alexander III was likely to lead to civil war, with Balliol and Bruce as the
main contestants. The guardians' initial task was therefore to preserve
peace, and it is often remarked that neither Bruce nor Balliol was chosen
as one of the six. But the guardians were hardly sage greybeards sitting
on the sidelines of the contest and attempting to influence its development. Bishop Fraser and the two Comyns were Balliol men, while Bishop
Wishart, the Steward, and the earl of Fife supported Bruce. Thus any
further crisis would divide the guardians; and already in 1286 they were
men trying to ride two horses at once.

   In the event, crises were not long in coming. Some time late in 1286,
Queen Yolande's pregnancy was known to be at an end; there would be no
posthumous heir to Alexander III. Around the same time (September
1286) the Bruces made the Turnberry bond with their Scottish allies and
two Ulster magnates, probably as a prelude to waging war on their
opponents. This obscure war, which occurred in the winter of 1286–7 and
was probably the first of the many Bruce attempts to acquire the Scottish
throne, apparently involved the seizure by the Bruces of the royal castles of
Dumfries and Wigtown and an assault on the Balliol castle of Buittle in
Galloway. The guardians – with what enthusiasm or reluctance we do not
know – summoned the host, made up of able-bodied men who were
required to serve in the country's defence for a maximum of forty days in
the year, and the Bruce rising seems to have failed or fizzled out. However,
the guardians were themselves severely weakened by internal rivalries; on
7 September 1289 the young Duncan, earl of Fife, was ambushed and
killed near Brechin, probably at the instance of Hugh de Abernethy, an
ally of the Comyns. If the elected leaders of the realm were engaged in
murderous feuds with one another, their chances of maintaining the
peace, finding a suitable husband for the Maid of Norway, perhaps even of
sustaining her rights as heiress to the kingdom, appeared slim.

   Crucial to the future of that kingdom was the attitude of Edward I of
England. The powerful English king, who would subsequently become
the great enemy of the Scots, and who would later be described as *Malleus
Scottorum*, the Hammer of the Scots, was undoubtedly a ruthless and
devious man who had learned his political lessons in a hard school; and
his spectacular coronation at Westminster in 1274 inaugurated a new age
of conquest – in the first instance of Wales – by a man determinedly
ambitious for his family and impatient of delays. Yet it is difficult to
escape the conclusion that, when he turned his attention to Scotland, he
was greatly assisted in pushing his claims by the ambivalence, naivety,
and internecine struggles of the Scots leaders.

Even Alexander III may have played a part in smoothing Edward's path. In 1284, after the deaths of his offspring and before he embarked on a second marriage, the Scottish king had written to Edward hinting at strengthening links between the two realms, and underlining the fact that the Maid of Norway was his heir. Perhaps we see in this correspondence the beginnings of the later scheme to marry the Maid to Edward I's son and heir, Edward of Caernarvon (the future Edward II). After Alexander's death, it was again the Scots who opened negotiations with the English king, sending an embassy to France to solicit Edward I's assistance as early as May 1286. The Scottish guardians' aims were understandable; in the weeks since King Alexander's death, the competing Bruce-Balliol claims to his throne posed the obvious threat of civil war, and they were presumably seeking Edward's assistance as mediator. Edward's response has not survived, though it seems likely that he made his acceptance as lord superior of Scotland – which he would revive famously in 1291 – a condition of his intervention. The English king's overlordship was unacceptable to the Scots at this stage; and so, as Professor Nicholson remarks, 'Edward allowed them to simmer for three years in their own juice'.

Their simmering came to an end in October 1289, when it became urgently necessary to send an embassy to Salisbury to take part in negotiations with Edward I; for the English king's aid and counsel in securing the Maid of Norway's position in Scotland had already been sought by the Norwegians; and the ensuing treaty of Salisbury (November 1289) placed the Maid under the custody of Edward I, her great-uncle. By the following March it was widely rumoured that the pope had granted a dispensation for the marriage of the Maid to Edward's son; and in the same month the Scottish guardians wrote to the English king giving their consent to the projected match.

Arguably the Scots had been bounced into this situation by the Norwegians; certainly their own internal problems appear to have been their major preoccupation between 1286 and 1289. However, by the spring of 1290 warning bells must have been sounding in the heads of some of their leaders. The doubts often raised about the independence of the Scottish kingdom – ruled as it was by a line of kings who were neither crowned nor anointed – seemed likely to surface once again, given that the Scots were dealing with an English king who had certainly once, and probably twice, already advanced the claim to be overlord of Scotland. And as recently as April 1289 the pope, Nicholas IV, had fulminated against the Scottish custom of admitting only native Scots to Scottish religious houses. The timing may be coincidental; but the leaders of the Scottish clergy – two of whom were guardians – were well versed in the history of English attempts to force the Scottish church to accept either the archbishop of Canterbury or York as metropolitan of Scotland. The robust rejection of these English claims was based on the authority of a papal bull granted to the Scots as long before as 1192, and which had made the Scottish church a 'special daughter' of Rome; but what one pope had granted, another might take away.

Scottish doubts and fears are clearly expressed in the Treaty of Birgham (July 1290), a full-scale marriage treaty in which the Scots guardians, while accepting that Edward of Caernarvon would eventually reign as King of Scots, included clauses stipulating that the kingdom of Scotland was to remain 'separate and divided from the kingdom of England', that Scots 'rights, laws, liberties and customs' were to remain inviolate, and that the kingdom was to be 'free in itself and without subjection'. These ringing endorsements of Scottish independence read well enough; but they jar with the English king's actions and perceived intentions around this time. In June of 1290 – a month before Birgham – Edward I had taken control of the Isle of Man, part of the Scottish kingdom since 1275; shortly after the treaty was made, Edward appointed Anthony Bek, bishop of Durham, as lieutenant in Scotland and ordered the Scottish guardians to obey him; and according to the contemporary annals of Waverley Abbey, Edward went further than this in 1291, announcing to his nobility and councillors that he intended to bring Scotland under his control, just as he had subjugated Wales.

The Treaty of Birgham was never put to the test. In September 1290 the Maid of Norway, en route for Scotland, died in the Orkneys. In modern parlance, all bets were off. The Canmore dynasty was extinct; the Treaty of Birgham was dead in the water; and the Kingdom of Scotland had no head. These were the circumstances in which Edward I was able to make good two centuries of English claims to the overlordship of Scotland. Early in May 1291 he arrived at Norham-on-Tweed, on the Scottish border, and declared that the Scots' acknowledgement of his overlordship over their kingdom was a condition of his acting as judge in what came to be known as the Great Cause – the competition for the Scottish throne. He may have been encouraged to assert his overlordship at this stage because he had already been lobbied on behalf of Balliol by Bishop Fraser of St Andrews, and – anonymously – by the elderly Robert Bruce on behalf of himself.

Nevertheless, Edward took no chances, and came to Norham with more than legal arguments to support his overlordship. A large army, provided by his magnates and levies drawn from northern England, would be supported, if necessary, by a fleet to blockade Scotland. In the circumstances, it is not surprising that Edward achieved the result which he wanted. The Scottish guardians, intimidated by the prospect of confrontation and war, first attempted to prevaricate by returning an evasive answer to Edward's claim, and then found themselves outflanked by the English king, who secured acknowledgements from the competitors to the throne – one of whom was bound to succeed – of Edward's 'sovereign lordship' over Scotland.

In all, a total of thirteen competitors submitted claims in the Great Cause (1291–2); but the great majority were doing little more than registering an interest with no real hope of success. The real contest lay where it had always been, between John Balliol and Robert Bruce as descendants of David, earl of Huntingdon, brother of William I (1165–1214). The legal arguments – about feudal law, Roman civil law, and 'natural law', about whether Scotland should be treated as a barony which might be divided among co-heiresses – need not detain us, for they have received very extensive treatment elsewhere. Arguably, Balliol's claim in law was superior to that of Bruce. In political terms, Balliol, with more support from the clergy and ultimately backed by one of the other competitors, his brother-in-law John Comyn, was certainly the better bet; and Edward I gave judgement in his favour in mid-November 1292. Balliol was inaugurated at Scone on St Andrew's Day, 30 November, and did homage to Edward for his kingdom at Newcastle just after Christmas.

John Balliol and the Treaty of Paris (1292–1306)

In some respects, the new king seemed an ideal choice. In his early forties, he was married to Isabella de Warenne, daughter of the earl of Surrey, and had two sons, Edward and Henry. There was thus the prospect of a continuing Balliol dynasty in Scotland (and indeed John's elder son, Edward Balliol, would be inaugurated as king at Scone in September 1332 – though in very different circumstances). Of more immediate importance to King John was the support of the Comyns, the most powerful Scottish baronial family, and his control of the lordship of Galloway, which he had inherited from his mother Dervorguilla on her death in 1290. Though Balliol was by birth and upbringing more English than Scots, his election as king was probably greeted with relief by many Scots as an alternative to civil war. Certainly he was a vassal king, and he had been created by Edward I, who had acted not as arbitrator but as judge in the Great Cause. However, the English king had given an assurance at the outset that he would require nothing more from the elected King of Scots than homage and the rights associated with it; and at the same time he had guaranteed the 'rights, laws, liberties, and customs' of the kingdom of Scotland. There was no reason to expect, lower down the social scale in Scotland, that much was likely to change.

War had been averted, and there was no imposition of English officials in Scottish localities.

In reality, however, King John was a man caught between a rock and a hard place. His internal problems were obvious: with little more than half the Scottish aristocratic community committed to his side, he was continually faced with the potential or real hostility of the Bruces and their allies. In 1293 the Bruce faction outflanked King John by marrying Isabella, sister of the youngest Robert Bruce (the future Robert I), to King Eric of Norway; and around the same time Eric claimed that the Western Isles, ceded to the Scottish crown by the Treaty of Perth in 1266, should be restored to Norway because the Scots were badly in arrears with the 'annual', the annual payment to Norway of a hundred marks in perpetuity agreed in 1266. John Balliol, perhaps anticipating trouble from Norway over Scottish possession of the Isles, had already attempted to extend royal authority in the west through the creation of new sheriffdoms in Skye, Lorn, and Kintyre; but in the south-west, the king was unable to prevent the election of a Bruce candidate, Thomas Daltoun, to the bishopric of Galloway in 1294.

However, the most ominous factor was external, namely the attitude of Edward I towards his new vassal king. As Michael Prestwich has observed: 'Edward did not live in an age when a man could be content with a mere recognition of his authority: he had to exercise his rights in order to establish them'. The English king took a very broad view of those rights: on 2 January 1293, little over a month after John's inauguration at Scone, Balliol had to acknowledge in writing that Edward I was now released from any restrictions imposed on him by the Treaty of Birgham or his subsequent promises in 1291. So much for the rights, laws, liberties, and customs of the kingdom of Scotland. In an important sense, the reign of John Balliol was over almost before it had begun.

The issue which had led to Edward I's annulment of the provisions of Birgham was that of Scottish protests against appeals to Edward beyond King John's jurisdiction. Judicial appeals from Scotland to England were both new and unwelcome in 1292, for the issue went far beyond legal technicalities; if King John's authority as lawgiver were undermined, how would he fare in other complex matters such as foreign diplomacy, trade, and defence? There were in fact only a few appeals beyond John's jurisdiction, and at least one of them – by the Bordeaux wine merchant John Mazun, who was suing for payment of Alexander III's wine bills and who arrested the bishop of St Andrews in Yorkshire in order to strengthen his case – came into the lunatic fringe category. But other cases, above all that of Macduff, brother of the slain earl of Fife, led to Balliol being summoned south to answer appeals in person at

Westminster. King John did the worst possible thing; he prevaricated, then went south in November 1293 and refused to answer in a matter relating to his kingdom without consulting his people. On being offered an adjournment to do so, he changed tack and denied the competence of the court. Charged with contempt, he had to back down or face war. Like a time bomb, the Macduff case moved inexorably from one adjournment to the next for the remainder of the reign.

Breaking point for the Scots came some time in 1294, and had its origins in a dispute between Edward I, in his capacity as duke of Aquitaine, and his feudal overlord, Philip the Fair of France. There is a certain irony in the fact that Edward as duke had long been forced to tolerate appeals from his vassals in Gascony to his overlord King Philip and the *parlement* of Paris; and Anglo-French tensions increased as a result of Philip the Fair's determination to assert his sovereignty over great French fiefs, especially Gascony and Flanders. Parallels between King Philip's treatment of Edward, and Edward's of John Balliol, are easy to make, if inexact; for Aquitaine was only a dukedom. Scotland was still a kingdom.

Two naval incidents, involving French and English fleets off the Breton coast in 1293, were followed by a series of unsatisfactory negotiations which ended with Philip the Fair announcing that Gascony should be forfeited, and that Edward should be summoned before the *parlement* of Paris as a contumacious vassal. Not surprisingly, on 24 June 1294 Edward renounced his homage as duke and sent his formal defiance to the French king.

Both sides now prepared for war, and both cast about for allies. Edward I hoped to find them in the Low Countries, Germany, and Spain; and he looked for support from his vassals, the Welsh and Scots. Summonses were sent out in June 1294 demanding the personal military service in France of the King of Scots, ten Scottish earls, and sixteen barons. In August the Welsh were also called on to fight in King Edward's war in Gascony, and the English king made the appalling error of distributing arms amongst them while they were still at home. The entire country exploded into revolt under the leadership of Madog ap Llywelyn, with the rebels seizing Edward's half-built Caernarvon castle and a number of baronial castles in North Wales. The rebellion, which was not crushed until the spring of 1295, required Edward I's personal intervention, which in turn meant a diversion of the levies summoned for the Gascon war.

The violent Welsh resistance may have encouraged the Scots, whose response to Edward's demand for military service in Gascony was equally dramatic, if rather more delayed. We do not know exactly when 'official' resistance was first mooted, but it may be that a Council of Twelve, four each of bishops, earls, and barons, to assist the indecisive

King John, and known to exist by the summer of 1295, had in fact been appointed some time before December 1294. For at some point in the preceding six months, the Scots appear to have been responsible for obtaining from Pope Celestine V absolution from any oaths exacted from them under duress. Admittedly the choice of Celestine V was unfortunate, as he was perhaps the least effective pope in the history of the office, and the only one to abdicate; but the message was clear. After years of evasion and prevarication, the Scots were now denying Edward I's 'superior lordship' in Scotland, and were preparing to fight.

This situation brings us back to our starting point, the dispatching of four commissioners – William Fraser, bishop of St Andrews, Matthew of Crambeth, bishop of Dunkeld, Sir John de Soules, and Sir Ingram de Umfraville – to Paris to conclude a treaty with Philip the Fair. All were experienced diplomats; indeed Soules had already been on embassy to Paris in 1285, when he had been involved in the negotiations for the marriage of Alexander III to Yolande of Dreux. Ingram de Umfraville was related to the Balliols, and Bishop Fraser had been a Balliol champion since at least 1290. During the Great Cause, however, both the bishop of Dunkeld and John de Soules had been auditors for (i.e. representatives of) Bruce. This might suggest that, in the interests of presenting a united Scottish front abroad, a balance was being struck between Balliol and Bruce commissioners, not only in those chosen for the embassy to Paris, but also in the composition of the kingdom's Council of Twelve. There must be some doubt, however, that this Council's function was to remove executive authority from King John. After all, the Treaty of Paris was designed, amongst other things, to provide John's son and heir with a prestigious French marriage and so ensure the continuance of the Balliol dynasty; and the Council of Twelve which sanctioned the treaty surely included Balliol's kin and allies, the Comyns.

The Treaty of Paris was made on 23 October 1295, and should be understood as part of a tripartite alliance engineered by Philip the Fair to further his struggle against Edward I. The third party was Norway, though King Eric, an ally of Edward I and recently married into the Bruce family, was no friend to John Balliol. But there was no direct treaty between the Scots and Norwegians; instead both made separate alliances with King Philip, the Norwegians on the day before the Scots, on 22 October. These two alliances were an undoubted success for Philip the Fair, who had turned the King of Norway, a former friend of Edward I, into that king's enemy; while the Scots, regarded by the French king as recently as March 1295 as his enemies – presumably as vassals of King Edward – had now become the friends and allies of France.

The Franco-Scottish treaty of 23 October provided for a marriage between Edward Balliol, King John's son and heir, and Jeanne, eldest daughter of Charles, count of Valois and Anjou, Philip the Fair's brother. The bride was to receive a dowry of 25,000 *petits livres Tournois* and dower lands worth £1,500 sterling annually and drawn from Balliol's French estates (Bailleul, Dampierre, Helicourt and Hornoi) and Lanarkshire and Ayrshire lands, Haddington and Dundee castle in Scotland. Otherwise the treaty was an offensive and defensive alliance between Balliol and Philip IV, directed against Edward I; the Scots were required to begin and continue the war against England at their own expense, while Philip IV would continue the war already started (i.e. in Gascony and Flanders). Not only the Scottish clergy and the earls and barons of Scotland, but also the communities of the towns, should make war, and letters patent should be directed to the French king in this sense, authenticated by their seals.

Philip IV's requirement was to assist the Scots, but only in a limited sense. If the king of England should invade Scotland, and provided the French king were given adequate notice by the Scots, then King Philip would give help to the Scottish king 'by occupying the said king of England in other parts, so that he shall thus be distracted from beginning the foresaid invasion'. The treaty concluded with an agreement that neither ally would make a peace or truce with Edward I without including the other in its provisions.

Whether the initial inspiration for the Treaty of Paris came from France or Scotland is not clear; it carried potential benefits for both. It is perhaps easier to see what Philip IV stood to gain – another ally to offset Edward I's military schemes in Gascony and Flanders, and no requirement on the French side to intervene directly in Scotland. Were the Scots, then, simply dupes of Philip the Fair, entering on an ephemeral alliance which carried great risks but few obvious benefits? Against such a view must be set the attractions of the marriage alliance and the importance of having as an ally the king who was Edward I's overlord in Gascony, a prince of enormous power and influence. The ending, however temporarily, of Norwegian hostility must have been attractive to a Balliol government which feared Bruce ambitions and King Eric's marriage into the Bruce family. Certainly that family may have appeared less of a menace following the death of the aged Robert Bruce, 'the Competitor', at Easter 1295; but in fact the smooth transition of his son into the lordship of Annandale, and his grandson (the future Robert I) into the earldom of Carrick brought new, younger, and more formidable opponents of the Balliols into entrenched positions in the Scottish south-west.

Thus the French treaty also had the virtue of enhancing the prestige of the harassed Balliol dynasty; and at the outset, a European alliance which carried a considerable threat to Edward I, both at home and abroad, must have appeared enticing to the Scots. Thus on 24 February 1296, at Dunfermline, Balliol ratified the Treaty of Paris; and as the French had required, the seals not only of several members of the First and Second Estates – clergy and nobility – but also those of six major burghs – Aberdeen, Perth, Stirling, Edinburgh, Roxburgh and Berwick – were appended to the ratification. The last-named, the largest and richest burgh in Scotland, would survive for only a few weeks more.

What went wrong? From a Scottish point of view, there was certainly a collective over-confidence in the alliance acting as a major restraint on Edward I's movements. There was also a failure to co-ordinate the planned attacks on England. In the event, the Norwegians, who had guaranteed a fleet of galleys to reinforce ships which Philip IV was bringing from the Mediterranean to the Channel, did not appear at all; and the French king's naval assault on southern England – a partial sack of Dover, with abortive raids on Winchelsea and Hythe – occurred in August 1295, two months before the Franco-Norwegian and Franco-Scottish treaties were made in Paris. Edward I, who had already scaled down his commitment to the war in Gascony, had dealt with the Welsh rising in the winter and early spring of 1294–5. Thus the timing of the Treaty of Paris could not have been worse from a Scottish point of view, simply because neither of Scotland's allies was in a position to assist John Balliol in any useful way.

By contrast, Edward I, though unable to intervene personally in Gascony, was able to muster huge forces to deal with the Scots. The English feudal host had in fact been summoned as early as December 1295 – long before the Scottish ratification of the Treaty of Paris – with orders to meet in Newcastle on 1 March 1296. In the first instance, the contentious issue was not the Franco-Scottish treaty, but the Scots' refusal to hand over the border castles of Berwick, Roxburgh, and Jedburgh to King Edward until the end of the Anglo-French war. Thus, as Barrow points out, the Dunfermline ratification of the Treaty of Paris was effectively a Scottish declaration of war.

The war which followed was short, bloody, and for the time being, decisive. The Scottish host had been summoned to meet at the traditional muster point of Caddonlea near Selkirk on 11 March. Edward I was already at Newcastle early in the month, having summoned an enormous army, possibly 25,000 strong. Unlike the Scots, whose host was unpaid and based mainly on the service of able-bodied men between the ages of sixteen and sixty for a very limited period, the English army could be paid daily wages of war, which made possible a campaign longer than the statutory forty days. Both armies, of course, contained feudal elements – mounted knights, squires, and men-at-arms – but England's population, perhaps five times or more greater than that of Scotland, together with her wealth, produced a more effective levy – and far more cavalry than the Scots could afford. When one adds that the English were battle-hardened in the Welsh wars, while the Scots, divided amongst themselves, had fought no recent campaigns, the outcome of the Anglo-Scottish struggle of 1296 appears a foregone conclusion.

Nevertheless, the Scots attacked first; headed by John Comyn, earl of Buchan, a force which included no fewer than seven earls came out of Annandale, crossed the Solway, and laid siege to Carlisle on Easter Monday, 26 March. The city was, however, held for Edward I by Robert Bruce senior, who with the earls of March and Angus had refused to join Balliol. At the end of the same week, while Scottish magnates defied each other in the west, Edward I arrived before the walls of Berwick. His offer of terms was rejected, whereupon his army took the burgh by storm on 30 March and the inhabitants were slaughtered in their thousands on Edward's orders. The Scottish response was a descent on Northumberland in April, burning and ravaging in Redesdale and Tynedale; as at Berwick, the civilian population suffered the most, and the tale of 200 schoolboys locked in a church and burned alive by the Scots at Corbridge was used as propaganda to impress Philip the Fair of France that he was backing the wrong horse.

The main theatre of war, however, was the Scottish south-east. The Scots having seized Dunbar castle through trickery – the earl of March, Dunbar's keeper, was with Edward I but his countess was on the Scottish side – the English feudal host arrived on 27 April to lay siege to the castle. Its leader, John de Warenne, earl of Surrey, was interrupted by the arrival of the Scottish host, and the first full-scale battle of the Auld Alliance followed. Accounts of the conflict vary; the Lanercost chronicler has Surrey and his men about to go to bed when the Scots appeared, which seems rather at odds with a battle fought in the afternoon. Perhaps Surrey was rehearsing for his role in the battle of Stirling Bridge eighteen months later. However, English accounts agree that the Scots, in the mistaken belief that the English were fleeing, shouted abuse at them, calling them tailed dogs and threatening them with death and the cutting off of their tails. In the event, the English held firm, and it was the Scots who were broken in what appears to have been little more than a skirmish, followed by a long and bloody pursuit of the Scottish rank-and-file. Amongst Scottish notables, however, only Sir Patrick Graham was killed fighting; the easy capture by the English of the earls of Ross, Atholl, and Menteith suggests not only inefficiency in the Scottish ranks, but perhaps also a reluctance to fight on the part of some of King John's commanders.

John Balliol was not personally present at Dunbar. About three weeks earlier, he had sent a formal renunciation of his homage to Edward I, conveyed to the English king at Berwick by two Franciscan friars, and arriving around a week after Edward's butchery of the burgh's inhabitants. In his remonstrance, John rehearses the English king's 'injuries, slights, and wrongs', comments that Edward had 'caused harm beyond measure to the liberties of ourselves and our kingdom', and in renouncing his fealty and homage he comments that these had been given 'by reason of the lands which are held of you in your realm' – a hint that even his homage of 1292 had been only for Balliol lands in England, and not for Scotland.

King John's stirring defiance of Edward I implies, at the very least, a remarkable over-confidence on Balliol's part. At the end of April, following the débâcle at Dunbar and with Edward I already advancing into the Lothians, Balliol moved north into Angus with his Comyn allies. By late June, with Roxburgh, Edinburgh, and Stirling all surrendered, there was no alternative but to ask for terms. On 2 July 1296 King John, less than three months after his defiance, sealed a letter in which he accepted that he had acted 'by evil and false counsel' in defying Edward I while he owed him fealty and homage, especially by making a marriage alliance with Edward's enemy, the king of France. Therefore, 'acting under no constraint, and of our own free will', John now surrendered to the English king 'the land of Scotland and all its people, with the homages of all of them'. This letter was sealed at Kincardine castle in the Mearns. A few days later, in the churchyard at Stracathro, John formally renounced the French treaty; and finally, on 10 July at Brechin castle, Balliol took part in the humiliating ceremony which followed his solemn resignation of the kingdom of Scotland to Edward I. The royal arms were stripped from his surcoat – hence the nickname 'Toom Tabard', or empty surcoat – and in August he joined the exodus of prisoners following King Edward south. The English king had punished a rebellious vassal; but somewhat inconsistently, he had also acted in the manner of a conqueror rather than a feudal lord recovering his fief by force of arms. Thus he removed from Edinburgh the Scottish regalia and the Black Rood of St Margaret, the holiest relic in the kingdom; while in Perth he ordered that the enthronement stone of Scone – the so-called Stone of Destiny – should be taken south to Westminster as a gift to his patron Edward the Confessor. By these actions, he was seeking to crush, not a rebellious feudal vassal, but an independent kingdom. And if he ever made his much-quoted riposte to Robert Bruce of Annandale, when after Dunbar the latter pleaded to be allowed to take the Scottish throne – 'Have we nothing else to do but win kingdoms for you?' – then he was not only giving notice of his intention to annul the kingdom and rule Scotland as a 'land', but also making a serious – possibly fatal – tactical error. It may also have been an understandable error for the judge in the Great Cause, who probably formed a very low opinion of the Scots at that time.

For the most part, the Scottish recovery of 1297 and continuing resistance to King Edward lie mainly outwith the scope of a study of the Franco-Scottish alliance. The risings of Andrew Moray and William Wallace, their victory over Surrey at Stirling Bridge in September 1297, the abortive rising of Robert Bruce, earl of Carrick, and his southern allies in the same year, and the temporary expulsion of the English from Scotland – all these events should be seen as internal struggles undertaken by a wide cross-section of Scots who would not accept Edward I's annulment of the kingdom. The alliance played a role in so far as Edward I was absent on campaign in Flanders during 1297; but he returned in the summer of 1298, with another huge army, to win the battle of Falkirk and put an end to Wallace's short-lived guardianship. But Scottish resistance continued for the next six years under new guardians – including, for a time, the ill-matched pairing of John Comyn and Robert Bruce – and with varying degrees of success. No easy analysis of the stance – or stances – taken by numbers of the Scottish nobility in this first phase of the Wars of Independence is possible. Almost all of them had, after all, given their homage to Edward I in 1296; many of them had English estates, and therefore much to lose by taking up arms against the English king. Perhaps the safest analysis is that of Professor Duncan, who remarked that those numbers of the Scottish nobility who were lukewarm patriots were 'not an Anglicised baronage betraying the nation, but men of wealth and political maturity and therefore careful, even cautious, patriots'.

In any event, committed patriots faced two seemingly insurmountable problems. First, such resistance as they offered had to be carried on, at least nominally, in the name of King John, a prisoner in England; and secondly, in defying Edward I the Scots faced not only an implacable enemy with a formidable war machine, but also a king who, more than any English king before or since, was determined to impose his will on Scotland irrespective of financial or human cost. In spite of constitutional and fiscal crises at home and wars abroad, he committed himself to his Scottish wars with a determination which amounted to obsession.

Balliol's career after his capture in 1296 suggests that he was not the leader who would redeem the lost kingdom of Scotland. His life in captivity was not harsh, for he was soon moved from the Tower of London to Hertford, and given a huntsman and ten hounds. His revealing view of the Scots at this time was expressed to Anthony Bek, bishop of Durham, at the bishop's lodging just outside London, and eagerly transcribed by the waiting notary. According to King John:

> he found in the men of that realm [Scotland] such malice, deceit, treason, and treachery, and . . . those who, as he had good grounds to believe were plotting to poison him . . . that it is not his intention to enter or go into the realm of Scotland at any time to come . . . or even to have anything to do with the Scots.

Such a statement may of course have been intended by Balliol to impress his English captors and secure an early release; and this at least was forthcoming. A Scottish embassy to the court of Philip IV in 1298 asked for support in terms of the Treaty of Paris; and the French king, while cautiously not promising military aid, indicated his support for the Balliol cause. In June 1299, the Anglo-French peace of Montreuil, bringing to an end some five years of war and providing for a marriage between Edward I and Philip the Fair's sister Margaret, also saw the release of John Balliol into the hands of a papal envoy. To this extent, the French king had not deserted his ally of 1295; and in the summer of 1301, Balliol was transferred from papal custody into the hands of Philip IV. Undoubtedly the French king regarded the former king of Scots as a useful pawn in his diplomatic games with Edward I and Pope Boniface VIII; and it may be significant that a Scottish delegation to Rome at this time, headed by Master Baldred Bisset, was concerned to submit the justice of the Scottish case in the struggle with Edward I to papal arbitration, but not specifically to argue for the restoration of King John. His name was used by the long-suffering Scots guardian John de Soules to authenticate the official business of the Scottish kingdom; but such a step hardly heralded the imminent return of the former king. Balliol lived out the remaining dozen years of his life at his ancestral château of Bailleul-en-Vimeu, in Picardy; at his death leadership of the Balliol cause in Scotland would be transferred to his able son and heir Edward, and in much-changed political circumstances.

The Treaty of Paris of 1295 was eventually made obsolete by the diplomatic and military re-alignments in turn-of-the-century Europe. Already the Anglo-French peace of 1299 had left the Scots vulnerable to much more consistent harassment by Edward I; a Galloway campaign in 1300 was followed – much more ominously – by lengthier expeditions, with the king wintering at Linlithgow in 1301–2, and at Dunfermline in 1303–4. Edward was able to give the Scots his undivided and unwelcome attention in the latter case because of the changed European situation. For on 11 July 1302 an army of Flemish urban foot-soldiers totally defeated the massed aristocratic cavalry of Philip IV of France at Courtrai. This was a bitter blow to Philip the Fair; and the Scots, fearing the withdrawal of their French ally's protection, sent an embassy headed by Sir John de Soules to France. The outcome was worse than had been feared. Philip the Fair, shaken by Courtrai and now at odds with Pope Boniface VIII, the Scots' former supporter, committed himself in May 1303 to a very different Treaty of Paris – a treaty of perpetual peace and friendship with Edward I of England. John Balliol, vegetating on his estates at Bailleul, had already roused himself sufficiently to consent that the French king should have a totally free hand in his negotiations with the English. King Philip responded by excluding the Scots from the treaty, as Edward I had requested; and the Scottish ambassadors in Paris found themselves both helpless and – temporarily – prisoners.

Deserted by the French, the Scots had to face the English king on their own in an unequal struggle. What appeared to be the end came in July 1304, with the surrender of Stirling castle, following a siege of three months during which Edward I employed fourteen war machines to batter the defenders into submission. Perhaps significantly, Sir William Oliphant, who had been charged with the defence of the castle by Sir John de Soules, the guardian, claimed to be resisting on behalf of the Lion, the symbol of Scottish kingship, rather than for King John Balliol.

Throughout 1305 there appeared to be only bad news for those who still held to the idea of an independent Scottish kingdom. In August William Wallace, the hero of Stirling Bridge and former guardian, was taken, judged and butchered at Smithfield; and in September Edward I, 'gracious towards time-servers, vindictive towards staunch opponents', produced an ordinance for the future government of Scotland. However, in February 1306 the Scottish political situation was transformed. One of the time-servers, Robert Bruce, earl of Carrick, killed his principal rival John Comyn of Badenoch in the Greyfriars of Dumfries, seized the throne as Robert I at the end of March, and gave the Scots the civil war which the guardians of the previous twenty years had sought assiduously to avoid.

Robert Bruce and the Treaty of Corbeil (1306–26)

Understandably a renewal of the French alliance was not at the top of the new king's priorities. He had to survive, and somehow to win the war, both against his Scottish enemies and a vengeful Edward I. After an appalling first year – promptly excommunicated by Pope Clement V for the act of murder and sacrilege which had preceded the reign, losing battles throughout central Scotland, becoming a hunted fugitive whose family and supporters were imprisoned or executed, temporarily taking

refuge in the Isles or Ireland, returning prematurely and surviving a
further encounter at Loudoun Hill in Ayrshire – Bruce at last enjoyed an
enormous stroke of good fortune. On 7 July 1307, Edward I, grimly
advancing towards Scotland, died on the shores of the Solway at the age
of sixty-eight. His death removed not only the most intractable enemy
the Kingdom of Scotland had ever faced, but also the king who had
made the treaty of 1303 with King Philip of France. The usurpation of
Bruce in 1306, and Edward I's death the following year, thus made
possible a new rapprochement between Scotland and France.

Acceptance abroad, most crucially from England and the papacy, was
of great importance to King Robert; and he achieved neither until the
very end of his life. So a renewal of the French alliance, drawing a line
under the unhappy pre-1306 diplomatic events, would be one useful
insurance policy for Robert I. At the very least, he would have in Philip
the Fair a powerful mediator in his struggle with England, a king who,
unlike Edward II, recognised Robert's title in Scotland and sent him a
message of 'extraordinary and peculiar affection' in 1308. Admittedly
Philip's letter had a purpose, to invite Robert to join him in a projected
crusade, an invitation which the Scottish king neatly side-stepped in an
eloquent and broadly sympathetic reply sent to the French king from
Bruce's first parliament, held at St Andrews in March 1309.

A formal renewal of the alliance was delayed for a further seventeen
years. In that time Robert I progressed from a usurper fighting for
survival and engaged in a constant search for security, to a ruler who had
forced the world to accept him on his own terms. His pursuit of
recognition from England and the papacy continued; but he was clearly
winning the military struggle, with a spectacular victory over Edward II
at Bannockburn in June 1314, from 1311 onwards a series of devastating
and highly profitable raids into northern England, and a 'second front'
developed in Ireland (together with Bruce's brother Edward) from 1315.
Underpinning all this military success was the effectiveness of Robert I's
propaganda, which created the myth in 1309 that Bruce the Competitor
had been the people's choice in the Great Cause and that John Balliol
was a puppet imposed on the Scots by Edward I. Early in 1314 news of
Balliol's death in France reached Scotland; and six years later, in Bruce's
most famous propaganda exercise, the 'Declaration of Arbroath' of April
1320, Balliol was not mentioned, even in a perjorative sense. He and his
supporters, many of them heroes of the first War of Independence, had
become, in an Orwellian sense, the non-persons of 1320. A massive
Balliol-inspired reaction, the so-called 'Soules conspiracy', was ruthlessly crushed by Robert I in August of that year.

Thus the Scottish political map had changed out of all recognition when the Franco-Scottish alliance was taken up again in 1326. In France, the Capetian dynasty was in crisis; Philip the Fair had died in 1314, to be succeeded by his three sons, Louis X (1314–16), Philip V (1316–22), and Charles IV (1322–28), all of whom died young without surviving male heirs. The last of these kings, Charles IV, renewed the Franco-Scottish alliance with Robert I in a treaty made at Corbeil, near Paris, in April 1326. Like its predecessor of 1295, the Treaty of Corbeil was an offensive and defensive alliance directed against England. It bound successive French kings to assist the Scots in peace and war with 'aid and counsel', while the Scots, in the event of war between England and France, were required to make war on the English. As in 1295, each ally contracted not to make peace or truce with England without including the other in it; and as in 1295, the Scots carried a heavier obligation – war rather than simply 'aid and counsel' – than their French allies.

Yet both sides needed each other, if only as insurance. In 1323 Robert I had concluded a thirteen-year truce with the weak and visibly failing government of Edward II of England; but that king still refused to recognise Bruce as king of an independent Scotland. And in 1324, King Edward had commanded Edward Balliol, son and heir of King John, to come from Picardy to England, an ominous gesture which in fact heralded the shape of things to come.

On the French side, Charles IV had resumed his father's struggle with England over the duchy of Aquitaine, and was concerned to recover the support of the Scots. While he still hoped to father a male child by his wife Jeanne of Evreux, he must have been acutely aware that failure to produce legitimate male offspring would mean the end of the Capetian dynasty. Worse still, his sister Isabella, who had come to France in 1325, abandoning her unsatisfactory husband Edward II of England, had a son Edward (the future Edward III) who would certainly have a claim, through his mother, to the French throne.

Thus the Treaty of Corbeil was made by two kings who probably sensed that their time was running out. Neither had time to benefit personally from its provisions; but its existence, in the transformed world of the 1330s, was to prove of vital importance to both allies, and especially to the survival of the independent Scottish kingdom.

2

Two Theatres of War: The Fourteenth Century

In March 1337 Edward III of England, the son of Philip the Fair's daughter Isabella, laid claim to the French throne of the first Valois king Philip VI. The English king's claim, subsequently reinforced by his assumption of the title of King of France in 1340, initiated the great European war, later described as the Hundred Years' War, which would sporadically engage the kingdoms of England and France, and the allies of both, until 1453. It would also have a salutary effect on the Franco-Scottish alliance.

The war had been a long time coming, and had its origins in the political and succession crises which afflicted France, England, and Scotland in the late 1320s and early 1330s. On 1 February 1328 Charles IV, the last Capetian king, died without male issue at Vincennes at the age of only thirty-four. On his deathbed he may have remembered the Templar curse laid on his father Philip the Fair and all his issue; and following Charles's death and the posthumous birth of a daughter rather than a son, Philip of Valois, Philip the Fair's nephew, was proclaimed king as Philip VI on 14 April 1328. The French were thus invoking the Salic Law, forbidding the inheritance of a woman; and the same law denied the claim of Isabella, Philip the Fair's daughter, and her son Edward III, who succeeded to the throne of England in 1327, at the age of fourteen.

The young King Edward's adolescent years were disturbed first by his father Edward II's deposition in 1327 at the instigation of his mother and her lover Roger Mortimer, then by a Scottish invasion of the English north-east during which, at Stanhope near Durham, the guy-ropes of the new king's tent were cut in a night attack by Sir James Douglas. This humiliation at Stanhope no doubt played its part in making Edward III view the Scots as his principal enemies at this time. Certainly he disapproved of the recognition of Robert I as the ruler of an independent kingdom in the Treaty of Edinburgh-Northampton of May 1328, an alliance engineered by Isabella and Mortimer and underpinned by the marriage at Berwick, two months later, of Bruce's son and heir David and Edward III's sister Joan.

This treaty and alliance was on the surface the crowning achievement of Robert I's long struggle. The kingdom of Scotland was to be 'separate

THE FRENCH SUCCESSION: CAPETIANS, VALOIS, AND PLANTAGENETS

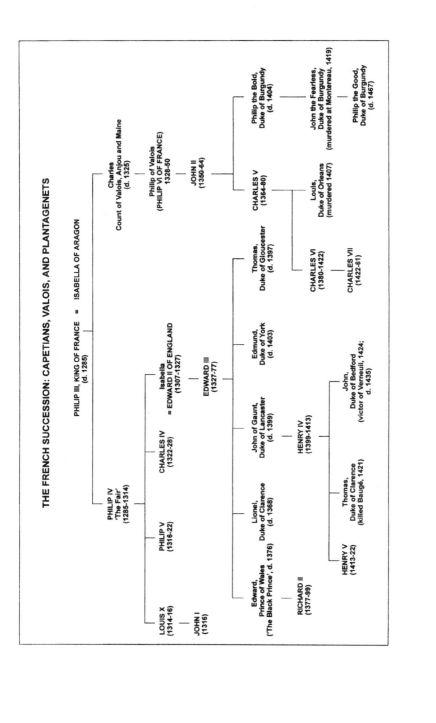

in all things from the kingdom of England . . . to remain forever free and quit of any subjection, servitude, claim or demand'. If the Treaty of Corbeil of 1326 had been intended by Bruce as an insurance policy to put pressure on the English government to recognise his status, there can be little doubt that the Scottish king set far greater store by the English treaty of 1328. A dying man, Robert I was looking to secure his heir's position and inheritance; and the Berwick wedding celebrations were appropriately lavish.

Edward III, Philip VI, and two Rival Scottish Kings
(1327–1337)

For all his achievements, above all the restoration of the power and independence of the Scottish kingdom and the enhancement of the status of its monarchy, Bruce's work was unfinished and his legacy ephemeral. For one thing, his distribution of lands among his principal supporters left a huge question mark over the future of the 'disinherited', those forfeited magnates who had remained loyal to Edward II and, in some cases, to the Balliol cause. The Treaty of Edinburgh-Northampton had made no reference to them; but they included claimants to the earldoms of Buchan, Atholl, and Angus. A more serious issue was the succession. Initially, the heir presumptive had been Bruce's grandson Robert the Steward (Stewart), born to Robert I's daughter Marjorie, the child of the king's first marriage to Isabella of Mar, and Marjorie's husband Walter the Steward in 1316; but in 1324 Robert I had a son David by his second wife Elizabeth de Burgh, who succeeded as David II in 1329, aged only five. Much of the political history of Scotland from the 1340s onwards can be written as a struggle between these two rivals once they had reached adulthood.

Initially, however, the linked problems of the disinherited and the succession made the Scottish kingdom extremely vulnerable on Bruce's death in June 1329. English recognition of Scottish independence rested, after all, on a treaty made by the Scots with one of the most unstable and short-lived governments in English history; and Bruce's land settlement in parts of Scotland owed much to his own forceful, ruthless character, and would not long survive his death. The shape of things to come was clearly indicated when, in October 1330, the young Edward III carried out a successful coup against his mother and Roger Mortimer at Nottingham, and took control of government in person. Edward's attitude to the Scottish treaty of 1328 was straightforward – it was a 'shameful peace' which he had no intention of honouring.

The Scots had little opportunity to mount an adequate defence against impending English aggression; for in the three years after Robert I's death, his principal commanders and supporters followed him to the grave. They included his long-serving chancellor, Bernard of Linton, Walter the Steward, and Bishop Lamberton of St Andrews. The 'good' Sir James Douglas was killed in Spain in March 1330, attempting to fulfil his royal master's last wish, to carry his heart on crusade to the Holy Land. The guardian for the boy king David II, Thomas Randolph, earl of Moray, died at Musselburgh in July 1332. In his short term of office, Randolph had managed to organise David's coronation, at Scone on 24 November 1331. For the first time in Scottish history, a ruler was both crowned and anointed; for a papal bull not only revoking the excommunication and interdict placed on Bruce and his realm, but also conferring the privileges of coronation and unction, had been issued at Avignon in the month of Robert I's death.

Thus the Scots at last had a ruler succeeding to an independent kingdom recognised not only by their allies abroad, but by England and the papacy. And their leaders may have reasoned that Edward III was unlikely to upset that settlement; for the Treaty of Edinburgh–Northampton had laid down a payment of £20,000 by the Scots to the king of England, payable at Tweedmouth in three annual instalments – that is, the final instalment payable in 1331.

Yet the Scots, bereft of clear leadership, had no reason for over-confidence. Within three weeks of Randolph's death in July 1332, an expedition led by Edward Balliol and containing the principal claimants among the disinherited, landed at Kinghorn and on 11 August won a shattering victory over the host of the new guardian Donald, earl of Mar, at Dupplin, near Perth. Mar, who had been guardian for a mere nine days, should have won the battle easily; but his own background – he had been sympathetic to some of the disinherited, possibly to Edward Balliol himself – made him an unsuitable commander, and he may have lost at Dupplin because Sir Robert Bruce, an illegitimate son of the late king, accused him of treachery before the battle and undermined morale in the Scottish host. Both men were killed, Edward Balliol occupied Perth, and on 24 September – less than two months after landing in Scotland – he was crowned as King of Scots at Scone. Little over three years after the death of Robert I, Scotland had two rival kings and a resumption of the Bruce-Balliol civil war.

Behind this disordered and dangerous state of affairs lurked a greater menace. Edward Balliol was not claiming to be king of an independent Scotland, but rather resurrecting the relationship which had existed between his father John and Edward I. In letters written to Edward III towards the end of 1332, Edward Balliol made it clear that he recognised the English king as lord superior of Scotland, to whom he had already performed homage and fealty. Thus, should Edward Balliol succeed on a permanent basis in Scotland, vassal kingship would be restored and Robert I's struggle would have gone for nothing; should Balliol fail, then Edward III would surely intervene in Scotland in person to restore him.

In one sense, the worst happened: Balliol failed, or at any rate could not sustain his position in Scotland unaided. A week before Christmas of 1332, he was surprised at Annan in a dawn raid led by the new guardian Sir Archibald Douglas (brother of the 'good' Sir James), and the sixteen-year-old Robert the Steward; Balliol's brother Henry was killed in the attack, and Balliol himself fled to Carlisle and called upon Edward III for assistance. In May 1333, ignoring the contrary advice of his English parliament, Edward III arrived to direct in person the siege of Berwick which his vassal had been conducting for two months. The hard-pressed Scottish defenders agreed to surrender if not relieved by 20 July, which forced the guardian and the Scottish host to march to Berwick's relief and to encounter Edward III in a pitched battle, an ominous reversal of English and Scottish roles prior to Bannockburn. On 19 July the battle of Halidon Hill soon developed into a carnage of the Scots in which Douglas, the guardian, and the earls of Ross, Sutherland and Carrick were all slain; Edward III entered Berwick the following day.

Further resistance to Edward Balliol's kingship seemed unlikely, and his allies among the disinherited came into their own. The Bruce cause, confined to the castles of Kildrummy and Urquhart in the north, Lochleven, Loch Doon in Ayrshire, and Dumbarton on the Clyde, was threatened with extinction. With benefit of hindsight, and with the Stewart dynasty firmly established, fifteenth-century chroniclers give us a moving account of the flight of the seventeen-year-old Robert the Steward in the final months of 1333; deprived of Cowal, Bute, and the Stewartry – which Edward Balliol had granted to David of Strathbogie, earl of Atholl, the most formidable of the disinherited – the young Robert fled by boat from Rothesay castle, bearing with him his family charters, and finally took refuge in the relative safety of Dumbarton castle, where the nine-year-old David II and Queen Joan were already lodged. This poignant tale is further enhanced by the naming of three of Robert the Steward's brothers as casualties at Halidon Hill. However, the reality of the political situation at the outset of 1334 was that the man who would be king and the boy who, according to Bruce loyalists, was king, were both skulking in Dumbarton while Edward Balliol held a parliament at Holyrood and confirmed the distribution of northern Scottish earldoms amongst his 'disinherited' supporters.

Early in 1334, then, the one useful remaining part of the Bruce legacy was the Treaty of Corbeil of 1326. Some time after the raid of Annan in December 1332, John Randolph, the young earl of Moray, had gone to France to seek aid from Philip VI, invoking the clause of the treaty which required the French to give aid and counsel to the Scots. Randolph appears to have been well received, for in 1333 the French king had sent money – £1,000 to be distributed amongst Bruce supporters – and probably also ten supply ships attempting to reach Scotland by the west-coast route but being blown off course to Flanders. With the Bruce cause visibly failing after Halidon Hill, Randolph clearly returned to Dumbarton with an invitation from Philip VI for David II and his queen to take refuge in France, where he would receive an annual pension of 2,000 livres from the French king. David and Joan duly sailed from Dumbarton in the spring of 1334, and by May had safely landed in Normandy and were promptly installed in the great fortress of Château Gaillard on the river Seine. The young couple were accompanied, among others, by Adam de Moravia, bishop of Brechin, Robert Keith, the Marischal, and Walter Twynham, abbot of Kilwinning, all men who had taken part in the Corbeil negotiations.

Philip VI had saved the boy king of Scots and established a Scottish court-in-exile in Normandy. He had honoured his predecessor's prom-ises in the Treaty of Corbeil, and indeed had gone further than that treaty, strictly interpreted, required of him. He had, however, the most obvious of motives for wishing to support the Scots; and these lay in rapidly deteriorating Anglo-French relations, above all over the posses-sion of Gascony.

Since 1294 the issue of successive English kings' homages to their French overlords for the dukedom of Gascony had created friction, and on occasions the threat of war, or war itself, between England and France. Philip VI, as the first Valois king, planned an invasion of Gascony in 1329, probably as a means of putting pressure on the English not to threaten French interests elsewhere. The English government of Isabella and Mortimer, recognising the threat, duly arranged for the adolescent Edward III to perform homage for Gascony to Philip VI, and a crisis was averted. Two years later in 1331, with Isabella and Mortimer gone and King Edward in charge of his own government, the English king again performed homage for Gascony, this time travelling to France in disguise and attempting, as his two predecessors had done, to find a formula whereby all outstanding disputes with Philip VI might be settled. This attempt took the form of the Process of Agen (1331), but it proved no more successful than the earlier Processes of Montreuil and Périgeux.

Gascony was a rich duchy, with annual receipts of £13,000 sterling and a flourishing wine trade with England. It was also part of Edward III's inheritance, which he was required to defend. Should the French invade the duchy, and the Scots be in a position to open a second front in the north, Edward might well be dishonoured, like his father another English king unable to protect his dominions. Hence his alarm when Philip VI, having established David II at Château Gaillard, went on to insist that any Anglo-French settlement must include the Scots.

Nor was Gascony the only source of Anglo-French friction. Another diplomatic running sore was Flanders, where the weaving industry depended for its existence on the regular import of English wool. The French, on the other hand, looked to destroy English economic interests there, and Philip VI had won a convincing victory over the Flemings at Cassel in 1328, a French revenge for Courtrai (1302). As the 1330s advanced, Edward III retaliated by building alliances with neighbouring rulers; and in 1336 the English government imposed an embargo on wool exports to Flanders. This had the desired effect of turning the screw on the Flemish weaving industry and so spreading dissension throughout the Low Countries. Tension mounted when, also in 1336, Philip VI moved the French Mediterranean fleet, assembled at Marseilles to take part in a projected crusade, into the English Channel. The vision of Western Christendom united in a war against the infidel, with Philip VI leading the crusade and Edward III taking part, was rapidly replaced by the spectre of a French naval blockade of England leading to the ruin of her commerce.

Anglo-French war was thus very likely in the later 1330s, and it was initiated by Philip VI's confiscation of Gascony in 1337. His reason for doing so was Edward III's reception in England, the previous year, of Robert, count of Artois, a disgraced vassal of the king of France, in Philip's eyes a forger and possibly also a poisoner. However, the most serious charge which could be laid against Robert of Artois was that he had persuaded Edward III to lay claim to the French throne. A contemporary anti-English poem describes Robert's attending a feast and placing a heron before King Edward, remarking that this coward among birds was appropriate fare for a king who did not have the courage to claim his inheritance. The poem may or may not have some basis in fact; but it seems unlikely that, by 1336, Edward III needed any prompting from Robert of Artois to claim Philip VI's throne. As Michael Prestwich has pointed out, Edward's claim transformed him from a rebellious vassal in Gascony into the French king's equal; and he would not lack support in some areas of France, not to mention the Low Countries. Thus a war which had many causes, including the vexed feudal relationship in Gascony, political and economic rivalries in Flanders, the Franco-Scottish alliance, and the continual English fear of encirclement by potential or real enemies, had as its justification in contemporary propaganda Edward III's assumption of the title of King of France, based on an allegedly superior claim to that of the incumbent, Philip VI.

For Scots supporters of the absent David II, the diversion of Edward III's warlike energies to the impending struggle in France must have come as a godsend. The Auld Alliance, initially created to meet the temporary needs of its two participants, would now achieve a permanence unimaginable only a generation before.

King David's War (1338–46)

Philip VI had saved the young Bruce king, but had he also saved the Scottish kingdom? Much has been said and written about the extent to which the Scots were saved by Edward III's personal abandonment of the war in Scotland to pursue his goals in France, and how far that war was already being won by Scottish supporters of David II even before King Edward's final withdrawal in 1338.

There can be no doubt that the Bruce cause had sunk to its lowest ebb in the first half of 1334. Not only had Edward Balliol been able to hold a parliament at Holyrood in February, but by June he had handed over to Edward III much of southern Scotland – the sheriffdoms of Berwick, Roxburgh, Selkirk, Peebles, Edinburgh and Dumfries, together with the constabularies of Haddington and Linlithgow and the forests of Ettrick and Jedburgh – to be annexed permanently to the English crown; and late in the same month Balliol did homage to the English king for the remainder of his kingdom, much of it lying in the west or north of Forth.

However, resistance to what Bruce Webster calls Balliol's 'Quisling' regime began to grow later in the year. The young John Randolph, earl of Moray, had emerged as an effective leader; together with Robert the Steward he assumed the guardianship and promptly overran many of the territories recently ceded to Edward III. They were aided by quarrels in the Balliol camp, principally over the allocation of Mowbray lands. There were some defections to the Bruce side, and even a temporary change of allegiance to David II by the formidable David of Strathbogie, earl of Atholl, in September 1334. Yet the overall impression conveyed by accounts of these years is of division and dissension amongst the leaders of the Bruce government; they might act together – as they did – to throw Edward Balliol and his English officials out of Scotland in 1334, but they were rivals within Scotland itself. Their alliances rarely lasted for any length of time, and there was always the danger of capture. Thus John Randolph, the joint guardian with the Steward, was captured in July 1335 and imprisoned in England for five years; and the Steward himself

submitted to Edward III in September 1335. This temporary power
vacuum allowed Sir Andrew Moray, son of Wallace's ally at Stirling
Bridge in 1297, to emerge as guardian, to challenge David of Strathbogie,
who had reverted to his Balliol/Edward III allegiance, and to kill
Strathbogie at the battle of Culblean on St Andrew's Day 1335. For three
years thereafter, Sir Andrew Moray was the principal leader of Scottish
resistance to the English king; but he died in the spring of 1338 at his
castle of Avoch in Easter Ross.

This tortuous power struggle amongst Scottish magnates is a reflection
of the kingdom's weakness. Bereft of many leaders at Dupplin and
Halidon, the realm was divided amongst rivals who could not face
Edward III in the field with any hope of success. Thus King Edward's
summer offensive of 1335, bringing an army of 13,000 into Scotland,
rapidly produced a host of Scottish submissions reminiscent of the days of
Edward's grandfather. The much-vaunted battle of Culblean, resulting in
the death of Strathbogie, can be viewed at one level as the turn of the tide
for the cause of David II; but perhaps it should be seen rather as a local
struggle, a showdown between two magnates with territorial interests in
north-east Scotland. After all, although the extension of a fourteenth-
century magnate's lordship might be achieved through marriage or a
royal grant of lands, it might equally be attained, as the striking cases of
the Black Douglases and Alexander Stewart, 'Wolf' of Badenoch, illus-
trate, through violence or the threat of it.

It is therefore not unreasonable to see the mid-to-late 1330s as a period
in which, when Edward III was not physically present, the Scottish
leaders conducted their own private wars over lands and offices, on
occasions changing sides to protect their inheritances. Even in the
struggle against the English, Scottish support for David II was rather
muted; those who broke the English truce in February 1336 claimed that
they adhered to the Lion – an ominous reminder of the siege of Stirling
Castle in 1304 – rather than King David himself. Writing with benefit of
hindsight in the 1440s, Walter Bower praises the heroic deeds of Sir
Andrew Moray and devotes chapters to a seemingly irresistible Scottish
recovery. Yet the two most famous tales of the period, though both
portraying the coolness under fire and courage of the Scots, point rather
the other way.

The first of these, which may be dated to July 1336, concerns Sir
Andrew Moray, who had blockaded Strathbogie's widow in the island
fortress of Lochindorb. Edward III came in person to raise the siege and
rescue the countess, hoping by a forced march to surprise Moray on the
way. The latter, who was hearing mass in the wood of Stronkalter, could
not be disturbed, even by the news of Edward III's rapid approach. Once

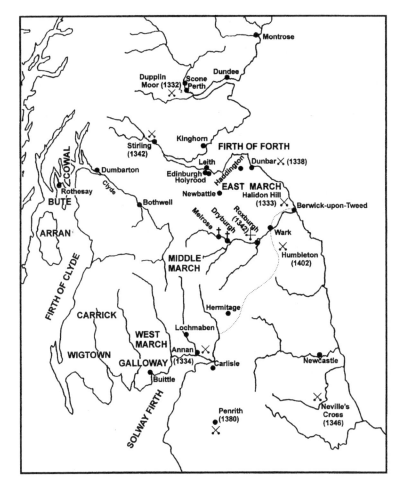

FRANCE'S SECOND FRONT: ANGLO-SCOTTISH WARFARE IN THE FOURTEENTH CENTURY

Major burghs, seaports, and strongpoints:	●
Battles and sieges:	✕
Abbeys:	✝
Anglo-Scottish border:	····························

Labels on map:

Montrose
Dundee
Dupplin Moor (1332)
Scone
Perth
Stirling (1342)
Kinghorn
FIRTH OF FORTH
Leith
Dunbar ✕ (1338)
Dumbarton
COWAL
Edinburgh
Holyrood
Haddington
EAST MARCH
Rothesay
Clyde
Newbattle
Halidon Hill (1333)
BUTE
Bothwell
Berwick-upon-Tweed
Melrose
Dryburgh
Roxburgh (1342)
ARRAN
Wark
Humbleton (1402)
FIRTH OF CLYDE
MIDDLE MARCH
Hermitage
CARRICK
Lochmaben
WEST MARCH
Annan (1334)
WIGTOWN
GALLOWAY
Carlisle
Newcastle
Buittle
Penrith (1380)
Neville's Cross (1346)
SOLWAY FIRTH

mass was over, and apparently at the last moment, Moray withdrew. A good tale, but the reality of the situation was that Moray did not – presumably could not – take on Edward III, and that the English king went on to relieve Lochindorb, for good measure adding a tour of Moray in which he burned Forres and Kinloss, and finished by heading south-east to raze the burgh of Aberdeen.

The second tale, which appears first in the chronicle of John of Fordun, concerns the 1338 siege of Dunbar castle by William Montagu, earl of Salisbury, and its heroic defence by Agnes Randolph – 'Black Agnes' of later legend – countess of March and sister of the imprisoned John Randolph, earl of Moray. Again, it is an inspiring story, with the countess resisting a blockade from the sea, and assaults from the landward side with siege machines shipped to Berwick from the Tower of London, for no less than five months, on occasions making appearances on the castle walls to hurl abuse at the besiegers. She was successful in that Dunbar was not taken, and that an Anglo-Scottish truce was made later in the year. But 'Black Agnes's' resistance makes the point that, as late as 1338, the Scots were still very much on the defensive. By contrast Edward III, though about to depart for Flanders, still had time to come personally to Whitekirk in East Lothian to confer with Salisbury; and the English government, although facing growing complaints about the expense of the Scottish war, could still spend close on £6,000 on this one siege. Altogether it is difficult not to agree with Fordun when he remarks: 'The same year, *happily for the kingdom of Scotland* [my italics], was begun a very fearful and savage war between the kings of England and France'.

The war conducted by Sir Andrew Moray had been a grim war of attrition: avoiding battle, going for scorched earth, and destroying castles as soon as he had taken them. While this may have been the correct policy given his limited resources, it was a blight to friend and foe alike. King David's war, when it came, would be fought in a very different way – even if it produced a depressingly similar result.

For in June 1341, David II and Queen Joan returned to Scotland. Landing at Inverbervie in the Mearns, the seventeen-year-old king displayed his piety by founding a Carmelite chapel there as an expression of thanks for his safe sea passage. Both Scottish and French chroniclers note the euphoria caused by David's return. Among consistent Bruce supporters during the hard times of the 1330s, this was understandable; but not everyone can have been glad to see the return of the king. Above all, David's nephew, Robert the Steward, guardian since Sir Andrew Moray's death in 1338, found himself not only unrewarded for his services but also mistrusted by the king; the combination of Bruce fears of a Stewart succession and the Steward's long pursuit of territory in central Scotland for himself and latterly for his sons was enough to create tension and antagonism. And David's rapid building up of royal support based on a process of removing reliable men from the affinities of magnates whom he considered to have too much power, and putting royal knights into sensitive or 'difficult' areas, only served to widen the political divide between the king and some of the great Scottish nobility.

King David was perhaps the victim of his own upbringing. He knew little of Scottish government, having fled from his kingdom at the age of ten. His formative years had been spent in France, grateful for Philip VI's continuing aid; and the small Scottish court at Château Gaillard included, or was visited by, Scots like Reginald More and Sir Alexander Seton, men who had connections with the Scottish Knights Hospitaller and an interest in Philip VI's projected crusade. David himself was probably trained in the use of weapons in France by Sir Robert Keith, a veteran of Bannockburn, sheriff of Edinburgh and justiciar north of Forth and marischal under Robert I. In 1339, at the age of fifteen, David flew his own banner in Philip VI's army – alongside the Kings of Bohemia and Navarre – at Buironfosse in Flanders, when the host of the French king and his allies came close to a major engagement with Edward III.

In sum, David II absorbed the main elements of European chivalry as a young man, and shared with his host Philip VI, and his rival (and later captor) Edward III, an obsession with royal chivalry, a passion for knight-errantry, and above all a desire to surround himself with knights and esquires with crusading reputations. He was also deeply grateful for Philip VI's support – not only for his annual pension but also for the French king's material assistance to Bruce supporters in Scotland during the late 1330s, for Philip's refusal to countenance Anglo-French truces if they did not include Scotland, and for his dispatch of small expeditions of French knights to assist the Scottish war effort between 1337 and 1341; two of the French king's future marischals, Eugene de Garancières and Arnoul d'Audrehen, gained their first experience of Scotland at this time, and French knights took part in the successful siege of Perth in August 1339.

Thus what is sometimes described as the 'first reign' of David II (1341–46) was largely taken up with the king's plans to aid his French ally by opening a second front in northern England. There were some successes: Edinburgh castle had fallen to the Scots shortly before King David's return, and an abortive raid on the Scottish south by Edward III in the following winter was promptly followed by the descent of David II on Northumberland in February 1342, a raid which paved the way for the recapture of the castles of Roxburgh and Stirling. These achievements were marred by internal dissensions which cast doubt on David's ability to provide firm rule; in June of 1342 Alexander Ramsay of Dalhousie, who had captured Roxburgh for the Scots, was attacked while holding his sheriff court at Hawick by William Douglas, the 'Knight of Liddesdale', and subsequently imprisoned and murdered in Hermitage castle. David II, significantly on the intercession of Robert the Steward, granted Douglas a remission for the murder. The issue, however, would not go away, and would not be settled by the king, but by the young William, lord of Douglas, whose ambition to control the middle march led to his organising Liddesdale's ambush and murder in 1353.

John of Fordun saw in the first of these murders an end to the good fortune which he claimed that the Scots had enjoyed since Culblean in 1335. The years 1346–7 would certainly provide support for such a view. King David was given the chance to assist his French ally when Edward III embarked on a major expedition to Normandy in July 1346. And there could be no doubt that Philip VI needed assistance. With varying degrees of success, English armies had made inroads into Flanders, Brittany, and Gascony in the previous year and the start of 1346; and Edward III's landing on the Cotentin peninsula was rapidly followed by the bloody siege and fall of Caen and a devastating inland raid by the English. Just short of Paris, Edward III turned north, forded the Seine and headed for Calais. Philip VI pursued the English army, whose commander was temporarily frustrated by the need to ford the river Somme; and at length, on 26 August 1346, the two armies met at Crécy in Ponthieu. The French king, his allies the kings of Bohemia, Navarre and Majorca, and a huge army were overthrown in a battle won by Edward III's good generalship and the deadly effects of the English longbow. Crécy produced the result that had not been achieved seven years before at Buironfosse; David II should have been there.

In fact, King David was busy masterminding his own individual disaster on the borders. He and Randolph had already raided Cumberland and Westmorland, and he might have left it at that. But the continued absence of Edward III, who had begun the siege of Calais on 4 September, and the summoning of English reinforcements to France, appear to have convinced David II that, with northern England militarily weak, he could achieve military success there, much in the manner of his father, the hero king. So he summoned the host to Perth for 6 October. There were the usual portents of disaster, both before and after the event: Ranald MacRuari was murdered in the nunnery of Elcho at the instigation of his rival William, earl of Ross, just before the muster – hardly a good omen for Scottish magnate co-operation in the field; and according to Walter Bower, St Cuthbert appeared in a dream to David

II, bringing 'the mild request' that the Scots should not invade or damage his lands.

However, King David, 'just as a snake foolishly closes his ears in response to a charmer', pressed on with his army, though it was late in the campaigning season and his ultimate objective is obscure; certainly the host was swiftly weakened by desertions. On the rainy morning of 17 October 1346, the Scottish host was surprised by an English force mustered by William la Zouche, archbishop of York, at Neville's Cross, a mile from Durham. In the ensuing mêlée, David II was deserted by both Robert the Steward and Patrick, earl of March; the earl of Ross had already defected. Well supported by those to whom he had given patronage since 1341, David fought on, and after being seriously wounded by an arrow in the face, he was captured by John Coupland, though not before the king had knocked out two of Coupland's teeth. Amongst the Scottish dead were John Randolph, earl of Moray; Maurice Murray, earl of Strathearn; Chancellor Charteris; Chamberlain Carrick; Sir Robert Keith, the Marischal; Hay, the Constable; and a host of David's favoured knights. Those captured included John Graham, earl of Menteith, who was subsequently executed by Edward III. Lost for ever was the Black Rood of St Margaret, which the king had brought to the field. The battle would later be mythologised by the chivalric French chronicler Jean Froissart, who saw it as an honourable occasion – 'celebrating the sport and participants regardless of the result', as Michael Penman puts it – which had occurred because David II had proposed to do 'some gallant deeds of renown' before returning to Scotland. The truth was rather more sobering: in the course of a single autumn, French and Scottish armies had been totally overthrown by those of England; and the King of Scots, who had lost his counsellors and aristocratic friends by death or capture, was a prisoner in the Tower of London.

New Solutions to Old Problems:
the Stewarts and the Alliance

David II had received his early schooling in chivalry in France. Now, following his capture at Neville's Cross in 1346, he would find a new chivalric mentor in Edward III of England, sharing his enthusiasm for Arthurian legends of the Round Table and the new Order of the Garter, and attending at least two St George's Day tournaments, at Windsor in 1349 and Smithfield in 1357. Though he was nominally King of Scots for twenty-five years after his capture in 1346, David spent eleven of these as a prisoner in England, lending himself to the chivalric ethos of his captor, and most of them concocting abortive plans for his release, and subsequently for the remission of his huge ransom and an English succession in Scotland if he should die without a legitimate heir. Thus the 'second reign' of David II (1357–71) stood in stark contrast to the first; and the Franco-Scottish alliance hardly figured in it at all.

To a large extent, the alliance was kept alive by the man who had deserted King David at Neville's Cross (though he was hardly alone in this), Robert the Steward. The heir presumptive's military experience – the sieges, raids, and scorched earth of the 1330s – was very different from that of his royal uncle. Warfare was no chivalric game in Scotland, more a grim struggle for survival. In this sense at least, the Steward was an appropriate replacement for David II; he had already been royal lieutenant in 1335 and 1338–41, and was to occupy the office again from 1347 to 1350, and from around 1354 to 1357. A far more astute diplomat than David, the Steward espoused a different, and more cautious, view of the Auld Alliance: it would continue to serve as a guarantee of the integrity of the independent Scottish kingdom, and the two allies would co-operate, as far as possible, in winning back territory lost to the common English enemy – in the case of the Scots the southern sheriffdoms overrun by the English and Edward Balliol a few months after Neville's Cross.

King David's position, whether as Edward III's prisoner or during his short periods on parole, did not improve. It may have been a demand by the English king in 1349 for David's recognition of Edward as lord superior of Scotland as a condition of his release which drove David to propose, as early as 1350, that a younger son of Edward III should be recognised as heir presumptive in Scotland. With such a proposal, of course, went the necessity of making concessions to the disinherited and the removal of Robert the Steward from the succession. When David was eventually released by the Treaty of Berwick of 1357, he was saddled with an enormous ransom of 100,000 marks (£66,666 sterling), to be paid in instalments over ten years; much of the remainder of his life was taken up with plans to have the ransom annulled in return for some form of English succession in Scotland. Apologists for David II have claimed that the king's policy was a wise one, achieving the double objective of undermining the Steward and cancelling the ransom. When this had been achieved, the argument runs, David would confound the English by producing a son and heir.

Perhaps; but there is no way of knowing that this is what was in David's mind, and in the event the king's second marriage, to Margaret Logie in 1362, ended not with an heir but with a divorce. It may be that David, a prisoner who had to watch the Steward's power in Scotland become more and more entrenched during his enforced absence, made a complete *volte-face* in diplomatic policy with no clear idea where it would lead, but in order to frustrate his rival and experiment with alternative settlements. He had, after all, inherited the French alliance from his father Robert I; he had done his best for it, and failed; and he never formally renewed it.

By contrast, Robert the Steward was a committed supporter of the alliance. His motives may have been cynical; obviously after 1346, and especially after King David's first proposals of an English succession, the Steward could further his own cause by wrapping himself in the national flag and adhering to the Auld Alliance. Scots were, and remained, divided over David's 'English' proposals and the political alternatives to these; but it seems that a majority – perhaps a large majority – would have no truck with David's various diplomatic schemes, especially as the 1360s advanced. The Steward, in pointing up the differences between himself and the king and taking advantage of David's temporary weakness, may be regarded as an unscrupulous opportunist; but he was also heir presumptive, a great magnate with a large family and huge affinity, and a man who had experienced the hard times – and French assistance – of the 1330s at first hand.

As lieutenant, the Steward wasted little time in showing his French sympathies. In November 1347, he issued acts under the captive David II's great seal banning all Flemings from Scotland and transferring the Scottish staple from Bruges in Flanders to Middelburg in Zeeland. The aim was probably political rather than commercial, as the Flemings had sided with Edward III against Philip VI of France. Less than a fortnight later, on 22 November 1347, the Steward requested – by way of the kings of France and Scotland – a papal dispensation for his marriage to the late Elizabeth Mure (the couple had been within the forbidden degrees of consanguinity) and the right to legitimise the sizeable offspring – by this stage four sons and two daughters – of the match. The dispensation, promptly granted by the French Avignonese pope Clement VI, former archbishop of Rouen and supporter of Philip VI of France, brought the Stewart dynasty a step closer; and the captive David II was apparently powerless to prevent what he must have regarded as the misuse of his seal in enhancing the status of his rival.

In August 1350 Philip VI died and was succeeded by his son John II, a man of similar chivalric ideals and impulses. In 1351, when a David II release deal seemed to be in the offing, and possibly on the prompting of the Steward, the French king wrote to the Scots warning that King David might be restored by force by the English; to avert this he offered the services of 500 men-at-arms and 500 archers. In subsequent letters, he offered to restore the French lands of Edward Balliol, who by this stage was clinging on to Buittle castle in Galloway and not much else. Balliol, John claimed, was in any case considering making peace with France and the Scots. Finally, in the summer of 1352, the French king offered the services of his fleet to protect Scottish merchant shipping, and promised to maintain the Franco-Scottish alliance.

David was not released at this time, so that John II's letters to the Scots were no more than diplomatic straws in the wind. In the spring of 1355, however, the French king sent Eugene de Garancières – a soldier already familiar with Scotland – with fifty men-at-arms, later reinforced with a gift of 40,000 gold *écus* (around 15,000 marks) to be distributed amongst the Scottish magnates on condition that they broke the English truce. The earls of Angus and March did so, joining with the French in a surprise assault on Berwick in November 1355. Edward III, just returned from France, was forced to intervene, coming north to relieve Berwick and to conduct the devastating raid on south-east Scotland which was later dubbed 'The Burnt Candlemas' (February 1356). It was certainly bad enough: the Franciscan friary in Haddington was burned, the pilgrimage church of Whitekirk was pillaged, and Edward III's armies laid waste the countryside in what was to prove his last Scottish campaign. Yet signs of a Scottish recovery were already underway; for at Roxburgh in January, Edward Balliol had at last given up the unequal struggle. He formally resigned his kingdom – now virtually lost – to Edward III in return for a fat English pension and an initial gift of 5,000 marks. Rivals for the Scottish throne had been reduced from three to two.

This see-saw of international diplomacy and war lurched violently in one direction in the autumn of 1356. On 19 September, at Maupertuis near Poitiers, a huge French host led by King John himself encountered an English force under the command of Edward, the 'Black Prince', Edward III's son. At the French council of war before the battle, the king knighted William, lord of Douglas (the future first earl), who had joined the army with his kinsman Archibald Douglas and a retinue estimated at 200–300 men, many of them archers. The French were confident of victory, and refused attempts to negotiate; but they were concerned not to charge headlong at the strong defensive English position and be mown down by archers in the attempt. According to the chronicler Froissart, it was the lord of Douglas who gave King John the advice that the French cavalry should dismount and advance on foot. The result, after trudging uphill *en masse* in full armour, was a hard-fought struggle in which the French were totally defeated; worse, King John was captured. To all appearances the Franco-Scottish alliance was in ruins: Edward III now had the kings of Scotland and France as his prisoners.

However, at this point the English king overplayed his hand in France.

In a misjudged expedition which was intended to place him on the French throne, Edward III laid siege to Rheims, where French kings were traditionally crowned. Stout resistance, followed by appalling weather, forced Edward to move on, and his encirclement of Paris produced no results. This was largely because the French had at last learned the lessons of Crécy and Poitiers; the young dauphin Charles (the future Charles V), proclaimed Regent for the captive John II and struggling to contain internal insurrection in France (the *Jacquerie* of 1358) and the indiscriminate pillaging of mercenary Free Companies, had the good sense not to engage the English king in a pitched battle. Edward III ran short of supplies, his campaign fizzled out, and the Treaty of Brétigny (1360) was the eventual result. This 'dishonourable peace' left Edward III with an enlarged Gascony, and in the north, Ponthieu, Calais, and Guines, all to be held in full sovereignty; but the English king had to give up using the title of King of France. Neither side had satisfactorily resolved the issues which had been at stake at the outset of the war, so Brétigny amounted to no more than an extended truce. Edward III's sizeable consolation was the agreed ransoms – £66,000 sterling already agreed for David II at Berwick in 1357, and ten times that figure for Jean II of France in 1360.

The Treaty of Brétigny had also stipulated the breaking of the Franco-Scottish alliance. However, the continuing popularity of that alliance had been demonstrated as recently as 1359. Michael Penman has argued convincingly that David II's efforts to impose an English succession deal in return for an annulment of his ransom came to a head in a general council at Dundee in April of that year; in spite of growing Anglo-Scottish trade, pilgrimage, and an English commitment to the establishment of a system of border tribunals to preserve the truce, King David had seriously underestimated the anti-English sentiment of the Scottish estates. This is strikingly revealed in the commission granted on 10 May 1359 to the Scottish ambassadors who were to proceed to France to secure a 'firmer alliance and confederation' between the two kingdoms. For the alliance, if renewed, was to be binding upon 'the king of Scots, *of his lieutenant, or others of sufficient power*' [my italics]. Previous, and indeed later, Franco-Scottish treaties were all made on behalf of the king of Scots and his heirs. Clearly David II faced strong Scottish opposition to his English schemes in the spring of 1359; thus in June, though the Scottish ambassadors in Paris spoke in the name of their king, they were in fact seeking to further the pro-French policy of Robert the Steward.

Franco-Scottish negotiations led to an agreement ratified by the Regent Charles on 29 June 1359. If it had been taken further, this new Treaty of Paris would have committed the Regent to paying the Scots

50,000 marks by the following Easter; in return the Scots would renew the alliance and – at some unspecified time – make war on the English.

This treaty of 1359, though ratified by the Regent Charles, was overtaken by the events of the following years. But it stands as an example of the growing strength of the alliance, for it was made, not by two kings, but by a tenacious lieutenant and a hard-headed dauphin, acting on behalf of, but probably not with the consent of, their chivalric masters. Certainly on the Scottish side, the French alliance had become closely associated with the wishes of a majority amongst politically active Scots.

Thus the 1360s proved to be no more than a temporary setback for the alliance. Within Scotland, there was undoubtedly 'intensive government', as Dr Nicholson calls it, on the part of David II, but no acceptable solution to the problems posed by the succession and the ransom was found. David's aggressive advancement of his friends and obvious hostility to the large and powerful Stewart affinity would probably have led, sooner rather than later, to civil war; but on 22 February 1371, King David suddenly died in Edinburgh at the age of forty-seven. The Bruce dynasty died with him. His nephew Robert the Steward, eight years David's senior, the man against whom the late king had struggled for a generation, became the first ruler of the Stewart dynasty as Robert II. Not surprisingly, the new king, who had fought with the French in the late 1330s and who was mainly responsible for the 1351–2 and 1359 negotiations, ordered an embassy to France within three days of his coronation. Its leader was Archibald Douglas, lord of Galloway (the future 3rd earl), who had fought at Poitiers; and the result was the Treaty of Vincennes of 28 October 1371, the first formal renewal of the alliance since Corbeil in 1326. For almost two centuries after 1371, every Stewart ruler would renew the Auld Alliance; and, unsurprisingly, most English rulers would seek to bring it to an end, by negotiation or, more frequently, by war.

Growing English concern over the Franco-Scottish alliance is understandable; for the high-water mark of Edward III's success in the Hundred Years' War was the late 1350s, after the battle of Poitiers. But from the late 1360s, a decline in English fortunes began to set in. Partly this was a result of Edward III's failure to evolve a coherent strategy when the war was renewed in 1369; but there was also the matter of vastly improved leadership on the French side. In April 1364, John II of France, having chivalrously re-entered English captivity after his hostage second son Louis, duke of Anjou, had escaped, died in London; he was succeeded by Charles V, who as dauphin had already acted as Regent and was an opponent of a much more formidable stamp. In 1369 Charles, by consenting to hear judicial appeals from lords within the

THE SCOTTISH SUCCESSION: BRUCES AND STEWARTS

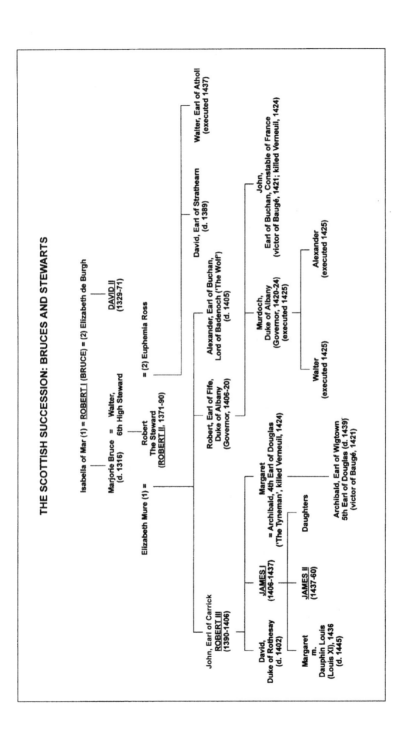

duchy of Gascony, whose duke was Edward, the Black Prince, effectively renewed the war with England. The French king had the advantage of the support of Henry of Trastamara, King of Castile; for the Black Prince had backed the wrong horse in the recent Castilian civil war, with the result that the French now had an ally with a powerful fleet. In 1372 an English fleet bringing reinforcements to Gascony was defeated in a sea battle off La Rochelle by the Castilian navy, and the English position in the duchy became increasingly precarious. Highly expensive English expeditions in 1369, 1373 and 1375 achieved little in any of the main areas of conflict, Gascony, Brittany, and the north; and the French refusal to be drawn into battle – a tactic of Charles V and (when the king could restrain him) his great Breton lieutenant, Bertrand du Guesclin – frustrated the English commanders and led to vociferous complaints at home, where the war was increasingly regarded as a costly failure.

The Franco-Scottish Treaty of Vincennes of October 1371 should therefore be seen in this European context of French revival and English decline. Some elements of the treaty were traditional: French aid and counsel to the Scots against England, Scots assistance to the French in the Anglo-French war once the short truce between the two enemies had expired or been annulled, and a Scottish requirement that the French would not conclude a truce or peace with the English without the kingdom of Scotland being included in its provisions. It is clear, however, that the French wished to go further than this; Charles V offered to pay off the substantial remainder of David II's ransom and to send a French expedition to Scotland to re-open the second front against England. Robert II, as the founder of a new dynasty less than a year old, rejected this French offer and chose to continue the payments of the late king's ransom to Edward III. Robert's caution is understandable; from his predecessor he had inherited not only a substantial debt but also a fourteen-year truce with England; and indeed there had been no fighting with the English since 1356. As king – rather than as a great magnate opposing the king – Robert was treading warily in his relationships with the warlike border magnates, the earls of Douglas and March and Archibald Douglas, lord of Galloway, for he was not in a position to dictate to them. Robert II, unlike the deceased David II, was a consensual rather than a confrontational ruler; he had to be.

So the official line in 1371 was to renew the Auld Alliance in the same terms as its earlier incarnations of 1295 and 1326; and twenty years later Robert II's son and successor, Robert III, would follow the same path in the Franco-Scottish treaty of 1391. This essentially defensive view of the alliance reflected the Scottish crown's initial weakness; but in the summer of 1377 Edward III, the Scottish kingdom's opponent over half-a-century, died, leaving Richard II, a boy of ten, as king. The Scots promptly ceased their annual payments of David II's ransom. As Ranald Nicholson succinctly puts it: 'The wars of independence were over. A war of chivalry on the borders was about to begin'.

That war would be conducted by the great border magnates, whose motives certainly included the recovery of territory lost to the Scottish kingdom during the Wars of Independence, but who were also moved by the prospect of extending their march lordships. Robert II did not attempt to stop, for example, the sacking and burning of Roxburgh by George, earl of March, in 1377, or William earl of Douglas's great raid through the west march as far as Penrith in 1380. The king may have approved; by August of 1383 he had gone back on his earlier refusal to receive French expeditionary forces in Scotland; but late in the following year he was removed from government by his son and heir John, earl of Carrick (the future Robert III), who publicly espoused a more aggressive approach to Anglo-Scottish relations.

Such was the context of one of the most famous of all the border raids of the 1380s, the Franco-Scottish expedition of the summer of 1385. Although this foray was later described by the Scottish chroniclers Wyntoun and Bower, the account of it most often cited is the highly coloured version of Jean Froissart. From this we have the enduring view of Robert II as a weak and ineffective ruler, arriving in Edinburgh late and reluctant to fight. Froissart, however, is a heavily biased source; he had visited Scotland in 1365, admired the chivalric approach to war of David II and the Douglases, and was not only anti-Stewart but anti-Scots in his outlook. 'In Scotland', he remarks, 'you will never find a man of worth: they are like savages, who wish not to be acquainted with any one.'

Froissart makes much of the unsurprising fact that when the French expedition of 1385, led by the Admiral of France, Jean de Vienne, had arrived and billeted itself in the Lothians, servants of the French knights were beaten up by the locals when they went out foraging for their masters. He also comments unfavourably on the Scots nobles' refusal to give battle to a superior English army, adopting instead the tactics of scorched earth, harrying and burning which should surely have been familiar to the chronicler from the strategy employed by Charles V of France in the 1360s and 1370s.

The raid of 1385 was in any case intended only as part of a grand design, a dual invasion of England with one French army joining with the Scots and invading from the north, while a larger French force would make the sea crossing from Sluys in Flanders and attack southern England. An advance party – around thirty French knights and squires – jumped the gun and landed at Montrose in 1384, subsequently conducting a raid on northern England. But the main event was the landing, at Leith and Dunbar in May 1385, of Jean de Vienne and his army. This was apparently of a decent size, perhaps around fifteen hundred men; and they brought some fifty thousand gold francs as a further incentive to their allies.

The grand design, however, fell apart because no French fleet was sent with troops to invade southern England, from Sluys or anywhere else. Its failure to materialise freed the young Richard II of England and his uncle John of Gaunt to intervene personally in Scotland with a huge army. Robert II's arrival in Edinburgh to summon the Scottish host provided a further opportunity for Froissart to castigate the king as 'no valiant man', and as having 'red bleared eyes, of the colour of sandal-wood'. No reference is made to the fact that the king was sixty-nine, that the Scots were facing almost certain defeat in battle, or even that Robert had been removed from power in a *coup d'état* the previous November.

Apart from the presence in the Scottish army of an unprecedentedly large number of French troops, the campaign which followed was depressingly familiar. The Scots could not risk encountering the host of Richard II in a pitched battle, and contented themselves with savage raids on the west march of England; the east border and the Lothians, virtually undefended, were plundered by the English. The great abbeys of Melrose, Dryburgh and Newbattle were burned, as was the burgh of Edinburgh and the church of St Giles; and Holyrood abbey would have suffered the same fate if John of Gaunt had not interceded on its behalf with Richard II. The English king was able to give monasteries to the flames with impunity, for in the Great Schism of the papacy in 1378, England had backed Pope Urban VI, while the French and Scots supported his rival Robert of Geneva, elected by eleven French cardinals and taking the name of Clement VII. Thus, very conveniently for the English invading army, the Scots clergy were in league with the anti-pope and could be regarded as schismatics who ought to be rooted out. The dismal summer war came to an end when the English, desperately short of provisions, withdrew and left the Scots to count the cost. Understandably the French were not popular in Lothian, and damages were laid against them; if Froissart is to be believed, Jean de Vienne was left as a hostage in Scotland until the money for his release was raised at Bruges. The departing French expedition, as Froissart has it, cursed the Scots, 'and wished the King of France would make a truce with the English for two or three years, and then march to Scotland and utterly destroy it'. One modern writer puts it more kindly when he suggests that 'the auld alliance was always more cordial when French and Scots were at a distance'.

Perhaps: but the alliance had survived throughout the fourteenth century because both kingdoms, to a greater or lesser degree, needed each other. Neither side could live up to Étienne de Conty's impossibly optimistic claim, made in 1400, that the Scots had always loved the French, and the French the Scots; but it would be difficult to deny that the Auld Alliance, in its first century of existence, had achieved much more than could reasonably have been expected of it, or that the French had helped to preserve the independence of the Scottish kingdom in the 1330s. The fifteenth century would see a reversal of roles, with the Scots being called upon to save the kingdom of France.

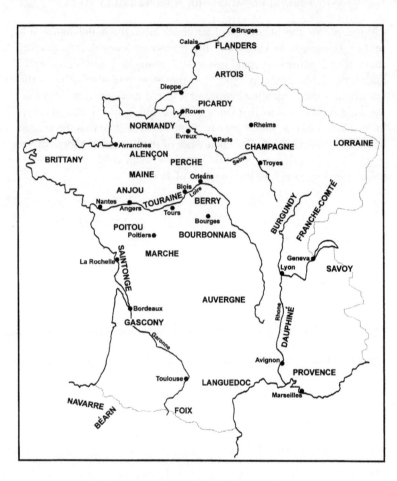

LATE MEDIEVAL FRANCE

Dukedoms and Counties: e.g. **PICARDY**

Major towns and cities:　　　　　●

'La Grande Armée Ecossaise': 1419–1429

Beginnings: Scots Abroad before 1419

In spite of his remote geographical location on the north-western fringes of Europe, the medieval Scot was a familiar figure within the European Continent. As early as the thirteenth century, he might be found as a trader in France, Flanders, the Baltic, or Norway; as a pilgrim, or crusader, a century earlier; as a student or scholar, both north and south of the Alps; and as a mercenary soldier in France and Flanders, in growing numbers, from the fourteenth century.

Scots abroad in medieval Europe could be identified either because they were known to be inhabitants of the Kingdom of Scotland and therefore vassals of the King of Scots, or alternatively by the European perception of the characteristics and mode of dress peculiar to the Scots. In the case of the latter, we have the evidence of a disapproving Premonstratensian canon from the diocese of Cambrai, commenting on the barbaric appearance of a party of western Scots travelling through Flanders in 1147, either as pilgrims or, more probably, en route for the Second Crusade. The Flemish witness noted that the Scots wore a general covering down to the knee, closed over at the front and back, but open at the sides; 'and it was clearly seen that some of these people . . . were not wearing drawers'. The Scots were presumably Highlanders, attired in some form of early kilt, 'producing', as Geoffrey Barrow delicately puts it when describing Highland elements in the Scottish host of 1296, 'an effect of nakedness about the lower quarters of the body which had long struck foreign observers with amazement'.

More revealing, in a rather different way, is a tale from around the same time narrated by Jocelin of Brakelond, the chronicler of the great Suffolk abbey of Bury St Edmonds. Around 1159–60 Abbot Samson of Bury undertook the hazardous journey to Rome – hazardous because a recent papal election had produced a schism, and while the English church had backed the eventual winner, Pope Alexander III, many of the Italian states had been slow to follow suit; and already some clergy carrying letters from Pope Alexander had been imprisoned, hanged, or mutilated. To avoid this fate and reach Rome in safety, Samson pretended to be a Scot – that is, by wearing Scottish dress and 'behaving like a Scot'. This behaviour consisted of brandishing a stick as though it were a spear, and

using threatening language 'as Scotsmen do'. Samson's attire suggests a
Lowland Scot rather than a Highlander, for his clothing, though tattered,
included breeches and boots, as well as old slippers 'which I carried over
my shoulders in the Scottish manner'. His crude impersonation seems to
have worked on the journey out to Rome, but on the way back his
performance appears to have been less convincing, for he was arrested
and robbed.

Taken together with much patchy evidence from the same period, the
observations of the Cambrai canon and the unfortunate Abbot Samson
suggest that, more than eight centuries before earnest souls committed
themselves to interminable conferences on the subject, Scottish identity
had made more than a passing impression on Europeans on both sides of
the Alps. The image of the Scot at this time is not, perhaps, an altogether
flattering one; but his distinctiveness is not in doubt.

By the fourteenth century, the number of Scots travelling to Europe,
and settling in France, had certainly increased, partly as a result of the
Franco-Scottish alliance. The rough edges of twelfth-century 'barbarism'
appear to have been smoothed out by this stage: in their place we find the
origins of the Scots College in Paris in Bishop David Murray of Moray's
1325 endowment towards the permanent maintenance of four poor
Moray scholars at the University of Paris. The Anglo-Scottish wars of the
period made it impossible for Scots students to attend Oxford or
Cambridge; and Murray, who had preached to his own flock that to fight
for the Kingdom of Scotland against the English was as praiseworthy as
crusading against the Saracens, would have been unlikely to send his own
students to England even in time of peace or truce. So Scots went to Paris
or Orléans universities, the latter the most important law school in
northern Europe, by 1336 housing enough matriculated Scots to form a
Scottish 'nation' within the university. When the refugee David II of
Scotland and his queen were briefly entertained by Philip VI of France in
Paris in the late spring of 1334, they were welcomed by the influential
Scottish expatriates Richard Lescot and Humphrey Kirkpatrick, the
latter soon to become abbot of the great Abbey of St Denis, the traditional
burial place of the French monarchy. By the following century the gradual
entrenchment of Scots in the French ecclesiastical hierarchy would
produce the Bishop of Orléans who welcomed Joan of Arc on the raising
of the English siege of Orléans in 1429; and at the outset of the sixteenth
century, an ambitious Scot, Andrew Forman, attained one of the greatest
prizes of all, the archbishopric of Bourges.

Probably, however, the most enduring image of the fourteenth-century
Scot in France is of the soldier rather than the scholar or ecclesiastic. The
Hundred Years' War, as much as the formal Franco-Scottish alliance,

drew Scots in sizeable numbers to fight in France, and we catch glimpses of them at various stages of the conflict. Foremost amongst these, as Michael Brown has shown, were the Douglases; probably both William, lord of Douglas (the future first earl), and his cousin Archibald (the future third earl, Archibald 'the Grim'), spent their youth and early manhood at David II's court-in-exile at Château Gaillard. Thus they considered themselves as much French as Scottish noblemen, and it was natural that both should fight for King John II at Poitiers in 1356. Scots were to be found in the marauding 'Free Companies' of the late 1350s and early 1360s, and in the army of Bertrand du Guesclin, Charles V's constable, in the Castilian civil war of the late '60s.

These Scottish soldiers, organised in companies of men-at-arms and archers under aristocratic leaders, were attracted by the prospect of pay and plunder; and they did not fight exclusively for the King of France. In the 1350s the earls of Angus and Mar agreed to provide troops, presumably drawn from their own estates, to serve Edward III of England in France; and Sir John Swinton, a prominent Berwickshire warlord, played the mercenary game very adroitly, taking the duke of Lancaster's money for himself and his following of sixty, only to use it later in border war against the English. For the most part, however, Scots appear to have adhered to the military alliance with France. This applied not only to the grim Anglo-Scottish border warfare, with its costly victory of Otterburn in 1388 and catastrophic defeat at Humbleton in 1402, but to the regular despatch to France, in terms of the official alliance, of Scottish soldiers. Thus in September 1390 we find Charles VI of France paying 600 francs to Guillaume de Cantiers and Audart de Brueil to go to Scotland for the purpose of raising soldiers to fight in France; those recruited may well have been the hundred Scottish archers paid 1100 francs by Louis, duke of Touraine, Charles VI's son, on their discharge the following June.

Links between Scotland and France's ally Castile seem to have been maintained after the initial assistance to Henry of Trastamara and Bertrand du Guesclin in the late 1360s. A decade later John Mercer, a Scottish seaman whose father was in the service of the first earl of Douglas, led a fleet of Scottish, French, and Spanish ships in an attack on English shipping; and this may have been the prelude to an alliance between Douglas and the Castilians in 1379, with a Castilian fleet being held ready to transport French knights and men-at-arms from Normandy to Scotland.

By the early fifteenth century, then, the Scots, either following their lords to France, recruited in Scotland by French agents, or forming part of a small but influential expatriate community in France itself, were committed allies of the House of Valois and had some maritime links with the Kingdom of Castile. In the autumn of 1419, these factors would prove vital to the survival of the French dauphin Charles in his darkest hour.

Charles the Mad

The last decade of the fourteenth century, and the first of the fifteenth, produced political, diplomatic and dynastic traumas for the Kingdoms of Scotland, France, and England. The Scots, saddled from 1390 with the feeble Robert III, removed him temporarily in 1399 to hand royal authority to his elder son David, duke of Rothesay, who ruled as lieutenant-general for three years before being arrested and dying, probably as the result of foul play, in his uncle's castle of Falkland in Fife. That uncle, Robert Stewart, duke of Albany, Robert III's brother, already the power behind the throne since 1388, took temporary control of government in 1402. The ageing and ailing Robert III now looked to protect his surviving son Prince James (the future James I) from Albany in 1406; in what may have been no more than a botched raid on the Lothians by the heir to the throne, things went badly wrong, and the prince took refuge on the Bass Rock; after a month's delay, James was picked up by a ship which should have taken him to France. However, he was seized by English pirates en route, and spent the next eighteen years as a prisoner, guest, or – latterly – companion-in-arms of the English king. His father, Robert III, died within a fortnight of James's capture, and Robert Stewart, duke of Albany, 'the uncrowned king of Scots', became governor of Scotland until his death in 1420.

Around the same time, the Kingdom of England witnessed an even more drastic change in the deposition of Richard II. King Richard, the son of the Black Prince, was unfortunate in that he was associated with failure in the Hundred Years' War and had to endure the inevitable problems associated with the greater nobility following a royal minority. However, he showed little talent for kingship, and his relentless pursuit of his uncle John of Gaunt, duke of Lancaster, led to the latter's son Henry taking up arms, deposing the king in September 1399, and taking the throne as Henry IV, the first of the Lancastrian line of kings. With remarkable speed, the new English king revived the ancient demand for superiority over Scotland – based not only on genuine documents drawn from the English records, but also on forgeries – and led a huge army north in August 1400. Henry's intentions have never been clear, largely because his host wasted a fortnight in the Lothians without doing much damage, and subsequently went home on the basis, apparently, of a Scottish promise to consider his claim to overlordship.

The Scots' response, though delayed, was predictable. Not only did

THE HOUSE OF VALOIS IN THE FIFTEENTH CENTURY

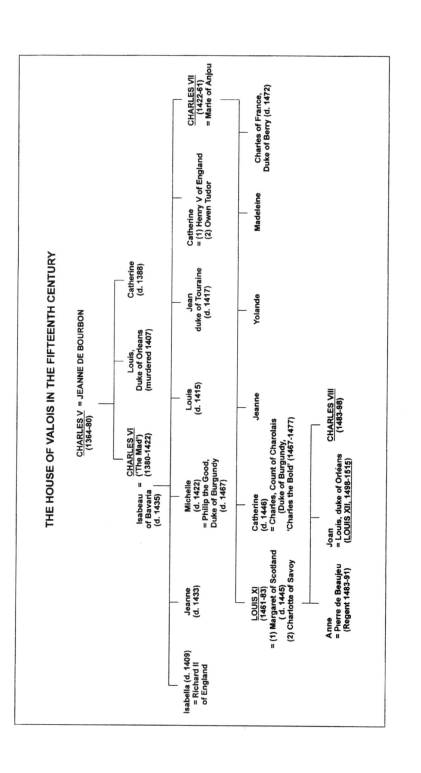

CHARLES V = JEANNE DE BOURBON
(1364-80)

Isabeau = CHARLES VI
of Bavaria   ('The Mad')
(d. 1435)   (1380-1422)

Louis,
Duke of Orléans
(murdered 1407)

Catherine
(d. 1388)

CHARLES VII
(1422-61)
= Marie of Anjou

Isabella (d. 1409)
= Richard II
of England

Jeanne
(d. 1433)

Michelle
(d. 1422)
= Phillip the Good,
Duke of Burgundy
(d. 1467)

Louis
(d. 1415)

Jean
duke of Touraine
(d. 1417)

Catherine
= (1) Henry V of England
(2) Owen Tudor

LOUIS XI
(1461-83)
= (1) Margaret of Scotland
(d. 1445)
(2) Charlotte of Savoy

Catherine
(d. 1446)
= Charles, Count of Charolais
(Duke of Burgundy,
'Charles the Bold' (1467-1477)

Jeanne

Yolande

Madeleine

Charles of France,
Duke of Berry (d. 1472)

Joan
= Louis, duke of Orléans
(LOUIS XII, 1498-1515)

CHARLES VIII
(1483-98)

Anne
= Pierre de Beaujeu
(Regent 1483-91)

they produce an impostor whom they claimed was the deposed Richard II, but they also launched a full-scale plunder raid into northern England in September 1402. It ended in total disaster at Humbleton near Wooler; the English, led by Henry Percy and the disaffected Dunbar earl of March, won a devastating victory, and the huge list of Scots captured included Murdoch Stewart, son and heir of governor Albany, and Archibald, fourth earl of Douglas. Humbleton brought to a decisive end the border warfare which the Scots had conducted with some success over a generation. There would be no further full-scale Anglo-Scottish border battles until Flodden in 1513. In the meantime, the Scottish governor's son went south as a prisoner, to be joined less than four years later by the uncrowned King of Scots, James I.

But it was in early fifteenth-century France that the worst disruption occurred. In the summer of 1392, while on a punitive expedition to Brittany, King Charles VI, aged 23, suddenly attacked his servants and his brother Louis, duke of Orléans. Thereafter, for the remaining thirty years of his life, he was afflicted by periodic lengthy bouts of mental illness. A regency was necessary, and it could only be supplied by the king's relatives, including his brother the duke of Orléans, and by Orléans' great rival (from 1404), John the Fearless, duke of Burgundy. Not only were these men deadly enemies, but they took different stances in their attitudes to England and the papal schism, with Orléans favouring war with England and adherence to the Avignon Pope Benedict XIII, while John the Fearless took a neutral position over the schism and looked to friendship and alliance with England. In 1407 John the Fearless had Louis of Orléans murdered in Paris; the result was a deadly feud between the Orléanist-Armagnac faction and the Burgundians, and for France a bloody civil war as the great feudatories struggled to acquire the inheritance of Charles the Mad.

France's civil war, like Scotland's a century before, provided an excellent opportunity for English intervention. The young Henry V, who had succeeded his father in March 1413 and who was briefly to become one of the greatest warriors of the age, revived the struggle with France by renewing the lapsed English claim to the French throne in 1415; and in the summer of that year he invaded Normandy with 9,000 troops. On 25 October he won a spectacular victory at Agincourt, attributable not only to his military skill but to poor French tactics and dissensions amongst the leaders of the numerically vastly superior French army. In the summer of 1417, Henry V returned to Normandy to conduct a systematic war of conquest, meeting resistance only from the fortresses which he besieged.

The principal opponent of the English and Burgundians finally emerged in the unlikely form of the adolescent Charles, eleventh child of Charles the Mad and his queen, Isabeau of Bavaria. The deaths in rapid succession of his elder brothers Louis and Jean made Charles dauphin in 1417 at the age of fourteen. The role was not an enviable one, for Charles was little more than a leader of faction, forced to flee Paris with his Armagnac/Orléanist supporters in May 1418, leaving the city to the Burgundians. The war which the young dauphin would conduct against the English and Burgundians would be directed from the south, from the valleys of the Loire and Cher. Charles's 'Kingdom of Bourges' embraced Berry, the Touraine, and Poitou, with its *parlement* at Poitiers and its *chambre des comptes* at Bourges, while in the south the Limousin, Auvergne, and Languedoc all remained loyal. In little more than a generation, the dauphin would have become King Charles the Victorious, the ruler who threw the English out of France. But in 1418, when at the age of fifteen he assumed the title of lieutenant-general, his problem was simply to survive. His mother, Isabeau of Bavaria, disowned him, claiming that he was not her child – which in view of her many extra-marital affairs was certainly possible – and for a time exercised the regency for her mad husband.

Excluded from Paris by the Burgundians, whose ally the queen was solicitously watching over Charles the Mad, with the English entrenched in Normandy – Rouen fell to Henry V in 1418 – and Guyenne, and relying entirely on dispossessed men whose survival was closely bound up with his own, the dauphin looked abroad for allies. In the summers of 1418 and 1419, he appealed to the Scots and Castilians for military aid.

Buchan and Baugé (1419–1422)

It was not immediately obvious that the Scots would respond to Charles's appeal. When the Sieur de Plusquallec, governor of La Rochelle, arrived in Scotland at the head of the dauphin's embassy, the ageing governor, Robert Stewart, duke of Albany, had the problem of reconciling Charles's pleas with those made by a rival Burgundian embassy which sought to enlist Scottish aid for John the Fearless of Burgundy and his puppet, the demented Charles VI of France. Albany's allies in government, Archibald fourth earl of Douglas and Alexander earl of Mar, had both taken large forces, drawn from their own affinities, to serve John the Fearless; Douglas had been contracted to produce 4,000 men in a stand-off with the English in 1413, while Mar had earned a warlike reputation in his service to duke John against the Liègeois five years earlier. Albany, as custodian of the Franco-Scottish alliance, was therefore in a position to deploy large troops of seasoned soldiers in the French civil wars. The problem lay in deciding which side to support.

The wily governor had another choice to make. His nephew and sovereign, James I, now in his early twenties, was a prisoner of Henry V of England; thus committed support for the French alliance on Albany's part would discourage the English king from considering James's release. It is probable, however, that Albany had already made up his mind on that matter; for in 1416, after protracted negotiations, he had secured the release of King James's fellow prisoner, Albany's son and heir Murdoch Stewart. Thereafter he made no further moves to negotiate the king's release; indeed, in July 1417, and at the age of 77, Albany took part in an abortive siege of Berwick, while the earl of Douglas launched an unsuccessful attack on Roxburgh. This 'foul raid', undertaken during Henry V's second Normandy campaign, was hardly calculated to ease Anglo-Scottish tensions; but Albany's long-term aim seems to have been to provoke, rather than to soothe, the Lancastrian dynasty. He continued to recognise the 'Mammet', a pseudo-Richard II, until the latter's death in December 1419, when the impostor was buried at Stirling with full royal honours; and he supported the anti-Pope Benedict XIII long after it made any diplomatic sense to do so.

It has been suggested that Albany, in pursuing a strong anti-English foreign policy, was deliberately condemning his sovereign to further long years of English captivity in order to further his ambition to acquire the Scottish crown for himself or his heirs. While it is true that his son Murdoch succeeded Albany as governor in 1420, and while Albany himself must have been very conscious of his closeness to the crown, there was no way in which he could dictate events. Release of the king, after all, required not simply Scottish negotiation on his behalf, but an English willingness to let him go. In the tense European diplomatic situation of 1418, there was no likelihood that Henry V would risk returning their king to the Scots. So Albany committed himself to a robust foreign policy: with the consent of the Scottish estates, he authorised the sending to France of an army which would be commanded by his second son John Stewart, earl of Buchan, Chamberlain of Scotland.

This seaborne force was probably the largest army to be sent abroad in Scottish medieval history. Bower, writing more than two decades later, claimed that it numbered 7,000 men, and while this has been disputed, it may not be much of an exaggeration; the dauphin Charles, who after all was the Scots' paymaster, claimed that 6,000 had come to France. The army sailed from Dumbarton to La Rochelle in a Castilian fleet of forty ships, each of which, according to the agreement reached between the allies, had to be at least 150 tons; for protection there was a total of 4,000 sailors and crossbowmen and 200 men-at-arms. Most impressively,

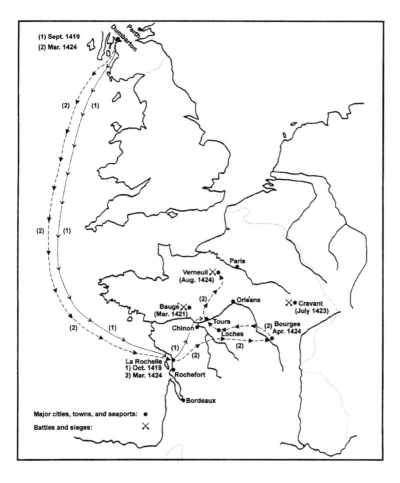

(1) Sept. 1419
(2) Mar. 1424

Perth
Dumbarton

(2) (1)

(2) (1)

(2) (1)

Paris

Verneuil ✕●
(Aug. 1424)

(2)

Baugé ✕●
(Mar. 1421)

Orléans

✕● Cravant
(July 1423)

Chinon ●

Tours

(2) Bourges
Apr. 1424

Loches ●

(1)

(2)

(2)

La Rochelle
1) Oct. 1419
2) Mar. 1424

Rochefort

● Bordeaux

Major cities, towns, and seaports: ●

Battles and sieges: ✕

1419-1424: SCOTTISH MILITARY ASSISTANCE TO THE DAUPHIN (CHARLES VII)

(1) The army of John Stewart, earl of Buchan and Archibald Douglas, earl of Wigtown (1419)

(2) The army of Archibald, 4th Earl of Douglas (1424)

wages of 119,000 *livres tournois* were paid in advance by the dauphin. This 'armée de mer' embarked towards the end of September 1419, and late in October, following a sea-fight with an English fleet off the French west coast, the Scots came safely to harbour at La Rochelle.

They were by no means the first to arrive. The dauphin had not confined his appeal to Scots and Castilian mercenaries; Savoyards and Lombards, many of them crossbowmen, were already in France by the autumn of 1418. It is, however, the Scots who predominate, albeit commanded by French captains: Michel de Normanville's hundred Scottish archers at Loches in November; a further twenty-nine at the siege of Tours, held by the Burgundians, in December; and an unspecified number of Scots under Louis d'Escrouilles in the dauphinist garrison of Melun, south of Paris. Some Scots commanders were already in Berry, at the heart of the 'Kingdom of Bourges', by May 1419; William Douglas of Drumlanrig and his lieutenant Thomas Kilpatrick headed 150 men-at-arms and 300 archers at Méhun-sur-Yèvre, near Bourges. They were involved in heavy fighting in the Sarthe district as the English advanced south through Lower Normandy and Maine during the summer of 1419; and on 4 September they were reviewed by the dauphin at Montereau-sur-Yonne.

This was the scene, six days later, of the event which made the dauphin's difficult position little short of desperate – the murder of the duke of Burgundy, John the Fearless, by former servants of Louis, duke of Orléans, on the bridge over the Yonne, and almost certainly with Charles's complicity. In June 1418, the dauphin had remarked ominously that 'those who get power should be careful how they rule, because one day we'll come back against them'. The murder at Montereau, which was brutally accomplished – the duke was surrounded by Charles's armed servants and hacked down – was an act of revenge, by those who perpetrated it for Burgundy's complicity in the murder of the duke of Orléans in 1407, and by Charles himself for the much more recent deaths of the constable Bernard of Armagnac and chancellor Henri de Marle, both killed during the Burgundian seizure of Paris in 1418.

The murder of John the Fearless at Montereau had the immediate result of throwing the English and Burgundians together in a military alliance, and 1420 proved an appalling year for the dauphin Charles. By the Treaty of Troyes (May 1420), Henry V of England was recognised as Charles VI's heir; the dauphin was disinherited and his sister Catherine was married to the English king, who now undertook to recover all the lands within the 'Kingdom of Bourges'. Just before Christmas 1420, Henry V, styled 'heir and regent of France', sat side-by-side in court with Charles the Mad in the hôtel of St Pol in Paris to hear the Anglo-

Burgundian charges of homicide laid against the disinherited dauphin and his accomplices. Clearly it was going to take much more than a few hundred Scots mercenaries to save the dauphin's skin.

However, if it did nothing else, the Montereau murder did help to clarify the issues in the French civil war. Yet the news of John the Fearless's death, which must have reached Buchan and the Scottish army shortly after they disembarked at La Rochelle in October 1419, can only have been daunting. The Scots, together with Italian and Spanish mercenaries who had responded to Charles's call, now faced the prospect of taking on the combined might of Henry V's war machine – which had made the English King recognised heir to France in less than five years – and the wealth and power of the Burgundians, baying for revenge.

In addition to John Stewart, earl of Buchan, the Scottish army's commanders were Archibald Douglas, son of the fourth earl of Douglas and styling himself earl of Wigtown, Sir John Stewart of Darnley and Thomas Seton. Having made their way north-eastwards from La Rochelle, Buchan and Wigtown reached Tours some time in late November 1419, being received with joy by the dauphin. The Scots leaders were showered with gifts – not only horses, but lands and castles; thus Buchan received Châtillon-sur-Indre in the Touraine, Wigtown was granted Dun-le-Roi in Berry, Darnley, Concressault (also in Berry, about thirty miles north of Bourges) and Seton the château of Langeais, west of Tours. In spite of predictable complaints amongst his French supporters in the Touraine, who apparently described the Scots disparagingly as 'mangeurs de moutons et sacs de vin', Charles valued them so highly that, little over a month after their arrival, he was considering sending their leaders back to Scotland for reinforcements; and around the same time, he had a letter sent to Alexander Stewart, earl of Mar, one of the Scottish governmental triumvirate, inviting him to come to France with as many recruits as he could provide.

In the event, Mar did not come; but in May 1420 Buchan duly returned to Scotland, probably accompanied by Wigtown and Darnley, and in the summer of that year he negotiated the sending of reinforcements of perhaps 4–5,000 men to stiffen the already sizeable Scottish army in France. That army, bereft of its commanders for at least part of 1420, was deployed by the dauphin in a number of ways: first, a small number (probably 100) were to serve as Charles's bodyguard, a role assigned to the Scots which probably dated back to 1418, and certainly to the Burgundy assassination at Montereau in September 1419; a larger number were sent to serve in dauphinist garrisons in Maine and Anjou, and – critically – in the Seine valley strongholds south-east of Paris.

Finally, it is likely that the greater part of the Scottish army went south with the dauphin in the spring of 1420; probably this journey should be understood as a progress by Charles, showing himself and confirming the loyalty of towns and nobility in the Auvergne, Languedoc, and Armagnac. Scottish units of the dauphin's army – mostly archers though including at least one trumpeter – are to be found at Carcassone, Le Puy, and Toulouse.

The main theatre of war in the campaigning season of 1420 – a grim one for the Scots – was to be found further north. For Henry V of England, armed with the new authority given him by the Treaty of Troyes in May, intended to campaign immediately against the dauphinist strongholds of Melun, Montereau, and Sens. To give his campaign greater credibility, he took with him not only the mad Charles VI of France, but also the captive James I of Scotland, now twenty-six, summoned from England for the purpose. They made an ill-matched trio – the conqueror and heir to France, no doubt exulting in the experience, like Edward III after Poitiers, of having the Kings of France and Scotland as his prisoners; Charles the Mad, who had already disinherited his son and signed away his kingdom, and probably had little idea of what he was doing; and the youthful King of Scots, who assuredly knew what he was doing. But how is James I's behaviour to be interpreted in 1420–21?

It could of course be argued that King James had no option: he was a prisoner, he was summoned by his keeper, and he had to go. He may have hoped, in modern parlance, for some remission of his imprisonment in return for his good behaviour; he had after all been in English custody for over fourteen years. Alternatively he may have been enthusiastic about the prospect of fighting in France. Certainly he went out with his own following, with banners and surcoats bearing the royal arms of Scotland generously provided by Henry V; and like David II in his relationship with Edward III, James I may have admired King Henry's success in war and his love of pageantry. Thus we find James, as King of Scots, at Henry V's marriage to Catherine of Valois in June 1420, at the new queen's coronation at Westminster in February of the following year, and at Windsor to be knighted by Henry V in April 1421. In the meantime, after a long and bitter siege ended with the fall of Melun in September 1420, James I was on hand in Henry V's army to witness the hanging of twenty Scots of the garrison as traitors for having supported the dauphin against their king. Whether through English coercion or of his own volition, or perhaps a combination of both, James I has the dubious distinction of being the only Scottish king ever found as one of the commanders of an English army challenging thousands of his own subjects in the field.

Early in 1421 Henry V crossed to England with his new queen, leaving his brother and heir Thomas, duke of Clarence, as his lieutenant in France. On the other side, the dauphin's forces had been reorganised, for the French accounts now refer openly to the 'army of Scotland', and to Sir John Stewart of Darnley as its Constable; the Scots would campaign together with French forces commanded by the Sieur de Lafayette. It was this combined Franco-Scottish army, presumably reinforced by the new levies brought from Scotland by Buchan and Wigtown, which would win the dauphin's first victory.

Accounts of the battle of Baugé, fought on Easter Saturday, 22 March 1421, vary in detail, but are unanimous in ascribing the English defeat to the rashness of Thomas, duke of Clarence. Clarence had mustered an army of some 4,000 men with the aim of locating and destroying the dauphin's forces on the Loire. After advancing as far west as Angers and finding the town too strongly defended to risk a siege, he moved east to Beaufort; it was while his men were foraging in the neighbourhood that the presence of the dauphin's army, led by Buchan, Wigtown, and Darnley, was discovered at Baugé, north of Beaufort and therefore blocking Clarence's line of retreat through the Sarthe to Normandy. However, the duke had no intention of retreating. If the Scottish chronicler Walter Bower is to be believed, both commanders agreed to a short truce 'out of reverence for the passion of Our Lord' at Easter. Thereupon Clarence, against advice, decided to surprise the Franco-Scottish army on Easter Saturday, and moved against them with his mounted men-at-arms, leaving his archers behind. The Scots were, however, alerted in time; accounts vary as to whether they were asleep or playing ball – presumably football, a sport to be vainly condemned by a Scottish parliament three years later – but they rushed to arms. A hundred Scots archers, commanded by Sir Hugh Kennedy and Robert Stewart of Ralston, held the only bridge between Clarence's cavalry and the Franco-Scottish army on the other side of the stream; when Clarence finally forced his way across, he and his men became literally bogged down and confronted by the assembled dismounted dauphinist men-at-arms, well protected by archers. In the confused mêlée which followed, Clarence (according to Bower) was wounded in the face by John Swinton, then hacked down by Buchan's mace. An alternative Scottish account states that Clarence was killed by a Highland Scot named Alexander Macausland, a native of Lennox; and predictably, the French chronicler Chastellain has the duke killed by a Frenchman. The duke's death turned an English defeat into a rout, with fleeing English troops pretending to be French in an attempt to gain the relative safety of the Sarthe.

The battle of Baugé was not a large-scale engagement, and its significance should not perhaps be judged by Pope Martin's comment on the
result which forms part of the title of this book; for the pope was
presumably moved to make the remark more by English resistance to his
efforts to secure the recognition of his right to dispose of religious
benefices within England than by any love of the Scots. However, Baugé
was a significant battle partly because of the scale of the victory. The Scots
lost only twelve men dead, their French allies only two notables, Charles
le Bouteiller and the brother of the sire de Fontaines; but English losses
were very heavy. They included not only the duke of Clarence, but also
Lord Roos, Lord Grey, Sir Gilbert Umfraville (who had advised the duke
not to give battle), and around 1,600 others. The earls of Huntingdon and
Somerset were captured by the Scots. Most writers agree that the battle
severely dented the English myth of invincibility. Henry V's heir presumptive and lieutenant in France had been killed, his banner sent to the
dauphin on the evening after Baugé; and Clarence's golden coronet, lost
in the battle, was sold for a thousand nobles to John Stewart of Darnley,
who used it as a pledge for his very considerable debts.

The dauphin was vindicated in his enlistment of so many Scots. Above
all he was delighted to receive such distinguished English nobles as
captives. Laurence Vernon, the Scot who had captured the earl of
Somerset, was able to sell him to the dauphin for the huge sum of 40,000
écus d'or, and he was granted the lordship of Montreuil-Bonnin in Poitou
for his services. Vernon went on to marry a Frenchwoman, Christine
Goupille, and the Vernon dynasty not only continued to hold Montreuil-
Bonnin, but became lords of Chatelier in Touraine, which they held
through six generations. Vernon is a spectacular example – though by no
means the only one – of a Scot who achieved his dream in France. As the
result of courage and good luck in the mêlée at Baugé, he became a
friend of the dauphin and an entrant into the nobility of France.

The Scottish leaders at Baugé were swiftly rewarded by the dauphin.
Buchan was created Constable of France, the highest military office in
the country, and was given the services of one of Charles's best astrolo-
gers, Germain de Thibouville; Wigtown became Count of Longueville
(though more as an enticement to further war on behalf of the dauphin
than anything else, for Longueville was held by the English); and a
month after Baugé, on 21 April, John Stewart of Darnley was granted the
castle and town of Concressault in Berry, to which was added, on 26
March 1423, the greater prize of Aubigny-sur-Nère, a few miles away.

The dauphin now felt himself strong enough to take the war to the
enemy, and with an army 6,000 strong moved north of the Loire into
Perche and laid siege to Alençon. The earl of Salisbury, taking the place

of the dead Clarence and in the absence of Henry V, had to call out the garrison troops in Normandy to defend the town, and he did not risk meeting Charles in open battle, instead retiring north with the loss of his rearguard. The dauphin thereupon stormed the fortress of Gaillardon and advanced upon Chartres. From an English standpoint, the return to France of Henry V with fresh levies in June must have come as a considerable relief.

The summer of 1421 saw Henry V attempting to remedy the considerable damage done by the Franco-Scots in his absence. Moving south from Calais to the Seine, he crossed the river and turned west to lay siege to Dreux. As in 1420, James I of Scotland was in the English army, which after the fall of Dreux in late August made a rapid march south towards the dauphinist force, assembled under Buchan at Beaugency on the Loire. In September Henry V, who was trying to force a battle, came close to Buchan's army; but wisely the dauphinists declined to engage Henry in open conflict and concentrated instead on stripping the countryside of supplies, leaving famine and dysentery in Henry's army to do the rest. Beaugency in September 1421 is one of the great 'might-have-beens' of the Hundred Years' War: James I of Scotland, in the company of Henry V, came close to fighting thousands of his own subjects. Perhaps it is fortunate that the issue was not put to the test.

For the dauphin, 1422 proved to be a crucial year, not because of the military campaigns undertaken in his name, but because of events beyond his control. The war itself presents the spectacle of two contestants, each unable to deliver a knockout blow, probing each other's defences and making short, jabbing attacks. Buchan moved through Perche and Alençon as far as the coast, where his army took Avranches, on the Normandy border. The dauphin spent a great deal of time recruiting Lombards to his service, and facing up to the problem of trying to finance a continuing war with only part of the resources of the Kingdom of France.

He was blessed with three great strokes of luck. Early in October 1422, Charles was holding court at La Rochelle, the landfall for all Scottish reinforcements, when the floor of the upper room in which he and his entourage were standing collapsed under them; the dauphin escaped with bruises, but Pierre de Bourbon, lord of Preaulx, who had been standing near him, was killed. The dauphin's survival was swiftly followed by the news of Charles VI's death on 21 October; with Charles the Mad gone, the dauphin, though as yet neither crowned nor anointed, was recognised by those who followed him as Charles VII of France.

But Charles's greatest stroke of good fortune in 1422 had come two months earlier. On 31 August Henry V died at Vincennes near Paris after

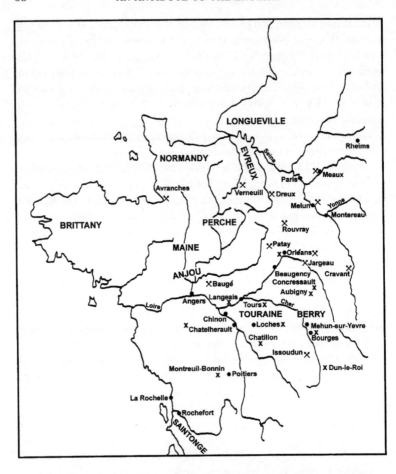

WAR AND SETTLEMENT: SCOTS IN FRANCE (15th AND EARLY 16th CENTURIES)

Battles and sieges:	✕
Major cities, towns, strongholds, and seaports:	●
Scottish settlement:	x
Counties: e.g. **SAINTONGE**	

a lingering illness which was most probably dysentery. His declining health is occasionally noted in the winter and spring of 1422, and he may have contracted the illness which was to kill him at the seven-month-long siege of Meaux on the river Marne, forty miles east of Paris, a place both resolutely defended and determinedly attacked. Writing a generation later, the chronicler Walter Bower made the most of Scotland's alleged contribution to the death of the Scots' implacable enemy. Henry V, he claimed, had been struck down with a cancerous illness known as 'St Fiacre's disease'. This, it seems, was the saint's revenge on the English king for sending out foragers during the siege of Meaux and violating the shrine of St Fiacre, whom the Scots identified with St Fergus, son of a former king of Scotland. The dying Henry V, in Bower's account, recognised the cause, though perhaps not the nature, of his illness in his grim comment: 'Wherever I pursue Scots alive or dead, I find them in my beard'.

The removal from the scene in quick succession of Henry V and Charles the Mad unquestionably aided the cause of Charles VII. However, there were limits to Henry's success during his lifetime. His swift conquest of Normandy was more impressive than his settlement of it, and the victor of Agincourt is perhaps best remembered as a very skilled, and remorseless, siege expert. Yet he failed, for example, to cut off reinforcements to the dauphin by blockading and laying siege to La Rochelle; perhaps he was never strong enough to risk doing so. By contrast, the dauphin's achievements in 1421–2 – taking the war to the English and Burgundians with some success – have probably been under-rated. In 1423, in spite of some dissension in his own ranks, he was looking yet again to Scotland for reinforcements.

The Tyneman Cometh (1423–4)

Archibald Douglas, fourth earl of Douglas, self-styled 'great guardian of the marches of Scotland', was unquestionably the most powerful magnate in early fifteenth-century Scotland, probably indeed the greatest of all late medieval Scottish nobles. Son of Archibald 'the Grim', third earl of Douglas, who had fought at Poitiers, the fourth earl was married to Margaret Stewart, daughter of Robert III, he acted as warden of all three marches and keeper of Edinburgh castle, and with lands and adherents stretching from Galloway to the Firth of Forth, he was the undisputed master of southern Scotland. He lacked luck or skill, or both, in pitched battles, and his nickname of 'the Tyneman' ('the Loser') may refer either to his defeats or to his habit of losing a portion of his anatomy at each of them. Nonetheless, his family had associations with France stretching back for two long generations, and his ability to bring thousands of men to the field was not in doubt. Early in 1424, on Charles VII's third appeal for Scottish levies, Archibald the Tyneman committed himself and his house firmly to the dauphin's cause.

The war in France had not gone well for Charles VII during 1423. Although the personal menace of Henry V was removed, the English government in France had fallen into the capable hands of John, duke of Bedford; and the dauphin was weakened by serious disputes in his own ranks, owing largely to French resentment of Buchan as a foreigner being Constable of the army. Added to this was the increasing problem of paying for the army of Scotland; as early as the summer of 1422, Charles had been forced to borrow from some of his French supporters to help defray the wages of the Scots. And it must be admitted that the Scots rank-and-file hardly made themselves popular with local people in the Touraine. The tax officials of Tours resorted to paying the dauphin's chancellor at Chinon for orders to move on huge numbers of Scots soldiers who were pillaging the area round the city. Buchan's countess was welcomed and richly entertained in Tours when she arrived with the news that her husband was gathering into the army Scots who were pillaging the neighbourhood; and on at least one occasion, saintly intervention was necessary to save a French peasant from the Scots. Jean de Pons, a partridge-hunter from Berry, was taken and hanged by a party of Scots because they had been having trouble with the locals; however, he had the good sense to pray for help to St Katherine of Fierbois, and his prayers were answered when the rope broke.

Stories such as these reflect the slow disintegration of the dauphin's military administration in general, and lack of wages in particular. Nevertheless there were some dauphinist successes, with the Scots under Darnley repelling an English move against Bourges at Issoudun in the summer, and playing a part in expelling the Earl of Salisbury from Vendôme, just north of the Loire, later in the year. However, by that time the Army of Scotland had sustained a shattering defeat at Salisbury's hands. At Cravant-sur-Yonne on 31 July 1423, Sir John Stewart of Darnley, rashly becoming involved in the schemes of a Burgundian defector, was totally defeated by Anglo-Burgundian forces in one of the few recorded instances of their effective co-operation. The dauphinist army, made up of Scots, Spaniards, and Lombards as well as French, was cut to pieces with very heavy losses amongst the Scots; Darnley, who lost an eye in the battle, was captured. Charles's cynical response to the news of Cravant has been much quoted. Remarking that no French nobles had been lost, the dauphin went on to comment that those killed had been 'only Scots, Spaniards and other foreigners who were accustomed to live off the country, and who are no great loss'.

But this remark should not be torn out of context. Charles VII valued the Scots: not only did he ransom Darnley in the following year, but also confirmed him in his possession of Concressault and Aubigny in 1425, and optimistically added the County of Evreux to these grants in 1427. And he had already dispatched an embassy, headed by Buchan and Wigtown, to Scotland in the summer of 1423, to take part in a massive recruiting exercise.

Far-reaching political changes had taken place since the sending of the first Scottish army to France in 1419. In September 1420, Robert, duke of Albany, the governor, had died, aged around eighty, to be succeeded by his son Murdoch. With Buchan active in France, the Albany Stewarts were firmly committed to the French alliance as a vital element of Scottish foreign policy; and in October 1423 Sir Walter Stewart, Murdoch's eldest son, swore at Stirling to abide by the Franco-Scottish alliance and to prevent any truce with England. His timing was unfortunate. The English government of the infant Henry VI was close to negotiating the terms on which James I would be released and allowed to return to Scotland; an apparently Anglophile king, with his new English wife Joan Beaufort – two of whose brothers had been captured at Baugé – was likely to disrupt the Auld Alliance.

Considerations such as these must have hastened the recruitment of the Scottish expeditionary force to France, and fuelled the English desire to finalise terms on which James I might return to Scotland. But if the Albany Stewarts sank all their credit in the French alliance – to their eventual heavy cost – Archibald, fourth earl of Douglas, pursued a subtler policy. As early as 1421, the Tyneman had hedged his bets by making an alliance with Henry V. Probably he had no intention of honouring it, and it was swiftly overtaken by events. But Douglas, though moved by vaulting ambition which steered him inexorably in the direction of the richest dukedom in France, had to secure his vast estates at home against any royal backlash on James I's return. The solution which he eventually adopted was to leave his eldest son Wigtown, one of the Baugé victors, in Scotland, while he himself, together with his second son Sir James Douglas, and the earl of Buchan, led a final 'armée de mer' to France.

Thus in March 1424, as James I made his long-delayed journey northwards towards his kingdom, his greatest subject, Archibald the Tyneman, sailed south and landed at La Rochelle, and with an army of 2,500 men-at-arms and 4,000 archers made his way east to Charles VII's court at Bourges. On 24 April, Charles received Douglas's army, and Darnley, released from captivity, appeared with his own contingent of 150 men-at-arms. Also present was the Breton commander, Arthur de

Richemont, a veteran of Agincourt and a deserter from the Anglo-Burgundian alliance; it is a measure of the importance of the Scots to Charles VII's cause that Richemont, a future Constable, brought with him a force of only 3,500, around half that of Douglas. Indeed, even allowing for heavy Scots losses at Cravant the previous July, there could still have been as many as 10–12,000 Scots in Charles's service. For any kingdom, let alone a remote one with a population of around half a million, this is a remarkable commitment.

On 17 April Archibald the Tyneman was given royal letters granting him the dukedom of Touraine, and ordering officials and vassals within the Touraine to obey him as their duke. The extent of Charles VII's generosity probably reflects hard bargaining before Douglas would consent to come; for Touraine was a wealthy dukedom, held by Charles's brother, the dauphin Jean, until his death in 1417, and subsequently by Charles himself. The idea of handing any French dukedom, let alone this one, to a Scottish earl was unheard of, and provoked fierce local opposition which had been simmering since the first arrival of the Scots in 1419. Moreover, the Tyneman had already been given the office of lieutenant-general, with the authority to wage war on Charles's behalf throughout the Kingdom of France. It was – briefly – the high water mark of Black Douglas success.

On 7 May 1424, Archibald the Tyneman, travelling from nearby Loches, made his formal entry into Tours to take possession of his dukedom. At three o'clock in the afternoon, having paused at the church of Notre Dame la Riche, he was presented with the keys to the city, together with suitable expressions of joy and promises of loyalty. These were undoubtedly more genuine when the duke took his army away from the city three months later, on 4 August, to fight the English; for in that short time the Tyneman had run up enormous debts and two formal complaints had been made to him by the city council about the behaviour of the Scots in Tours. Gifts were showered on the duke, on Buchan, and on Adam Douglas, the Tyneman's cousin and captain in Tours, the inhabitants of the city breathed a collective sigh of relief, and the fourth earl of Douglas embarked on what was to prove his last campaign. Buchan, the victor of Baugé and Avranches, and tireless Scottish recruiting officer for Charles VII, should certainly have consulted his astrologer Germain de Thibouville before committing himself to a campaign as the Tyneman's companion-in-arms.

In the event, the campaign lasted only thirteen days. The Scots, who began by marching north-east to Châteaudun to join up with a French force led by the duke of Alençon and count of Aumale and a group of Lombard mercenaries, then turned north-west towards the Norman town of Ivry, which was under siege by John, duke of Bedford, the English regent in France. But Ivry surrendered, by arrangement with Bedford, on 14 August, before the huge Franco-Scottish army could reach it; and the allies turned instead to the town of Verneuil-sur-Avre, which was weakly held and which swiftly surrendered. Bedford, who was at Evreux when he heard the news of the fall of Verneuil, hurried south with an army which, including reinforcements brought from England by the earl of Salisbury, seems to have numbered around 9,000-10,000 men. The dauphinist army under Douglas and Buchan was certainly much larger, possibly 12-14,000 strong, though it can hardly have been four times the size of Bedford's force as Bower suggests. On the afternoon of 17 August, the battle of Verneuil was fought.

For once, Scottish and French chroniclers are in agreement that the battle was lost through the 'vain arrogance and reckless haste' of the Scots. The Tyneman refused to take the advice of Alençon and Aumale, which was to avoid battle and conduct an invasion of Normandy while it was sparsely defended. Possibly, as Michael Brown suggests, Douglas felt that he had to make an immediate impression as Charles VII's new lieutenant-general by inflicting a heavy defeat on the English. In any event, he instructed the Scots that they were to give no quarter to their enemies, an order which had fatal consequences. In an extremely bloody battle, which lasted around an hour, the Franco-Scottish forces at first seemed likely to prevail; but Bedford's men rallied, and the Lombard mercenaries on the dauphin's side rapidly plundered the baggage in the English rearguard and then vanished, taking no further part in the battle. Because no quarter was to be given, the death toll on both sides was appalling. When Bedford and Salisbury finally emerged as the victors, they had lost over a thousand dead; but the carnage on the Franco-Scottish side ran to many more, and the Scottish section of the army, upwards of 6,000 men, was all but wiped out. Amongst the French, the Count of Aumale and the Viscount of Narbonne were killed, and the prisoners included the duke of Alençon, who was found alive under a pile of corpses. The Tyneman, having enjoyed his dukedom of Touraine for exactly four months, died fighting together with his second son James and his son-in-law John Stewart, earl of Buchan. All three were buried together in the cathedral of St Gatien in Tours, 'almost clandestinely', as Professor Chevalier remarks. The Tyneman's dukedom, his lieutenant-generalship, his kin, friends, most of his servants and almost all of his army had been lost in less than a fortnight.

James I and the Treaty of Perth-Chinon (1424–9)

Unsurprisingly, neither Charles VII nor the French inhabitants of the
Touraine showed much solicitude for their defeated Scottish allies. Two
months after Verneuil, the king gave the Touraine to Isabel of Anjou, his
sister-in-law, and all attempts by Douglas's widow Margaret to assert her
family's rights to her husband's inheritance were in vain. Three days
after receiving news of the battle, the Tours city council agreed to pay the
Scots garrison to depart, and stipulated that no Scots should come in to
take over the city. This injunction was clearly ineffective, for by July of
1425 a census was ordered of all Scots living within the walls of Tours,
and all of them (including a friar) were to be expelled during the current
emergency. Eighteen Scots are listed, including the 'Lord of Polloc' –
presumably Maxwell of Pollok; and the emergency was probably caused
by Scottish demands for debts which they claimed were owing to them,
together with damages done to them by the people of Tours, with a
captain named Turnbull resorting to threats and extortion. This local
friction, which was to continue well into the '30s, not only reflects the
perennial problem of relationships between civilians and soldiers –
especially foreigners – in the aftermath of war, but makes clear that there
were many Scots survivors who continued to live on in the Touraine
and – as we shall see – elsewhere.

As Bedford was not in a position to follow up his victory at Verneuil,
Charles VII had time to make the changes necessary to shore up his
position. The dead Buchan's constableship went to Arthur de
Richemont, and efforts were made to reunite the French princes around
the Crown, above all by attempting to detach Philip the Good of
Burgundy from the frequently shaky Anglo-Burgundian alliance. But
dissension, jealousies and faction persisted at the court of the 'Kingdom
of Bourges', largely because Charles was still surrounded by irreconcil-
able Armagnac leaders. However, with the exception of his personal
bodyguard, he was no longer surrounded by Scots.

In fact, the real significance of Verneuil lay not in France, but in
Scotland. James I, returning to his kingdom in 1424, aged thirty and
after an absence of eighteen years, modelled his style of kingship not on
that of his consensual Stewart predecessors but rather on the ruthless
and aggressive royal government of Henry V of England, with which he
was of course very familiar. There is little doubt that, from the outset of
his personal rule in May 1424, King James regarded the immense power
of the Albany Stewarts, headed by Murdoch, duke of Albany, the
governor since 1420, as an unacceptable restraint on his power as king.
The existence of the large Scottish army under Buchan and Douglas in

the Touraine was probably the major factor in preventing James I from launching an assault on his Albany kin. Buchan was duke Murdoch's brother as well as the Tyneman's son-in-law, and the Scottish army in France was largely composed of the affinities of both these magnates. Thus if James were to make a premature move against the Albany Stewarts, the army which had sailed from Dumbarton to France in the spring might swiftly return with the king as its target.

Verneuil removed that possibility. Bereft of his powerful father and kinsmen, Wigtown, who now inherited the Douglas estates as fifth earl – and who vainly styled himself duke of Touraine and count of Longueville for the rest of his life – made an accommodation with James I, probably in October 1424, and lent his support to the king the following spring when James arrested and subsequently executed duke Murdoch and his family, enriching the crown with the revenues of the earldoms of Fife, Menteith, and Lennox. While this near-annihilation of the Albany Stewarts was an important factor in King James's assassination twelve years later, in the late 1420s the temporary removal of checks on royal authority allowed James to present to the world the image of a king in full control of his kingdom, admired even by the English for his apparent mastery.

But the Scottish king's admiration of Lancastrian government in England did not blind him to his own needs. He was saddled with a large ransom, described as 'expenses' by the English, while wanting the freedom to play an independent role in Europe. It may be added that he was the first Scottish king since David II to have any personal experience of France, albeit campaigning in an English army. Above all, he needed greater financial resources and prestige abroad. He was thus happy to receive an embassy from Charles VII of France at Perth in July 1428.

Charles's choice of ambassadors reflects the importance he attached to securing a renewal of the Auld Alliance. The embassy was headed by Regnault de Chartres, archbishop of Rheims and chancellor of France, and also included John Stewart of Darnley, styled Count of Evreux, and Charles's poet-secretary Alain Chartier, the most experienced of the French king's ambassadors. Chartier, who arrived first, launched into a Latin oration to James I; the text survives, and although Chartier has been much criticised by modern writers for his 'laboured and pedantic medley of biblical texts and classical allusions', much of what he had to say appears both eloquent and moving. Recalling the ancient Franco-Scottish alliance, Chartier remarked that it had been handed down through the generations as an eternal covenant, not made on a sheet of parchment, but written on the skin and flesh of men, not with ink, but with the mingled blood of both allies. Darnley and the archbishop of

Rheims, more prosaic souls, were not present to hear these flights of oratory, preferring instead the delights of a night out in Linlithgow at the cost of £6. 9s. 10d.

The French ambassadors, well aware of the continuing negotiations between Scotland and England, urged James I not to forsake old friendships in the pursuit of dubious new ones. However, they needed the King of Scots more than he needed them, and King James was prepared to drive a hard bargain. An agreement was quickly reached at Perth, and ratified by Charles VII three months later, at Chinon in the Touraine. James I's eldest daughter Margaret was to marry the dauphin Louis when both reached a suitable age – in 1428 she was four and he was five – and bring a dowry of 15,000 livres. James promised Charles the services of 6,000 troops to help in his wars against the English, and expected in return to receive the county of Saintonge on France's west coast, with its key port of entry, La Rochelle, together with the great castle of Rochefort, further down the coast.

Only part of the treaty was effective. Eight years later, the twelve-year-old Scottish princess would sail from Dumbarton to La Rochelle, en route to her marriage to the dauphin Louis (the future Louis XI) in Tours on 25 June 1436. But no fourth Scottish 'armée de mer' would use this route. King James preferred to wait, possibly to see how the war in France developed. It could be argued that he waited too long, and that he wasted a real chance to acquire an accessible French county from a grateful ally; and the issue of the cession of Saintonge to the Scots would drag on for almost a century.

In the event, Charles VII was saved – if he needed saving – not by the Scots, but by a very different phenomenon. In May 1428 Joan of Arc, the sixteen-year-old daughter of a tenant farmer from the village of Domrémy, on the borders of the duchies of Bar and Lorraine, arrived at Vaucouleurs castle, held for Charles VII by Robert de Baudricourt. She demanded an escort to the king, and showed herself both confident and well informed, stating that 'nothing in the world, neither kings nor dukes, nor daughters of the King of Scots, nor others, can recover the kingdom of France; there is no help for France but myself'. Nine months later she arrived at Chinon and was received by Charles VII, who was sufficiently impressed by her promise to raise the siege of Orléans – begun by the English earl of Salisbury in October 1428 – that he allowed her to proceed. She had, of course, influential friends – not only her companions-in-arms, Jean, duke of Alençon (a survivor of Verneuil), and Arthur de Richemont, but also probably Charles VII's Angevin relatives, one of whom, Yolande of Aragon, examined Joan for virginity at Chinon. And Charles VII himself may have been aware of the prophecy of Marie of Avignon, which foretold that France would be saved by a virgin.

Whether Charles VII was as desperate as is sometimes claimed just before Joan of Arc's arrival at Chinon in February 1429 may perhaps be doubted. The stories which claim that he contemplated flight to Spain or Scotland, or perhaps to the Dauphiné in southern France, are of a later vintage; and although the English reappearance on the Loire at Orléans was an unwelcome development, they were achieving little there. The earl of Salisbury had been struck in the face by a French cannon ball while conducting the siege, and died on 3 November 1428; thereafter the English had not been able to maintain a strict blockade of Orléans.

But they did have one conspicuous success. On 12 February 1429, around a fortnight before Joan of Arc arrived at Chinon, the Army of Scotland formed part of a French force which attempted to interrupt an English provision convoy (including flour and herrings) en route to supply the besiegers of Orléans. In the 'battle of the Herrings' which followed at Rouvray Saint-Denis, John Stewart, Lord Darnley, lord of Aubigny and Concressault, and titular count of Evreux, the last of the original commanders of the Scots in France, was killed together with his brother William. Darnley was buried in Orléans cathedral, and three months later another Scot – John Carmichael, former chaplain to the Tyneman and now bishop of Orléans – was on hand to welcome the victorious Joan of Arc when the siege was finally raised. Thereafter stunning victories over the English at Jargeau and Patay led swiftly to Charles VII's crowning and anointing, in Rheims cathedral on 17 July.

Reviewing the Scots involvement in 1420s France more than sixty years ago, Balfour-Melville remarked severely that the Scottish change in tactics from border warfare to the sending of large armies to France was 'another instance of the exaggerated individualism of Scottish nobles getting the better . . . of the national interests'. Apart from the fact that it was Scottish government policy to assist France in this way, Balfour-Melville does not seem to suggest any alternative other than a continuation of massacres like Halidon Hill, Neville's Cross, and Humbleton. He goes on blithely to assert that 'the Franco-Scottish alliance was always more cordial when the two nations remained apart'. Perhaps: but in the hour of his greatest need, the years 1419–21, the dauphin Charles had been saved by the Scots. And in spite of Cravant, Verneuil, and Rouvray, there were still hundreds, if not thousands, of Scots active in the Touraine, Berry and elsewhere at the end of the decade. This, surely, is the true legacy of the 1420s.

4

Diplomacy and the Scottish Diaspora: The Mid-Fifteenth Century

The Franco-Scottish alliance inevitably underwent a substantial change in the middle years of the fifteenth century. In 1453 its apparent *raison d'être*, the Hundred Years' War, came to an end; and eight years later Berwick, the last major border stronghold still held by the English, was ceded to the Scots. Clearly, therefore, Scottish expeditionary forces to France had become both unnecessary and unacceptable, while in the other major theatre of war, the Anglo-Scottish frontier, the war had gradually declined in status from a large-scale struggle mounted by national governments to become little more than the intermittent, if violent, clashes of local families.

In the circumstances, it might seem remarkable that the Auld Alliance survived at all. It did so partly at a diplomatic level, with first James I and then those acting for his young son and successor pushing for foreign marriages for James's six daughters – four were married abroad – and Charles VII of France, more and more the likely winner in the Anglo-French wars but still requiring dependable allies, playing host to the Scottish princesses, acting as marriage broker, and giving the Stewart dynasty a European reputation for the first time in its history. But the decade of the great armies had come to an end in 1429; and Franco-Scottish diplomacy settled into a kind of routine, with – for the time being – no life-or-death commitments on either side.

Underpinning and strengthening Franco-Scottish diplomatic intercourse was the Scottish diaspora in France, the survivors of Verneuil and Rouvray, who settled in large numbers in the Touraine, Berry and Poitou. Many of them were trusted by Charles VII and helped to maintain diplomatic links with Scotland; some of them kept a keen eye on political events in their native land. Those who made successful careers in France provided openings for their kin and allies to join them; and a number of influential Franco-Scottish family dynasties – Stewart (or 'Stuart') of Aubigny, Monypenny, Vernon, Cunningham, Kennedy, Chambers, Lyle, Cockburn, and Gray – had their origins in their leaders' service to Charles VII in the 1420s, together with their good fortune in surviving that decade.

Back to Diplomacy (the 1430s and 1440s)

The adult James I had pursued an equivocal foreign policy after returning to his native land in 1424. Arguably he had no option but to do so, for he came with an English wife Joan Beaufort (whose brothers had been captured at Baugé), with a sizeable ransom to pay to the English, and with a long Anglo-Scottish truce negotiated before his return. He had to consider the fate of the noble hostages sent south as surety for the payment of his ransom, and also the simple fact that Burgundy, England's ally in the wars in France, was also the principal outlet for Scotland's North Sea trade. And the king would have little or no political rapport with the survivors of the Scottish armies in France, against whom he had taken the field with Henry V in 1420–21, and whose kin and allies he had judicially murdered in the removal of the Albany Stewarts in 1425.

For some or all of these reasons, James I did not rush to fulfil the terms of the 1428 Treaty of Perth-Chinon. Possibly he missed the boat, for Charles VII would never again be so desperate for Scottish military assistance; and there was at least a chance that the Scots could have acquired a French county – initially Saintonge, with the prospect of a later exchange for Evreux or, even better, Bourges – which successive Scottish kings would have held of the French crown in the same manner as the English held Gascony.

It was not to be. For some years during the 1430s, James I dithered between the Auld Alliance and the new; and in 1433 the English, keen to break the former, sent north an embassy headed by Edmund Beaufort, offering King James very attractive terms – a lasting Anglo-Scottish peace and the restoration to the Scots of Roxburgh and Berwick. Early the following year there appear to have been proposals for a marriage between the twelve-year-old Henry VI of England and one of James I's daughters, possibly Margaret herself. Had any of these schemes found acceptance with the Scots, then the Franco-Scottish alliance might have come to an end in the early fifteenth rather than mid-sixteenth century. But in two days of stormy debate held in the Blackfriars of Perth, to which King James had summoned a general council, the English peace plan was thrown out, and the clear opinion of Scottish council and estates was that the king should honour his diplomatic obligations to the French. The outcome of this debate, extensively reported by the chronicler Bower who took part in it himself, can hardly have pleased the king who, though he affected not to take sides, had his confessor John Fogo, abbot of Melrose, acting as spokesman for the English peace proposals. Both in its substance and in its conclusions, the 1433 debate strikingly recalls the efforts of David II, some seventy years before, to produce an English peace plan which would be acceptable to a majority within the Scottish estates.

The alternative – assiduously advanced by the French – was to proceed with Margaret's marriage to the dauphin Louis. After more than a year's delays, with both Scots and French prevaricating in order to obtain better terms, the twelve-year-old dauphiness-to-be set sail from Dumbarton on 27 March 1436 in a fleet of eleven ships, Margaret herself sailing in the Spanish ship of Pierre Chepye – the fastest – accompanied by the Earl of Orkney and 140 attendants, while the entire fleet boasted a force of over a thousand men-at-arms and was commanded by Hugh Kennedy, a veteran of Baugé. In spite of contrary winds, an abortive English attempt to kidnap Princess Margaret en route, and a violent storm at the end of the journey, the prospective bride arrived safely at La Rochelle on 18 April; and a subsequent slow progress east, by way of Poitiers, brought her to Tours, which she entered on Midsummer Day at four o'clock in the afternoon. On the following day, her wedding to the dauphin Louis took place in the castle of Tours.

Appropriately, the wedding was a sumptuous affair, and contemporary French and Scottish chroniclers loyally and conventionally paid tribute to Margaret's beauty: she was 'belle et bien formée', 'a handsome and good lady', and she had 'a very lovely face'. Probably she presented a more striking appearance than her thirteen-year-old husband. The future Louis XI, who had little interest in pageantry and who would later order that a portrait painted to serve as an effigy for his tomb should faithfully display even his less pleasing features, has been memorably characterised by Louis Barbé as possessing 'a hooked nose of disproportionate length, and piercing, but shifty, close-set eyes, overhung with shaggy beetle-brows', which 'imparted a sinister expression to a face which had no air of distinction to redeem it'. Barbé is of course describing the adult Louis, with benefit of hindsight and centuries of a developing legend of the 'Spider King', ruthless, cunning, and conniving. But he slams the door on any alternative view of the dauphin Louis by adding that 'it is hardly conceivable that he can have been otherwise than unprepossessing as a boy'.

Unprepossessing or not, the dauphin arrived for his wedding in a suit of bluish-grey velvet, embroidered with leaves of gold, and carrying a sword which had been sent as wedding present by James I. This elaborate weapon was adorned on the pommel on one side with the figure of the Virgin Mary, and on the other with an impression of the Archangel St Michael. The sword survived Louis' lifetime, as it is recorded in a 1489 inventory of the armoury at the Château of Amboise, eloquently described as 'l'espée du roy d'Escosse qui fust fort hardy'. Barbé assumes that the Scottish king referred to as 'very brave' must be Robert Bruce, and that the dauphin wore Bruce's sword at his wedding. (In view of the fact that James III of Scotland would bear Bruce's sword to his last battle at Sauchieburn in 1488, this seems highly unlikely.)

The wedding promised much, in diplomatic terms, for the Scots. But the young couple were ill-matched. In a marriage of convenience this was hardly surprising; but the dauphin's neglect of his wife for the remaining nine years of her short life meant that the marriage produced no issue, and the dazzling prospect of a future half-Scottish Valois king of France never materialised. Margaret's life in France, flitting about the Loire with her small household, has been described at length by Barbé and others. A lonely and unhappy life, relieved only by the writing of poetry, came to an end on 16 August 1445, when Margaret died of tuberculosis at Châlons; she was buried, according to her wishes, in the abbey of Saint-Laon at Thouars, in which she had founded a chapel. Six years later, and against Charles VII's wishes, the widowed dauphin married his neighbour Charlotte of Savoy, who bore him seven children.

The marriage of Margaret to the dauphin in the summer of 1436 may be seen as part of James I's overdue commitment to the Auld Alliance. Clearly the king was moved to take sides by two momentous events in the previous year. On 21 September 1435, Charles VII of France and Philip the Good of Burgundy were at last reconciled in the Treaty of Arras; sixteen years of Franco-Burgundian enmity, which had its origins in the murder of Duke John the Fearless on the bridge at Montereau, had come to an end. The English had lost their most powerful ally in France; worse still, in the same month of September 1435, their most able commander in France, the victor of Verneuil, John, duke of Bedford, died at Rouen. The tide of war turned decisively in favour of Charles VII. Certainly he had had to pay dearly, in terms both of lands and authority, for his reconciliation with Burgundy at Arras; but the treaty allowed him to plan the systematic recovery of French territory from the English without fear of intervention; and in April 1436, after an enforced eighteen years of absence, Charles VII entered Paris in triumph.

The Franco-Burgundian alliance, and Charles VII's growing stature, seem to have convinced James I to come off the fence. The Anglo-Scottish truce expired on 1 May 1436, and the Scottish king planned a major assault on Roxburgh, probably to coincide with a Burgundian attack on English Calais, in order to stretch English resources to the limit. Thus King James's military intervention in 1436 was a throwback to the earlier days of the alliance, working at long distance by opening a second front on the borders.

Less than six weeks after his daughter's marriage to the dauphin Louis at Tours, James I assembled the Scottish host, stiffened by a large contingent of archers and his Burgundian cannons, outside Roxburgh. His confidence in his ability to take the castle is reflected in his creation – before the event – of a new herald, Marchmont. But the siege itself, which lasted for around a fortnight from 1 August, was a humiliating rebuff for the king. Not only was Roxburgh well defended by its garrison, but there were rumours of dissension within the Scottish camp – later tales expanded these to suggest that the king was in danger of assassination – and at length James's English queen Joan Beaufort arrived and took the king away, leaving his entire artillery park to fall into the hands of the English. This dangerous episode led to what Professor Duncan has described as 'a first class row' between king and estates in parliament in Edinburgh at Hallowe'en 1436, when an attempt was made by Sir Robert Graham to arrest King James for tyranny; and on the night of 20–21 February 1437 Graham was among a small band of conspirators – some of them former Albany Stewart adherents who had never forgiven King James for his annihilation of that family in 1425 – who broke into the Blackfriars of Perth, wounded Queen Joan, and on discovering the king hiding in a drain under the royal apartments, killed him, leaving his corpse with sixteen wounds. The assassination plot, the brainchild of James's uncle Walter Stewart, earl of Atholl, succeeded only in the removal of an unpopular king. But the subsequent attempt by Atholl, his kin and supporters, to seize control of the government of the new king James II, only six years of age in 1437, failed largely because the conspirators had not killed queen Joan, who became, with her son, a focus for immediate resistance. The assassination had however removed a ruler whose support for the Franco-Scottish alliance had been equivocal, tardy, and ineffective.

Contemporary French writers had a different view of James II (1437–60). A short 'cronique descoce' describes the king as 'un vaillant chevalier et homme de grant corage', while the poet François Villon commented on the birthmark which gave King James his nickname 'James of the Fiery Face' – a huge blotch covering much of the left side of his face, 'Vermaille comme une emastiste depuis le front jusqu'au menton' ('Vermilion like an amethyst, from the forehead to the chin'). Most writers emphasise James II's qualities as a warrior, sometimes indeed to the exclusion of anything else. They are right to do so, for King James, condemned by the circumstances in which he succeeded to a long, politically fraught minority, spent much of his life in the saddle. But the wars which he fought – until at least the last five years of his short life – were undertaken against his own subjects. Succeeding aged six in 1437, and controlled successively by his mother, factions of Livingstons and Crichtons, and by three earls of Douglas, the king emerged from his minority in the late 1440s. By the early '50s, James II had taken on those who had controlled him during his minority; and in February 1452 he personally stabbed to death his greatest subject, William eighth earl of Douglas, at Stirling castle, plunging the country into a civil war which he won only with great difficulty, and a fair measure of luck, in 1455.

By contrast, Franco-Scottish diplomatic intercourse during the reign was fairly conventional. The alliance was formally renewed at Tours on 31 December 1448, and subsequently ratified by James II at Edinburgh on 20 December 1449. The Scottish embassy to Tours, led by King James's Chancellor William, Lord Crichton, altered the conventional terms of the alliance by stipulating that the Scots might have the option of accepting or rejecting comprehension within any truce between France and England. But the objectives of the alliance remained the same: Charles VII wished to recover Normandy and Gascony from the English, while the Scots looked to acquire Roxburgh and Berwick. And the Auld Alliance was renewed in the wake of a major Scottish victory in the West March; on 23 October 1448 an English force under the earl of Northumberland crossed the Solway to raid Annandale, but was routed by Hugh Douglas, earl of Ormond, at the water of Sark.

If the events of the late '40s suggest 'business as usual' in the conduct of the alliance, there were also some striking changes, above all in the clutch of prestigious European marriages negotiated for James II's sisters. The leaders of the Scottish government during the king's minority – Douglases, Crichtons and Livingstons – were quick to exploit the opportunity to marry Stewart princesses to the allies of the king of France, at the same time strengthening the Franco-Scottish alliance and shifting the burden of providing for the princesses to someone else. There may also have been an element of speculation in all of this; for William, eighth earl of Douglas, who succeeded to the title in 1443, still styled himself duke of Touraine and made an unsuccessful effort to reclaim part of the duchy in 1448. It has been suggested by Fiona Downie that Douglas's negotiation of continental marriages for Stewart princesses may have been inspired primarily by his desire to enhance his own family's reputation in France, badly shaken since Verneuil. Perhaps: but pushing Stewart princesses on to the Continental marriage market surely adds lustre to the Stewart name, rather than that of Douglas. In any event, in February 1452 the issue of Stewart and Douglas prestige was permanently settled at Stirling by James II himself.

The foreign marriages spanned the entire decade of the 1440s. The first of them may have been the result of a Breton initiative in 1441. A

Scottish embassy to Brittany, consisting of Sir George Crichton, William Foulis, archdeacon of St Andrews, and Sir William Monypenny, the expatriate lord of Concressault in Berry, drew up a marriage contract with John, duke of Brittany, by which Isabella, James I's second daughter, would marry John's son and heir Francis, count of Montfort. In the event Francis succeeded to the dukedom of Brittany two months before his marriage to Isabella, which took place at Auray on 30 October 1442. Some time in the next eight years, Isabella bore her Breton husband two daughters, both of whom are portrayed at their devotions with their mother on a folio of the duchess's sumptuous Book of Hours.

Less than two years after the Breton marriage, the princess Mary Stewart, James I's third daughter, was married to Wolfaert van Borselen, son of Henric, lord of Veere and admiral of Philip the Good, duke of Burgundy. As Fiona Downie has recently argued, Philip the Good must at the very least have approved of this marriage, and in view of his later role in finding a wife for James II in 1448–9, he may well have inspired it. Indeed the presence in France and Burgundy of two powerful rulers – Charles VII and Philip the Good – who lacked daughters of marriageable age, may largely explain the attraction abroad of the Stewart princesses in the 1440s. In every case, it was not so much Stewart prestige as the needs of Philip the Good and King Charles to forge European marriage alliances which dictated the ultimate destinations of James I's daughters.

Thus both king and duke were probably the initiators of the unusual marriage proposal for James I's daughter Annabella, who was betrothed at Stirling to Louis, count of Geneva, second son of the duke of Savoy, on 14 December 1444. A marriage link between Scotland and Savoy is strikingly unusual, and at first sight no clear benefits would seem to accrue from such an alliance. However, both France and Burgundy had strong links with the dukes of Savoy, and so the use of one of their Scottish ally's sisters in the marriage market is probably explained. Annabella left Scotland in 1445, possibly aged no more than nine, and significantly her journey to Savoy was organised by the duke of Burgundy and began with a visit to Annabella's newly married sister Mary in Veere. Thereafter, in the autumn of 1445, Annabella travelled to Geneva and spent the next eleven years in the household of the duchess of Savoy.

In the same year, 1445, Charles VII of France came into his own in the role of marriage broker for Stewart princesses. On 19 August, Eleanor and Joanna Stewart arrived in Tournai en route for the French court at Tours, only to be greeted with the news that their elder sister Margaret, the dauphiness, had died three days previously. Nevertheless they were well received by Charles VII at Tours, and were rapidly established at court with their own households while the French king negotiated for suitable husbands. A scheme to marry Eleanor off to Emperor Frederick III fell through, as did a tactless suggestion by James II that Eleanor might take her dead sister's place as a wife for the dauphin Louis. At length, in June 1447, Eleanor was found an Austrian husband, archduke Sigismund, who had been betrothed to Charles VII's daughter Radegond, who had died in 1445. Enlisting the help of his surrogate Scottish family, the French king dispatched Eleanor to Innsbruck late in 1448, and early in the new year she was married to Sigismund. James II, who had initially protested to Charles VII about the Austrian match, finally accepted it with a good grace; for he was looking to use the French king's services to find a bride for himself.

From the point of view of Scotland's prestige in Europe, however, these foreign marriages achieved little. Isabella's husband, duke Francis of Brittany, died in 1450; and when her brother James II proposed that she should remarry and raised the whole issue of the Breton succession, Isabella rounded on him, claimed that he had failed to pay her dowry in the first place, that she was happy and well loved in Brittany, and was in any case too frail to travel elsewhere (though she lived for another forty years). Eleanor's marriage to Sigismund lasted thirty-one years, but produced no children; and after her death at Innsbruck on 20 November 1480 – followed by a state funeral in which both French and Scottish representatives were conspicuous by their absence – Sigismund rapidly took a second wife, Katharine of Saxony. Annabella Stewart's eleven-year sojourn in Geneva came to an end in 1456, when the betrothal to Count Louis was at last broken off, probably on James II's insistence; and both Annabella and Joanna, for whom the French king had been unable to find a husband, were escorted back to Scotland in 1458, subsequently being married respectively to the Earls of Huntly and Morton. For a short time, Scotland had become enmeshed in Franco-Burgundian diplomacy; but in the last analysis, the exodus to Europe of five Stewart princesses had done little more than provide constant ambassadorial work for the indefatigable Sir William Monypenny.

Early in 1448, however, James II had written to Charles VII asking for assistance in finding a bride for himself. The French king recommended that a Scottish embassy should be sent to the Burgundian court, and in 1448–9 Scottish ambassadors headed by William Lord Crichton went back and forth to Burgundy with full powers to negotiate a marriage alliance for James II with Burgundy, Gueldres, or Cleves. The choice eventually fell on Gueldres, and on the daughters of duke Arnold of Gueldres, Philip the Good of Burgundy's nieces. Burgundy conducted the negotiations himself; and it may be significant that his original scheme was to marry Mary, the elder daughter of duke Arnold, to duke Albrecht of Austria, the Emperor's brother, while the Scottish king would be married to Mary's younger sister Margaret. The fact that these projected marriages were reversed suggests hard negotiating on the part of the Scots ambassadors, and argues for some Scottish diplomatic clout at the court of Philip the Good. The resulting Treaty of Brussels, drawn up on 1 April 1449, ratified by the Scottish king at Stirling on 25 June, and subsequently endorsed by a very full Scottish parliament on 22 January 1450, duly provided for a marriage between James II and Mary of Gueldres, the elder of duke Arnold's daughters. On 3 July 1449, following Mary of Gueldres' journey to Scotland in a fleet of fourteen Burgundian ships, the royal marriage took place at Holyrood. Certainly it had been inspired by a suggestion of Charles VII of France, and may in that sense be seen as an offshoot of the Auld Alliance; but the man paying the dowry was Philip the Good of Burgundy.

The Outbreak of Peace?

By the mid-1450s, it was clear that the mutual dependence which had forged and sustained the Franco-Scottish alliance had come to an end. Charles the Victorious had expelled the English from every part of France apart from Calais and the county of Guines in the north-east. James II had survived his assault on the Black Douglases; if he ever contemplated flight to France, as the sixteenth-century chronicler Pitscottie suggests, it can only have been for a very short time following his killing of the eighth earl of Douglas in February 1452. Certainly by the summer of 1455 the Scottish king was able to write confidently to Charles VII of France describing his siege and capture of the great Black Douglas stronghold of Abercorn in West Lothian. James II had overthrown the most powerful magnate family in his kingdom, a family moreover whose fame had spread throughout France in earlier generations and whose head, William, eighth earl of Douglas, had visited Charles VII's court as recently as 1450. In the kingdoms of France and Scotland, peace had at last been imposed following ruthless and ultimately successful warfare waged by the Crown.

The victories of Charles VII and James II in their own kingdoms were paralleled by governmental collapse in the realm of their mutual enemy England. Since 1453 Henry VI had been showing signs of mental instability, and a challenge to the Lancastrian dynasty was aggressively advanced by Richard, duke of York, and his sons. By May of 1455, around the same time that James II gained his final victory over the Black Douglases, England was plunged into civil war between Lancaster and York – the so-called 'Wars of the Roses', and the kind of struggle from which both France and Scotland had only recently emerged.

What, in these changed circumstances, was the future for the Auld Alliance? Its aims had largely been accomplished: the English had been cleared out of France, and a weakened England represented no real threat to the independence and integrity of the Kingdom of Scotland. The Franco-Scottish alliance diminished in stature to become little more than, in modern parlance, a 'special relationship', with Charles VII and James II writing friendly but distant letters to each other. Thus King Charles was prepared to act as mediator in disputes between James II and the Danes, at Chinon in 1459 and Bourges in 1460; King James for his part joined with the King of Castile to mediate between France and Burgundy (where Charles VII's rebellious son Louis had fled for protection) in 1458; and Charles neatly side-stepped the Scottish king's request for the cession of Saintonge in 1458. When in 1460 James II sought to take advantage of English weakness to recover Roxburgh, however, he was on his own, not part of a second front to assist his French ally; for the Hundred Years' War was over. Roxburgh was duly captured in early August 1460; but James II was killed at the siege, mortally wounded by the explosion of one of his own cannon. He was twenty-nine.

Scottish diplomacy had now become, in Alexander Grant's words, a 'complex quadrille' involving Scotland, England, France, and Burgundy, further complicated by the alignment of the victorious Yorkist king Edward IV of England with the Burgundians, while the defeated Lancastrians, represented by Henry VI and his formidable wife Margaret of Anjou, looked to France for succour. And not only to France. Following the Yorkist victories of 1460–1, Henry VI and his queen became refugees in Scotland; and the astute Mary of Gueldres, James II's widow, obtained Berwick for Scotland in April 1461 as the price of her support for the Lancastrian cause, swiftly changing sides when it became apparent that the Yorkists had won the day in England. By the early 1460s, the last Scottish strongholds lost to England during the wars of independence had been regained by war or negotiation, and the most obvious motive for war between the two kingdoms had been removed.

However, the 1460s also witnessed a rapid turnover in the *dramatis personae* who ruled in France, Burgundy, England, and Scotland. As we have seen, Henry VI became first a fugitive in Scotland, and was subsequently captured and spent almost the rest of his life in the Tower of London as a prisoner of the Yorkists; Edward IV, the first Yorkist ruler of England, confirmed his kingship with a shattering victory over the Lancastrians at Towton in March 1461. Four months later, on 22 July 1461, Charles VII of France, who had spent more than forty years fighting for survival, the expulsion of the English from his kingdom, and an accommodation with the great feudatories of France, died at Mehunsur-Yèvre near Bourges. He was succeeded by the dauphin Louis, whose rebellions against his father had been supported by the Burgundians, but who, as Louis XI of France, would look on the destruction of Burgundy as his most important mission in life. And in Burgundy Philip the Good, the most successful of the great dukes, and certainly the richest, died in 1467, leaving the duchy in the unstable hands of his son and heir, Charles, count of Charolais, who as duke of Burgundy acquired the nickname of Charles the Bold ('le Temeraire') or Rash.

Growing to manhood in this rapidly changing European landscape was the new King of Scots, James III (1460–1488). This aloof and enigmatic ruler, who undoubtedly possessed greater initial advantages than any of his Stewart predecessors, took control of government in 1469 after a minority in which Scotland had been ruled first by his mother, Mary of Gueldres, then by Bishop Kennedy of St Andrews, and finally by the Boyds of Kilmarnock, who had advanced their family fortunes by seizing the king's person in 1466. In 1469 James was seventeen, and initially he showed himself a true son of his warlike father. In 1471–2 he contemplated leading an army abroad to seize part of Brittany from its duke, a scheme apparently instigated by the crafty Louis XI of France as a means of obtaining the army of 6,000 Scots first denied to, and then unwanted by, his father. The ubiquitous William Monypenny, now a Scottish lord of parliament as well as lord of Concressault in Berry, was pressed into service by Louis XI to negotiate with James III; but the first prospect of a Scottish king leading an army abroad since the early 1420s (when James I, in a rather different fashion, had campaigned in France) was scotched by a Scottish parliament whose spokesmen were reluctant to give the king his expenses and reminded him of his duty to provide for the succession.

The projected dismemberment of Brittany was one of the three Continental schemes which preoccupied the Scottish king during the years 1471–3. Another was James III's claim to the duchy of Gueldres, his interest lying in the fact that his mother, Mary of Gueldres, had been the eldest daughter of duke Arnold of Gueldres; but Arnold had been deposed by his son Adolphus, who by the early '70s was in the custody of Charles the Bold, duke of Burgundy. Thus although the Scots had a clear interest in the succession to Gueldres – James III's brother, Alexander, duke of Albany, had spent part of his youth there, and the Scottish king may have been asked to intervene in Gueldres by duke Arnold – little or nothing was likely to be achieved without Burgundy's support; and the truth was that Charles the Bold intended to acquire the duchy for himself.

It is conceivable that the crisis in Gueldres had been engineered by Louis XI of France. The 'Spider King', whose complex diplomatic webs were mainly woven to weaken or isolate his great rival Charles the Bold,

Beginnings: The Treaty of Paris, 23 October 1295, between Philip IV (the Fair) and John (Balliol), King of Scots. *Paris, Archives Nationales,* J. 677 (1).

John Balliol performs homage to Edward I of England. Royal MS 20C, VII F. 28
British Library.

Edward I of England performs homage to Philip the Fair of France, the ally of the Kings of Scots. *Grandes Chroniques de France:* Ms. Fr. 6465, f. 301v. *Bibliothèque nationale de France.*

Silver groat of Robert II, the founder of the Stewart dynasty. *National Museums of Scotland.*

The siege of Orléans (1428). *Chroniques du temps de Charles VII:* Ms. Fr. 2691.
Bibliothèque nationale de France.

bride for the dauphin: Margaret of Scotland enters Tours on Midsummer Day
436. *Chroniques du temps de Charles* VII: Ms. Fr. 2691. *Bibliothèque nationale de France.*

Adoration of the Magi, attributed to Jean Fouquet, from *The Hours of Etienne Chevali*
This illumination, painted between 1452 and 1461, depicts Charles VII, attended k
the *Garde Ecossaise*, as the first of the Three Kings. In the background his troops m
be seen laying siege to a well-defended castle. This may be a mock battle staged
part of the Epiphany celebrations.

Bérault Stewart, Lord of Aubigny, counsellor and chamberlain of the King of France, knight of the Order of St. Michael, captain of the *Garde Ecossaise*, hero of the Italian Wars, Renaissance patron and diplomat (died Corstorphine, June 1508). *Bibliothèque de l'Arsenal*, Paris, Ms. 5062, f. 203v.

The remains of the Château of Concressault in Berry, one residence of William, Lord Monypenny, Franco-Scottish diplomat and soldier. *Author's photograph.*

The more impressive pile of La Verrerie, a few miles from Concressault and Aubigny, built by Bérault Stewart and his successor Robert. *Author's photograph.*

The chapel at La Verrerie. The interior is decorated with painted roundels containing Aubigny Stewart and French royal and noble portraits against a background of
thistles and fleurs-de-lys. *Author's photograph.*

Diplomacy rewarded: the west front of the cathedral of Bourges, centre of the archbishopric obtained for Andrew Forman, bishop of Moray, by a grateful Louis XII of France. *Author's photograph.*

Imperial imagery: James V with his second wife Mary of Guise. An anonymous and probably contemporary portrait, showing an imperial crown between the royal couple. James V's premature death in 1542 would severely damage the Auld Alliance; Mary of Guise's death in 1560 would destroy it. *Scottish National Portrait Gallery.*

'A French château set down in Fife': Falkland Palace from the north. The palace was remodelled from 1537 onwards. James V, newly returned from his French holiday, employed French masons to re-design the north, east and south ranges of the palace. *Crown Copyright: Royal Commission on the Ancient and Historical Monuments of Scotland.*

Mary, Queen of Scots around the age of thirteen. This chalk drawing with water
colour, attributed to François Clouet, provides a striking image of the queen a fe
years before her marriage to the dauphin Francis. *Library of the Ossolinski Nation*
Institute of the Polish Academy of Science, Wroclaw.

was a past-master at stirring up trouble in territories neighbouring Burgundy, or directly under the duke's lordship. His Breton scheme, if carried through, would have involved others – namely the Scots – in an invasion of a duchy which Louis also wished to acquire for himself. Similarly Charles the Bold might be weakened by a dispute in Gueldres. The French king was, in a sense, endeavouring to put the clock back and invoke the Auld Alliance – one amongst many – as a counter to the formidable coalition of Burgundy and England, a menace to France which had not been seen since the 1430s. It must be said that Louis XI, for all his cunning, had brought much of this on himself; for in 1470 he had backed a Lancastrian revival in England in the person of the feeble Henry VI. Henry had been briefly restored, and the Yorkist Edward IV chased from his throne to become a temporary refugee in Burgundy. But Edward's triumphant return to England in 1471, winning the battles of Barnet and Tewkesbury and eliminating Henry VI, left Louis XI dangerously exposed as the enemy of Yorkist England and Burgundy. Throughout the early 1470s the French king fearfully anticipated an Anglo-Burgundian invasion, and sought to protect himself through renewal of familiar leagues, including the Franco-Scottish alliance.

Ultimately James III was unimpressed. During his minority Scotland had already been deserted by its fickle French ally when in October 1463 Louis had made a truce with the Yorkists from which the Scots were excluded. Now, in the 1470s, King James clearly reckoned that he was in a good bargaining position with Louis; and he was negotiating for a very tangible return, in territory or money – or both – for his support. Thus in 1472 the issue of the cession to the Scots of the county of Saintonge was brought up yet again, together with offers to open a second front against Edward IV, if the English king landed in France, in return for a pension of 60,000 crowns a year. A period of intensive diplomacy followed, with James III sending John Murray to Louis in the spring of 1474, warning the French king that Edward IV of England was pressing the Scots to break the Franco-Scottish alliance and instead to negotiate a treaty with England; Louis XI countered by sending the first of the next generation of Monypennys, Alexander, son of the lord of Concressault, to Scotland, offering 10,000 crowns to James III if he could launch an attack on England and divert Edward IV from his projected invasion of France. It was very much old-style alliance diplomacy, to which Louis added a sweetener by making Lord Monypenny seneschal of Saintonge.

It was all too little and too late. The astute Louis had miscalculated once more, possibly believing that Scotland and England were on the brink of war, as some unreliable Milanese reports of the time suggested.

James III, who summed up the essence of Scottish foreign policy in a sentence at this time by remarking that the king of England was the only European ruler who made war on Scotland, opted in October 1474 for the first firm Anglo-Scottish alliance of the century. This brought the Scottish king immediate material gains: his son James (the future James IV), born at Holyrood the previous year, was to be married to Edward IV's daughter Cecilia when both infants reached an appropriate age. In the meantime, the English would pay instalments of Cecilia's dowry in advance. And the dowry was substantial – 20,000 marks sterling, or around £35,000 Scots.

Too late in the day, in the late summer of 1474, Louis XI must have got wind of the impending collapse of the Franco-Scottish alliance and the threatening prospect of Anglo-Scottish amity as an alternative. As a last attempt to swing the diplomatic situation round, he wrote to Gian-galeazzo Sforza, duke of Milan, suggesting a marriage between one of the duke's daughters and the prince of Scotland. Sforza caustically replied that while he was quite prepared to muddy the waters by opening negotiations, he would not wish to marry off any of his daughters 'so far off as Scotland would be', or, in the less diplomatic language of his ambassador, 'in finibus orbis' ('at the ends of the earth'). So much for the growing reputation of the Stewart kingdom within Continental Europe.

The Anglo-Scottish treaty of 1474, though in some ways the logical outcome of a growing rapprochement between the two kingdoms since the mid-1460s, turned traditional Scottish foreign policy on its head. The Auld Alliance, which had not been formally renewed since 1448, was shattered; for Edward IV's main purpose in allying with Scotland was to ensure her neutrality during his invasion of France, which occurred in the summer of 1475. However, the wily Louis XI, whose skill in extricating himself from crises of his own making was legendary, turned aside the Anglo-Burgundian threat to his kingdom by detaching Edward IV from the alliance before the Burgundians could take the field. The Treaty of Picquigny (July 1475), made following a personal meeting between Louis XI and Edward IV, left the latter with a sizeable annual French pension which he enjoyed for most of the rest of his life. At a stroke, the Yorkist threat was removed, and King Louis was left free to concentrate on the Burgundians.

The knock-on effect of Picquigny for the Scots was that Edward IV had no further pressing need for the Anglo-Scottish alliance of 1474. His enthusiasm for it clearly dwindled in the late 1470s, although he continued to pay regular instalments of his daughter's dowry. By contrast, James III's enthusiasm for maintaining, and even extending, the English alliance remained undiminished. In the late 1470s, he pressed for a marriage between his sister Margaret and Edward IV's brother George duke of Clarence, a proposal quashed by Clarence's arraignment for treason and bizarre execution in February 1478. Nothing daunted, James III suggested an alternative bridegroom in the English king's brother-in-law, Anthony Lord Rivers; and in March 1479 the Scottish estates voted a tax of 20,000 marks as the expenses of sending Margaret to England for her marriage. Only a fraction of it was ever collected; and in the following year James III found himself in the appalling position of having to go to war with the ally whom he had obsequiously pursued, against the odds, since 1474.

The truth was that the Scottish king had done himself a serious disservice in his single-minded pursuit of the English alliance. It was not popular with powerful elements in Scotland, especially in the south; the English rapidly tired of it; and James had omitted to provide himself with insurance by formally renewing the French alliance. Thus as the '80s loomed, James III not only found himself at war with his former ally Edward IV, but also opposed by an influential group amongst his own subjects; and France, far from being an ally to whom he could turn in need, had become a refuge for dissident elements in his own kingdom, above all his brother Alexander, duke of Albany.

Winners and Losers: Scots in France and Franco-Scots

Scots mercenaries who survived the carnage of the 1420s and opted to remain in France thereafter experienced mixed fortunes. Some initially remained part of the Army of Scotland under its successive constables, Patrick Ogilvy and Alan Stuart of Darnley (son of the John Stuart killed at Rouvray in 1429); others formed independent companies whose presence in central France became a growing menace to the French and to the Scots' former employer Charles VII; and some were employed either in Charles's bodyguard, the *Garde Ecossaise*, or in one of the ordonnance companies formed by the French king in 1445.

In spite of the setback at Rouvray, the Army of Scotland, under the command of Patrick Ogilvy, styled 'sheriff of Angus' in the French records, still contained seven Scottish captains and at least 500 Scots archers and men-at-arms, all of whom acted as Joan of Arc's companions-in-arms on her entry into Orléans in May 1429. Describing the advent of Joan some two decades later, Abbot Walter Bower remarked that she 'conferred many benefits on France and struck terror among the English'. Her Scottish companions-in-arms were perhaps less easily overawed. When Joan rebuked a Scottish soldier for looting food in Orléans, he retorted that she had been eating some of it herself.

After the tremendous drama of the 1420s, the progress of the Army of

Scotland becomes less easy to discern. Its records, which were kept separate from Charles VII's other military outlays, have not survived; but there can be little doubt that there were occasions when the Scots, like other soldiers in French service, were paid late or not at all. Furthermore, as the '30s advanced – and especially after the Franco-Burgundian rapprochement of 1435 – King Charles had less need of the foreign troops in his service; and when they turn up in the records, it is frequently as criminals or extortioners. As early as July 1433 we find an agreement between the city council of Tours and an individual styling himself 'James Stewart, bastard of Scotland', who was clearly the leader of a company of Scots in the vicinity. The agreement indicates the existence of a lucrative protection racket. Grandly affecting the royal 'we' ('Nous Jacques Stewart chevalier bastart descoce'), Stewart demanded to be paid 6,000 *écus* by Tours, in return for which none of his captains would claim lodgings within five leagues of the city, or damage property; and all travellers in the area would be taken under his protection. The agreement would be valid for only three months. It was no new thing for the citizens of Tours to have to pay for foreign mercenaries to move on, or at least not to rob them; but Charles VII could hardly claim to be liberating France from the depredations of the English and Burgundians if he had no effective control over marauding bands of Scots, Lombards, and Spaniards.

The French king eventually tackled the problem in the summer of 1445 by promulgating the 'ordonnance', a measure designed to divide military forces under royal control into fifteen companies, each composed of a hundred 'lances' – that is, 400 armed men. If this was the original concept, it was not followed in practice; Professor Contamine has identified 24 captains who held command at this time, over companies of varying sizes. However, the creation of new companies 'à l'ordonnance du roi' officially spelled the end of the independent companies – the *Ecorcheurs* – and tightened up French royal military administration. Initially there were two Scottish captains, Robert Cunningham and Robin Pettylow (described as 'Petit-Loup' in the French accounts), each in command of a company of 400 men. Subsequently these two Scottish ordonnance companies were amalgamated, and a single company continued to serve successive French kings down to the end of the fifteenth century and beyond. Its leaders included both Cunninghams, Robert and his son, John, Pettylow and – later – Bérault Stuart of Aubigny; it played a prominent part in such ventures as Charles VII's siege of, and triumphant entry into, Rouen in 1449 and Louis XII's entry into Milan fifty years later; and in general, probably due to their proximity to the king, soldiers in the Scottish ordonnance company appear to have had better opportunities for advancement than their French counterparts.

Set apart from the ordonnance companies, and unaffected by the ordonnance of 1445, was the royal bodyguard, the *Garde Ecossaise*, which had protected Charles VII from the very outset of the reign. Some of them had probably been with Charles on the bridge at Montereau in 1419; subsequently, in 1442, they had to save the king from burning to death when his lodgings at La Réole in Gascony were set on fire, though his sword of state, the sword of St Louis, was apparently lost in the blaze. Towards the end of the reign the *Garde Ecossaise* remained consistently loyal to King Charles in spite of the dauphin Louis' efforts to subvert them. When the dauphin duly became Louis XI in 1461, he was in a position to appreciate the loyalty of the Scots, and retained them as his bodyguard throughout the reign.

Distinctive in the royal livery colours of red, white, and green, the members of the *Garde Ecossaise*, like the papal Swiss guard, lived a life which alternated between boredom and terror – hanging about the entrances to royal apartments for much of the time, and then being suddenly called upon to frustrate attempts on the king's life, or to defend him in war. The Scots guards, immortalised in Sir Walter Scott's *Quentin Durward*, are described in the French records as 'soldiers of the nation of Scotland, continually about the person of the king'. According to Professor Chevalier, they appear to have numbered 106, including a small corps of 24 archers and a larger group consisting of both men-at-arms and archers. The heyday for the Scots in this élite corps was the entire reign of Charles VII and much of that of his successor Louis XI. However, by the end of the latter's reign in 1483, the Scots were only one element in the small army employed to protect the king and the royal household; the bodyguard had increased in numbers to 540 men-at-arms and archers, of whom only around a hundred were Scots. The commanders of the *Garde Ecossaise*, however, remained expatriate Scots or their descendants – Christy and Nicol Chambers, Patrick Folcart, the Cunninghams, father and son, Bérault Stuart and his nephew Robert.

There were, of course, winners and losers amongst the Scots. The latter included those who had not been incorporated into the ordonnance companies, or who simply continued to take an independent line on the wrong side of the law. In some cases, their fates may be discerned in contemporary judicial records – for example, in a remission to a labourer at Vivier near Tours, who had murdered a Scots soldier who had stolen his wheat and beaten up his brother; or in the rather sad case of the remission granted to the notary Pierre Buyon and his son Yves, both from Azay-le-Rideau in Touraine, who had insulted a neighbour and murdered a Scot, John Gray or Gras, who had tried to intervene. What eventually became of 'James Stewart bastard of Scotland' is, however, unrecorded.

If some lost out, many prospered. Service in the ordonnance companies automatically conferred gentle birth; and many Scots thus employed looked beyond their military service to establish themselves and their families in France. To achieve this, they sought and obtained from the royal chancery letters of naturalisation which would allow them to endow goods and property to their descendants. In the later fifteenth century, thirty such letters were granted to Scots – not only to career diplomats like Sir William Monypenny, who had served James II and James III of Scotland as well as Charles VII and Louis XI of France, but to lesser known but highly successful expatriates. As we have seen, the Vernon dynasty in Poitou and Touraine acquired their wealth and influence through Laurence Vernon's capture and subsequent ransom of the earl of Somerset at Baugé in 1421. Of comparable status, also in Poitou and Touraine, were the Cunninghams: John Cunningham was wealthy enough in 1489 to acquire the lands and Château of Cangé in Touraine; not only did he rebuild the castle, but he also paid for the reconstruction and endowment of the neighbouring parish church of St Avertin. Another father-son team, Christy and Nicol Chambre or Chambers, were well rewarded for their captaincy of the *Garde Ecossaise:* the latter not only became Lord of La Guerche and Chédigny in Touraine in 1448, but his French wife, Catherine Chenin, was employed by the king to escort the princess Eleanor Stewart from Chinon to Innsbruck late in 1448. Nicol and his wife received 5,000 *livres* from the Crown around this time; and on Chambre's retirement from the guard in 1451, he became lord of Villeneuve-la-Comtesse with a generous pension from Charles VII. Patrick Folcart, Chambre's successor at the head of the *Garde Ecossaise*, had an income of no less than 4,300 *livres* at the outset of the 1470s, not counting gifts; for both Charles VII and Louis XI understood that loyalty from their closest servants could best be guaranteed by frequent acts of generosity.

Advancement for ambitious Scots in France, then, was most frequently achieved through service to the crown in the royal bodyguard or one of the ordonnance companies. The guard was also replenished with newcomers arriving from Scotland in the late fifteenth century, presumably by invitation; for example Andrew Kynnimond, arriving at Plessis-les-Tours from Fife in 1478 to take service in the royal bodyguard under Robert Cunningham, married Jeanne de Nepveto, lady of St Senoch and La Roche Aymer in Touraine, and founded what became one of the most important families in the duchy, with 'Kynnimond' rendered into French as 'Quinemont.' Two generations sion of Scots from Tours following the disaster of Verr Franco-Scottish families of Hay, Gray and Drem Drummond), all headed by soldiers of the royal bodygu property in the neighbourhood, at Azay-le-Rideau and La Chapel Blaise. And before the end of the century there are examples of Franco-Scots buying and selling to each other: in 1489, Henry Crawford, lord of Longchamps, and his wife Mariette Deriam, are to be found selling property to Simon Ferré, a man-at-arms in the company of Bérault Stuart of Aubigny.

But it is in Berry, at the heart of France, that the most concentrated and influential group of expatriates and Franco-Scots is to be found. Within Bourges itself, no fewer than eleven Scots owned town houses in the later fifteenth century; these included William Henryson, John Stud and his son-in-law Gilbert Cunningham, lord of Sollier, John Dodds, archer of the royal bodyguard, and John Chambre, 'natif du païs d'Ecosse'. These men lived in the parishes of St-Fulgent and St-Pierre-le-Guillard, close to the royal palace of Bourges, which would suggest that, whether or not they were so designated, they were all employed by the Crown. Further afield in Berry, we find Franco-Scottish dynasties established through fortunate marriages, like the Stutt or Estuard family, who included the mother of Guillaume de Cambray, archbishop of Bourges; David de L'Isle, of a Glasgow family, archer in the *Garde Ecossaise*, who married Guillemette Bastard; on his death Guillemette remarried, choosing another Scot, John Cockburn, whose father George was captain of a hundred Scots in Louis XII's army entering Genoa in 1502. And so it goes on – Aitchisons, Houstons, Johnstons, Langs, all arriving in France as mercenary soldiers and subsequently settling in Berry, many making local marriages and not a few acquiring considerable wealth. The family of Monypenny stand out from all of these, as their fortunes were earned not through war but through diplomacy; they possessed not only the lordship of Concressault, north of Bourges, but the lands of Kirkandrews in Galloway, the office of seneschal of Saintonge, and an annual pension of 1200 *livres* from Louis XI. In the early sixteenth century, one of the family, William Monypenny, abbot of Saint-Satur, even went so far as to seek election as archbishop of Bourges, which would have made him one of the most powerful men in France. He failed; but as we shall see, another Scot, Andrew Forman, bishop of Moray, succeeded.

The Monypennys were a family who never lost touch with their roots, looking for advancement not only in France but also in their native land. By far the most important family of this kind – indeed the most influential of all Franco-Scottish dynasties in the late fifteenth century –

was that of Stewart of Aubigny in Berry. The family's fortunes were securely based on the service of Sir John Stewart of Darnley, who as we have seen fought consistently for Charles VII throughout the 1420s, receiving the lordship of Aubigny-sur-Nère from a grateful king as early as March 1423, losing an eye at Cravant but temporarily acquiring the county of Evreux in 1427; serving – probably rather warily, in view of what James I of Scotland had done to his kin in 1425 – on the French embassy which negotiated the Treaty of Perth-Chinon in 1428; and finally losing his life as Constable of the Army of Scotland, at the 'Battle of the Herrings' at Rouvray in February 1429.

John Stewart was succeeded by his elder son Alan, who though named as Constable of the Scots, does not seem to have received much favour from Charles VII in the early 1430s. In 1437, within a month of James I's assassination, Alan Stewart of Darnley made elaborate preparations to return to Scotland. With James I dead, he may have reckoned that he was safe to lay claim (through his mother) to half the earldom of Lennox; and a letter of Charles VII, dated 4 August 1437, refers to Darnley's imminent departure for Scotland, apparently on the king's business as well as his own. However, Darnley had misjudged his time: on 20 September 1438 he was treacherously killed by Sir Thomas Boyd of Kilmarnock during a meeting held by the two men to resolve the Boyd/Darnley family feud. The following summer Alexander 'Bucktooth' Stewart, the dead Alan's brother, had his revenge; enlisting his family and friends, he killed Boyd and put an end – at least temporarily – to the feud. Viewing the volatile politics of south-west Scotland with a cool eye, John Stewart, second Lord of Aubigny, stayed in France and enjoyed a distinguished career under Charles VII and Louis XI, as captain of the *Garde Ecossaise* for both kings. He married Beatrix d'Apchier; and around 1452–3 the couple had a son Bérault, whose fame was to eclipse that of all other Scots in France.

5
Renewal: 1484-1517

In the early 1480s, the Franco-Scottish alliance must have seemed only a distant memory to the rulers of both kingdoms. It had not been renewed since 1448, and by the mid-fifteenth century, the wars which had sustained the alliance for so long had come to an end. Louis XI of France had been especially cynical about the alliance, and James III of Scotland abandoned it altogether in pursuit of a rapprochement with Yorkist England. Yet in the space of little more than thirty years from 1484 onwards, the Auld Alliance would receive formal renewal no less than four times, and the commitment of France and Scotland to each other's military, naval and diplomatic needs would prove stronger than at any earlier time.

No Safety Net: the Crisis of 1482–3

The renewal of the alliance in the spring of 1484 occurred largely because James III badly needed some foreign insurance to offset his inept diplomacy and deeply unpopular domestic policies. As we have seen, towards the end of the 1470s King James was eagerly pursuing an English alliance about which Edward IV was unenthusiastic, while successive parliaments were criticising the Scottish king for his efforts to levy taxation and his failure to staunch feuds throughout the country. James III's committed Anglophile stance was clearly deeply resented by power-ful magnates, especially in the south, where his brother Alexander, duke of Albany, earl of March and lord of Annandale, became a focus for resistance to Crown policies. Albany, an aggressive magnate whose wardenship of all three Scottish marches gave him very extensive powers, clearly preferred fighting the English to upholding King James's peace on the borders; and he was compared with the king, his brother, to the latter's disadvantage. Blind Harry's epic vernacular poem 'The Wallace', which was written in the late 1470s and was to become enormously popular a generation later, is an indictment of James III's pro-English policy and, by implication, a vindication of Albany's resistance to it.

The response of the neurotically suspicious James III to his brother's popularity was to play the old Stewart game of attempting a pre-emptive strike against opponents. Albany, however, neatly sidestepped a huge parliament in March 1479, at which he would probably have been arrested, and when a royal army arrived to lay siege to his castle of Dunbar at the end of April, he had probably already taken ship for France. James III's siege of Dunbar was followed in the autumn by his attempt to have Albany forfeited for treason by an assize of parliament; but the indictment was so unconvincing that no sentence was passed, with the case being continued again and again over the next two-and-a-half years.

The escape to France of a man considered by many Scots to have a far greater aptitude for ruling the kingdom than James III underlined the dangers for the king of failing to maintain good relations with Louis XI; and worse was to follow. The wily French king was quick to recognise Albany's value as a diplomatic pawn. He paid for the duke's lodgings at the 'Sign of the Cock', and swiftly arranged a prestigious marriage for him; on 19 January 1480 Albany, with Louis' blessing, was married to Anne de la Tour, daughter of the Count of Auvergne and Bouillon. Thirty-five years later their son would become Governor of Scotland.

It seems likely that, on his arrival in France, Albany was met by sympathetic expatriate Scots close to King Louis. The Stewarts of Aubigny, as kin of Albany's ally in the west march, John Stewart, Lord Darnley, were probably present at the French court on the duke's arrival there – Jean Stewart the father as captain of the *Garde Ecossaise*, and Bérault, his son and successor in Aubigny in 1482 and in the guard in 1493, would be described as counsellor and chamberlain of Louis XI as early as 1482. In his late twenties in 1479, Bérault was already a seasoned soldier, having been a man-at-arms in Robert Cunningham's ordonnance company at the age of sixteen.

Bérault Stewart can also be linked to another expatriate Scot who played a major role in Franco-Scottish diplomacy at this time. A surviving copy of a chronicle of Scotland from its mythological beginnings to 1463, the 'Vraie Cronicque d'Escoce', includes a note to the effect that its former owner was Bérault Stewart and that its author was 'ung grant clerc escosois nommé irlandia'. This 'great Scottish clerk' was John Ireland , who had left his home university of St Andrews without a degree in 1459, and subsequently had a distinguished academic career in Paris, where he had become a Doctor of Theology at the Sorbonne by 1476. This was the Scot whom Louis XI employed in 1480, perhaps not without a hint of irony, to go on embassy to Scotland with the ostensible aim of mediating between James III and Albany. Bérault Stewart and John Ireland were subsequently to act together as ambassadors in 1484, and their relationship may date from that year; but it is tempting to envisage an earlier association, dating from Albany's arrival at the French court in 1479.

The Spider King's more likely motive in sending John Ireland to
Scotland was to provoke trouble between James III and Edward IV, so
that the latter would be in no position to give any assistance to
Maximilian of Burgundy. Ireland, however, may have had his own
agenda, namely finding a new patron in James III. If so, he was
remarkably successful. By the summer of 1480, he was already sitting
with the royal judicial body, the Lords of Council; and though he went
back to France thereafter, and was probably there from late 1480 to 1483,
he may have been moved by Louis XI's failing health to seek a
permanent return to his native land; for while still in France, and at
James III's request, Ireland wrote the treatise *De Speciali Auxilio*, and sent
two Latin hymns to the Scottish king.

None of this laudable activity made the slightest difference to the
events of 1480–82. Probably before Ireland's first embassy to Scotland,
James III had become involved in a war with a belligerent and increasingly insecure Edward IV. The projected royal marriage was off, and the
English king looked to a return of the advances already paid on Cecilia's
dowry, to which he added a demand for the cession of Berwick and a
string of other unacceptable points in what amounted to an ultimatum.
King James, though dangerously isolated, continued to take advice from
unpopular counsellors, including William Scheves, whom the king had
elevated from a court servant to archbishop of St Andrews (and who may
have been responsible for John Ireland leaving St Andrews without a
degree in 1459); he had his other brother, John Stewart, earl of Mar,
arrested – probably in December 1479 – and subsequently forfeited and
executed in mysterious circumstances early the following year; and he
had no answer to the menace posed by Albany, and the continuing
reluctance of parliamentary assizes to forfeit the duke.

Thus in the spring of 1480 James III became embroiled in a war with his
former ally Edward IV not only without the support of France, but in the
knowledge that the French king was providing succour to James's dissident
brother Albany; and at home the king would have to rely on the Scottish
host, made up of men who had criticised him openly for a decade, to
defend him in his *volte face* from Anglophile to abuse of Edward IV as 'the
reiver Edward, calling himself King of England'. At first, however, the
dismal failure of his diplomacy did not affect James III as seriously as
might have been expected. 'King Edward's war', as David Dunlop calls it,
was initially something of a phoney war, confined to English naval raids on
the Firth of Forth and the 'scaling' (disbanding) of the English and Scottish
hosts without coming to blows in 1481. One ominous omen, however, was
the loss at sea during a violent North Sea storm of a gift of cannon
thoughtfully sent to James III by his uncle, Sigismund of Austria.

Another kind of storm broke over James III's head in 1482; for in that year Edward IV clearly meant business. Initially he intended to lead an army north in person; but when he handed the command over to his younger brother Richard, duke of Gloucester, he was doing the Scots no favours. For Gloucester, in Alexander Grant's view the most powerful northern English magnate since the Norman conquest, was a seasoned commander and a man of seemingly limitless ambition; worse, he was devoted to the Northumbrian St Cuthbert, whose intervention had proved disastrous to Scottish military enterprises in the past, and would do so again in the future. And Gloucester would not be coming alone. At the end of April 1482 Alexander, duke of Albany, armed with Louis XI's dubious blessing and sailing in a Scottish carvel, the *Michael*, commanded by one James Douglas, landed at Southampton; within six weeks he had made the Treaty of Fotheringhay with Edward IV, styling himself 'Alexander, king of Scotland' and promising to do homage and fealty to the English king for Scotland once James III had been removed. He would set off immediately for the north, sharing command of a huge army – possibly as many as 20,000 strong – with Gloucester.

At one level, it is difficult to take the Treaty of Fotheringhay seriously. On Albany's part, it may simply have been a device – perhaps the only one open to him – of acquiring control of Scottish government while James III was vulnerable. But it is hardly likely that Albany would genuinely countenance a restoration of the Black Douglases, or that he would be able to make himself 'clear of other women' to marry Cecilia in place of his nephew, as he had recently contracted a prestigious French marriage; yet both these courses were proposed in the Fotheringhay treaty. Clearly, however, the Scottish invasion scheme was the brainchild of Albany's two patrons, Louis XI and Edward IV, in the autumn of 1481, and Albany had to go along with their proposal that he should seek James III's throne as 'Alexander IV'.

Arguably, however, Albany's ambitions should also be seen in the context of an unofficial Franco-Scottish alliance, involving powerful Scottish magnates, possibly even some members of James III's council, on the one hand, and Albany and Scottish expatriates in France on the other. While Albany was still in France, a Scottish parliament, meeting at Edinburgh in March 1482, had put the country on a war footing, with elaborate (if inadequate) provisions for the defence of the borders. Despite the three estates' high-flown language, with a promise to live or die with the king, there was a strong undercurrent of opposition. An embassy sent to France to seek aid contained three of James III's most committed opponents – 'Hearty James' Stewart, earl of Buchan, the king's half-uncle and a born intriguer; Archibald, fifth earl of Angus; and

James Livingston, bishop of Dunkeld. These men would have had time – just – to confer with Albany in France before his departure for England, and to indicate to him how much support he might expect in a governmental coup in Scotland; certainly all of them were major political players in the Albany government of the autumn of 1482. In sum, there was probably a French end to Albany's intrigues; and the image of a treacherous and unpatriotic duke returning to his country at the head of an English army, destroying his reputation in Scotland in the process, is not wholly convincing in view both of Albany's past patriotic record and of subsequent events.

Closer to home, in the summer of 1482 the unpopular James III – who, whatever else he may have been, was no coward – was prepared to launch the Scottish host into battle against the rapidly advancing army of Albany and Gloucester. But the king had run out of allies; the dukes moving against him were coming at the behest of Louis XI and Edward IV, and with the potential or real support of many Scots. There is some irony in the situation; for in 1482 the Scottish king was doing his job as leader in war, calling out the host to Lauder to defend his country against the English. It was his hopelessly inept diplomacy which had left him friendless. The idea of following him into battle against 20,000 English can hardly have been popular with many in the Scottish host; and a plot to seize the king and avoid what must have seemed inevitable disaster may have existed for some time.

Thus at Lauder Bridge on 22 July 1482 the leaders of James's host – including his Master of Household, Colin earl of Argyll, his half-uncle Buchan and his cousin John Stewart, Lord Darnley – seized James III, hanged a few of his familiars over the bridge, and hurried the king back to Edinburgh, where they incarcerated him in the castle with Darnley as his gaoler. Whether intentionally or otherwise, the Lauder lords had saved King James from the consequences of his own folly. For when the English army of Albany and Gloucester arrived in Edinburgh, James III was inaccessible in the castle, and the only Scots available to negotiate were the king's displaced counsellors and understandably frightened burgh representatives. This stalemate came to an end in early August, when Gloucester had to disband his army, using a smaller force to take Berwick later in the month as the only tangible English gain in a highly expensive campaign.

The various Scottish factions were left to work out their own political solutions. James III, initially in fear of his life, was eventually released from Edinburgh castle following a siege by Albany in late September; and for the remainder of the year the duke, having quietly dropped his untenable claim to the throne, claimed the office of lieutenant-general.

There were of course Scottish precedents for appointments to this office, most recently in 1399 and 1437; but these had been made because the king was senile in the one case and a minor in the other. In 1482 James III was a presumably sane adult king, aged thirty, arrested by his own subjects while attempting to perform one of a Scottish king's most vital duties. Thus when Albany attempted to have his lieutenant-generalship confirmed in parliament in December 1482, there was clearly a sharp division of opinion amongst the estates; and James III, though not yet a free agent, would not budge on the issue.

Shortly after Christmas, both sides cast about for military support, with Albany retiring to Dunbar and planning another coup, while the king, still in Edinburgh, summoned loyal lords, headed by the Gordon earl of Huntly, from the north-east. Thus the early months of 1483 witnessed something approaching civil war in Scotland, a struggle which was uncannily reminiscent of James II's contest with the Black Douglases thirty years earlier; for neither James III nor Albany had the strength to deliver a knock-out punch. The duke, having advanced on Edinburgh in early January, was soon back in Dunbar calling for English support; and in mid-March 1483 the king and Albany sealed an indenture which, like the James II–Douglas bond a generation before, was no more than a respite to allow both sides to improve their positions.

The vital difference between 1453 and 1483 was that, in the former case, there had been no danger of English intervention in Scotland's affairs. In January 1483, however, an English parliament conferred on Richard, duke of Gloucester, a hereditary grant of the wardenship of the west march, extensive powers in Cumberland, and all the lands which Gloucester could conquer for himself in the Scottish west march – Liddesdale, Eskdale, Ewesdale, Annandale, Wauchopdale, and Clydesdale – with all these Scottish conquests to be held as a palatinate, virtually independent of English royal control. As parliament also awarded Gloucester 10,000 marks sterling as initial finance, there was an immediate danger that the Scottish kingdom, hopelessly divided against itself, would be invaded by a formidable soldier who on this occasion, unlike 1482, would be coming on his own account; for Albany's lordship of Annandale was among Gloucester's projected conquests. In the early months of 1483, then, the kingdom of James III faced as grave a crisis as any thrust upon his predecessors during the wars of independence – and without the benefit of the safety net of the Auld Alliance.

As had often happened in the past, Scotland was saved by external events. On 9 April 1483, possibly as the result of apoplexy brought on by excess, Edward IV died at the age of forty. He left a thirteen-year-old heir Edward V; and the late king's brother Richard, duke of Gloucester, hurried south, first to assume the role of Protector, and then, on 26 June, to seize his nephew's throne as Richard III. The removal of Albany's former paymasters left the duke vulnerable and no longer able to play the patriot; he admitted an English garrison to Dunbar castle and took refuge in the south. James III, whose luck had been extraordinary, found the strength to arraign Albany for real rather than imagined treasons; and the duke was duly forfeited in July 1483.

Within five months of Edward IV's death, his rival, sometime pay-master, and diplomatic nemesis Louis XI followed the English king to the grave. The Spider King had for the most part been no friend to the Scots, apart, that is, from the *Garde Ecossaise*, who remained loyal to the aloof and mistrustful monarch in his last days at Plessis-les-Tours. Louis' death on 30 August 1483 left France, like England earlier in the year, with a thirteen-year-old heir, Charles VIII; unlike his English counterpart, Edward V, however, King Charles was fortunate to have an honest and capable regent, his sister Anne of Beaujeu. However, the deaths in rapid succession of Edward IV and Louis XI provided the opportunity for the eternal diplomatic triangle of France, England and Scotland to be resumed in time-honoured fashion. James III was confronted by a hostile English ruler, Richard III, who had benefited from Scottish crises to acquire Dunbar and Berwick; the regency government for Charles VIII of France looked to absorb Brittany and to provide a refuge for the Lancastrian Henry Tudor, the claimant to Richard III's throne. It was time to forget the recent past and to renew the Auld Alliance for the first time since 1448.

The Lord of Aubigny and the Treaties of 1484 and 1491–2

The initiative for renewal came from the French. It was characteristic of James III that, in spite of his recent experiences, he looked first to England for a renewal of the truce and, if he could manage it, a full-scale alliance based on the return of Dunbar and Berwick. But Richard III's initial replies to James's letters, in the autumn and early winter of 1483, were unenthusiastic; and King James reverted instead to the classic pattern of Scottish diplomacy, responding at last to appeals for a renewal of the Franco-Scottish alliance. The way may well have been prepared by John Ireland, who following the death of his other patron Louis XI, returned to Scotland and is to be found in James III's service as early as November 1483.

In the early spring of 1484 Charles VIII's ambassadors, Bérault Stewart of Aubigny and Master Pierre Millet, arrived in Edinburgh. This was Stewart's first recorded visit to the country which, despite his French birth and upbringing, he described as his native land. In his early thirties, Lord of Aubigny since his father Jean's death in 1482, Bérault already bore the imposing titles of counsellor and chamberlain of the King of France; and as a kinsman of the Lennox Stewarts he must have been well acquainted, even at long distance, with recent Scottish politics, and certainly with the crisis of 1482–3 in which his cousin John Stewart, Lord Darnley, had played a major role.

The French aim in 1484 was clearly to convince James III that the old alliance was preferable to his recent dubious English experiments, a cogent argument in 1484 when Richard III, to bolster his own shaky throne, was conducting a naval war against Brittany, France, and Scotland. To lend weight to diplomatic rhetoric, Bérault Stewart may also have brought with him the collar of the Order of St Michael, a gift from the government of Charles VIII to James III. The Scottish king took little convincing; with remarkable speed, on 13 March he confirmed the 1448 alliance at Edinburgh – an offensive and defensive Franco-Scottish pact of friendship directed against England, with neither ally sheltering the rebels of the other. John Ireland was one of the ambassadors who crossed to France bearing James III's seal and signature on the treaty, which was duly ratified by Charles VIII on 9 July.

Having taken out his French insurance policy, King James was in a stronger bargaining position in his dealings with Richard III. He was further strengthened by the failure of his brother Albany, who together with James, the forfeited ninth earl of Douglas, had made an incursion into the Scottish west march in the summer of 1484. On 22 July the Albany/Douglas force was defeated at Lochmaben by an army of local lords and lairds. Douglas, a relic of a previous age, was captured and imprisoned for the remaining seven years of his life; Albany escaped and remained a menace, though he was unlikely to receive further official support, either from France or England. Thus at the Anglo-Scottish peace talks at Nottingham in September 1484, Richard III was very much on the defensive. He had lost his only son in the spring; the Franco-Scottish alliance, directed against him, had been renewed; and worst of all (though Richard may not have been aware of it when he met the Scots at Nottingham) Henry Tudor fled – just in time – from Brittany to France in September 1484, and would henceforth receive the protection and active support of the greatest power in Europe.

Thus the Anglo-Scottish truce negotiated at Nottingham failed to produce the peace that James III no doubt wanted, for he also wanted the return of Dunbar and Berwick; and the masterly Latin oration which the senior Scottish ambassador, James's secretary and former tutor, Archibald Whitelaw, delivered to Richard III in person, combined compliments on the English king's martial prowess – in spite of his small physical stature – and warnings that kings should not take over each others' lands: in other words, as Alexander Grant convincingly suggests, that Dunbar and Berwick should be restored to the Scots. Richard, very much on the back foot, did the negotiating in person; and the end result was a three-year truce and a projected marriage between the Scottish king's son and heir and Anne de la Pole, Richard III's niece.

Further negotiations between James III and Richard III failed to materialise. On 22 August 1485 the last Yorkist king was defeated and killed at Bosworth, and Henry Tudor became King of England as Henry VII. Richard III probably failed mainly because he had so many enemies at home and because many of those on whose support he depended did not turn up, played no active role, or worse, changed sides at the last moment. But Richard was also in some sense a victim of the Franco-Scottish alliance. For it appears that, following the Edinburgh treaty of March 1484, Bérault Stewart returned to France with 'bon nombre de gens de Guerre' – Scottish reinforcements, probably for the ordonnance company, to fight against the English. The Beaujeu government in France, fearing an Anglo-Breton alliance, even an English invasion, used Franco-Scottish troops under Bérault's command in the following year, when the refugee Henry Tudor crossed to Wales; estimates of the number of Scots in Henry's army vary, but there may have been as many as a thousand, including a large number of archers. Apart from Bérault himself, the principal Scottish commander appears to have been Sir Alexander Bruce of Earlshall, who would be rewarded by Henry VII a few months later.

So Richard III's fulminations before Bosworth – reported in contemporary official sources, and later immortalised by Shakespeare – that he was defending the English realm against the incursions of foreigners, above all her ancient enemy France, have some truth in them; and Grant is surely right to see King Richard as a man who had put the clock back to the early fifteenth century in terms of Anglo-Scottish-French diplomacy. Given time and support, he might well have re-started the Hundred Years' War.

James III, a committed representative of the new order of Anglo-Scottish friendship, had shown much more diplomatic skill in the early '80s than he had done in the previous decade; and he might have been expected to be able to do business with a grateful Tudor king. To some extent he was successful. In 1486 he was able to recover Dunbar by siege without causing Anglo-Scottish tension; in the same year and the following one, he negotiated a series of English marriage alliances, first for his sons and then – following his wife Margaret of Denmark's death – for himself. His choice was bizarre – Elizabeth Woodville, the widow of

Edward IV. It is difficult to imagine what conceivable diplomatic value James imagined his prospective bride might possess in Tudor England; but the matter was never put to the test. In what proved to be his last months as king, James III was negotiating hard to secure the return of Berwick, a burgh of which he had always been inordinately proud; and he had scheduled a meeting on the subject with Henry VII for July 1488.

However, a reputation of sorts abroad is of little value to a king who cannot rule effectively at home. An over-confident James had spent much time since his narrow escape in 1482–3 pursuing those whom he regarded as real or potential enemies; and he may have been encouraged in this course by his final encounter with Albany. Early in 1485 the duke had made his way back to Scotland in a last effort to win support or effect a reconciliation with his brother. Arrested and imprisoned in Edinburgh Castle – perhaps an act of grim humour by James III, whose unwelcome stay there in 1482 was fresh in his mind – Albany narrowly escaped with his life; his steward, Sir James Liddale of Halkerston, was executed. The duke fled to France, to his second family and to an early death, killed by a splinter from the lance of Louis, duke of Orléans (the future Louis XII), while spectating at a tournament in Paris. At the age of thirty-one, Albany had met his end in his adopted country; he was buried with the honour due to his rank beside the high altar of the church of the Celestines. Louis, duke of Orléans, soon to become much better acquainted with Bérault Stewart, was present at the funeral.

James III might reasonably have concluded from all this that parts of the French alliance of 1484 were of little value to him; in terms of the treaty the French should not even have received Albany, a forfeited rebel, far less given him an imposing funeral. So the Scottish king's reversion to the pursuit of English alliances may in part be explained by James's rapid disenchantment with the Auld Alliance. And he may also have misinterpreted Albany's death as the removal of the last threat to his kingship. He should have looked even closer to home.

In the early months of 1488, with James III in hot pursuit of the powerful border family of Hume for defying his efforts to suppress the priory of Coldingham, the storm broke. The king's son and heir, James, duke of Rothesay, aged fifteen, became the nominal leader of an ominously large number of disaffected lords, many of them taking arms as a means of resolving unstaunched local feuds, others fearing for their safety if James III continued to live and reign. The end came on 11 June 1488 at Sauchieburn, a battlefield close to the site of Bruce's great victory of Bannockburn in 1314. The king had distributed money in advance to buy support, he had called for military aid from Henry VII of England, and – conscious of past history – he brought Bruce's sword to the field with him as a talisman. But the royal standard flew above both armies, and by the end of the day James III was dead and his son was king as James IV. John Ireland, who had become James III's confessor in the 1480s, had lost two royal patrons in the space of five years. He may have consoled himself with the fact that he had been able to shrive the king before the battle, and in the knowledge that he could present his *magnum opus*, 'The Meroure of Wyssdome', originally intended for James III, to his successor; the work's conventional wisdom on the business of royal government would no doubt suit the one as well as the other. As for the victors of Sauchieburn, they were swift to distance themselves from the actual killing of the king, and in their famous parliamentary apologia of October 1488 claimed that James III 'happened to be slain'; however, he deserved it, for he had been guilty of 'inbringing of Englishmen . . . to the perpetual subjection of the realm'. It was a statement which contained just enough elements of truth for it eventually to gain widespread acceptance.

It also dictated the initial direction of foreign policy under the new régime. The parliamentary apologia of 1488 was to be sent to the pope, and to the kings of France, Spain and Denmark; ambassadors were to be sent to the Continent to look for a suitable bride for James IV, and to renew the alliance with France. Relations would soon be renewed with Henry VII of England, but the shadow of James III hung heavily over Anglo-Scottish intercourse in the late '80s and early '90s; and it was to France that the Scots would first turn in search of a matrimonial alliance.

The embassy to France was delayed, partly by the rebellion which swept the country in 1489 and was not resolved until a 'reconciliation' parliament in February 1490; and partly by the reluctance of the three estates to find the money for the matrimonial tax. At length, however, towards the end of July 1491, the Scottish ambassadors sailed for France aboard the *Katharine*. It was a high-powered embassy – Patrick Hepburn, the new earl of Bothwell, the mastermind behind the 1488 coup; Robert Blacader, archbishop of Glasgow, who had crowned James IV; the earl of Morton, Lords Glamis and Oliphant, the Prior of St Johns, and Richard Muirhead, soon to succeed Whitelaw as royal secretary. They were accompanied by two French envoys, the indefatigable Monypenny, Lord of Concressault, and Champagne Herald. According to a later satirical poem, the poet William Dunbar also sailed with the embassy, but was violently seasick before the *Katharine* had passed the Bass Rock; he apparently 'spewit . . . faster than all the maryneris could pomp', and had to be put ashore.

When the Scottish ambassadors finally reached the Loire valley, around mid-September, they were met by Bérault Stewart. The Lord of Aubigny's fortunes had continued to climb since his embassy to Scotland in 1484. Named royal baillie of Berry in 1487, he had been entrusted with the custody of the rebel Louis, duke of Orléans, at Bourges, and his subsequent release and escort to Charles VIII's court at Montrichard. Orléans, later Louis XII, became a friend of Bérault Stewart at this time, and would show himself a very generous patron of the Lord of Aubigny in the future. As for Bérault, in the first half of 1491 he had crossed the Alps on Charles VIII's business, to Ludovico Sforza, duke of Milan, to Genoa, and to Turin; by September he was back on the Loire, at the Château of Langres.

How well informed the Lord of Aubigny was about political events in Scotland is not clear; certainly he would have been aware of the 1488 coup and the advancement of his kinsman, John Stewart of Darnley, to the title of earl of Lennox under the new government of James IV. He may even have been aware that Lennox and his son Matthew had rebelled against that government in 1489, though both had subsequently been pardoned. In any event, the consistent Francophile stance of the Scots since 1488 must have made a welcome change for expatriates and Franco-Scots like Bérault Stewart.

Having conducted Bothwell and his fellow ambassadors to Tours, Bérault formally presented them to Charles VIII in the church of St Martin on 15 September. That same evening, after dinner and during a royal audience at Montils-les-Tours, Bérault introduced the Scots to the Milanese ambassador, Erasmus Brascha, and suggested that Blanche, the daughter of Giangaleazzo Sforza, would be a suitable bride for James IV of Scotland. Charles VIII, who did not approve of the proposed match, roundly abused Bérault; but Brascha was not prepared to give up, and together with the Lord of Aubigny, he tried to take the matter further. The earl of Bothwell had fallen ill and had to return to Scotland, but in his place the archbishop of Glasgow was sent to Milan to continue the marriage negotiations. Bérault Stewart accompanied him on his way as far as Montrichard; but thereafter he was sent to Picardy while the French court moved to Orléans, and the projected Milanese marriage, lacking a forceful advocate, foundered early the following year.

Thus the Scots accomplished less than they had hoped for in France. However, Bothwell returned home on 29 November 1491 with a treaty, signed by Charles VIII, which was more or less identical with its predecessor of 1484. But it was not a marriage alliance; the days of Charles VII acting as an honest broker for the Scots were long over. This was recognised by parliament in February 1492, when the estates authorised the raising of a further matrimonial tax. The hunt for a European bride for the king would continue; and in the meantime, on 4 March 1492, James ratified the French treaty.

As for the Lord of Aubigny, his disagreement with Charles VIII over the Milanese match did not damage his career in royal service. On the contrary: in December 1493 the French king made Bérault Stewart captain of his bodyguard of Scots archers, a post which Stewart was to retain till his death in 1508, when he was succeeded as captain by his nephew John Stewart, lord of Oizon in Berry. In 1494, Charles VIII embarked on his greatest and most costly adventure – the invasion of Italy at the invitation of Ludovico Sforza of Milan, the first step, as Charles proclaimed, on a crusade to Jerusalem. Bérault Stewart was sent ahead as diplomat to Milan, Florence, and Rome; and when the French army finally went in, the Lord of Aubigny was named constable of the kingdom of Naples and sent to Calabria. His subsequent career in the Italian wars made him one of France's foremost commanders. In keeping with his status he began the construction of a château at La Verrerie, a few kilometres from Aubigny. The chapel of La Verrerie, with its interior of fleurs-de-lys and thistles surrounding roundels bearing painted portrait heads of contemporaries, both Scots and French, would well repay further study; and the château itself, with its mixture of French and Italianate Renaissance styles, is a remarkable commentary on Bérault's diplomatic and military career. He would not see Scotland again for many years; yet he takes his place, in Brantôme's later work on the lives of great French captains, unequivocally as a Scot: 'M. d'Aubigny, escossois et grand seigneur, qui fit grand honneur à sa nation . . . nos annalistes françois l'ont appelé grand chevalier sans reproche'. (Monsieur of Aubigny, a Scot and great lord who brought great honour to his nation . . . our French writers have described him as 'great knight beyond reproach.)

'Perpetual Peace' or 'Auld Alliance'? (1502–1513)

Bérault Stewart's younger contemporary, James IV, had developed during the same final decade of the fifteenth century from the lonely and frustrated adolescent who had seized his father's throne to become the most formidable of all the Stewart rulers of Scotland. Probably he never forgot his first grim lesson in kingship. On 24 June 1488 (a conscious choice as the anniversary of Bannockburn?) he had been crowned at Scone, the traditional centuries-old site for royal inauguration ceremonies, and the magnates of the realm had duly sworn solemn oaths to support him as king; the following day, 25 June, they took their new sovereign south to shovel his father James III into his grave at Cambuskenneth Abbey. The young king was no doubt left with food for thought.

In the event, he proved himself a ruler of remarkable skill and subtlety.

Whether consciously or not, he was a late developer, making no attempt to remove the various competing factions who ruled in his name, instead allowing reconciliation between the victors and vanquished of Sauchieburn to emerge gradually, stepping in personally to take charge of affairs only in 1495, at the relatively advanced age of 22. His success as an adult ruler was based on a combination of hard work, enormous energy, an avoidance of regular taxation, a balanced distribution of royal patronage, an abandonment of regular parliaments, the invoking of a variety of sources of casual income to screw money out of his subjects (while, remarkably, remaining personally popular), and, like all successful rulers, a sizeable slice of good luck. By the turn of the century, James IV was in full control of his realm; when the revolts in the Isles ended a few years later, he was its undisputed master.

In the field of foreign diplomacy, the long quest for a bride for the Scottish king finally came to an end when James IV married Henry VII's elder daughter Margaret Tudor, at Holyrood on 8 August 1503. The match had been a long time coming, and was only achieved as the result of some extremely aggressive diplomacy on the part of the Scots. In 1493 Henry VII had been prepared only to offer Katharine, daughter of the Countess of Wiltshire, as a bride for the King of Scots. The Scottish response was to explore other possible European sources, with bishops Elphinstone and Blacader being dispatched to the Empire and Spain respectively. More ominously, James IV threw his support behind the Pretender to Henry VII's throne, Perkin Warbeck, broke the English truce, and invaded Northumberland in 1496 and 1497. It is unlikely that King James had a higher opinion of Warbeck than any of the European rulers who had temporarily sheltered the Pretender in order to cause Henry VII diplomatic embarrassment; significantly, when the Scottish king went to war over the border, he did so in the east, where his armies could enjoy plundering in the Tweed and Till valleys, rather than in the west, where Perkin Warbeck might have received some English support.

Henry VII's initial furious response – plans were drawn up for a massive invasion of Scotland in 1497 – was frustrated by a Cornish rising which forced the English king to reconsider his position. The Scots abandoned Warbeck to his fate, and left Norham Castle scathed by balls from the great bombard Mons Meg, but still in English hands. A truce was followed by negotiations for a firm Anglo-Scottish peace and marriage alliance. And James IV was to be allowed to marry Henry Tudor's daughter.

The grandly named Treaty of Perpetual Peace, concluded in London in January 1502, laid down elaborate rules for the maintenance of peace between England and Scotland – including the threat of excommunication

by the pope should either sovereign break the treaty – and stipulated a
dowry for Margaret Tudor of 30,000 angel nobles (around £35,000
Scots), to be paid in three annual instalments. As to the wedding itself,
James IV was determined to put on a good show: more than £2,000
Scots was spent on wine alone, and a solemn entry into Edinburgh by the
thirteen-year-old Margaret Tudor led to five days of pageantry – singing,
dancing, tournaments, and the creation of new earls and knights by the
king – following the wedding itself, which took place in Holyrood Abbey,
adjoining the Scottish king's newly constructed Renaissance palace. The
court poet William Dunbar celebrated the happy event in the com-
memorative poem 'The Thistle and the Rose'; and a sumptuous Book of
Hours, produced by the Ghent-Bruges school of illuminators and
containing, amongst much else, portraits of James IV and Margaret
Tudor, was most likely completed around this time as a wedding gift for
the royal couple. On the face of it, then, the Treaty of Perpetual Peace of
1502 and its follow-up, the Union of the Thistle and the Rose in 1503,
might have been expected to herald a new era in Anglo-Scottish
relations, with a solemn peace treaty leading to long years of profitable
intercourse between the two former enemies, while the Auld Alliance,
which after all had failed to produce a European bride for James IV as
recently as 1492, was quietly laid to rest.

Yet nothing of the sort happened. In fact the decade following the
Anglo-Scottish peace of 1502 was marked by gradually deteriorating
relations between England and Scotland, while the Franco-Scottish
alliance grew stronger each year and culminated in the formal renewal of
1512. For the truth is that the Treaty of Perpetual Peace, although it
produced momentous consequences for both kingdoms in the union of
the crowns a century later, was in its day a brittle alliance made between
two temporarily exhausted enemies and providing little by way of
improved relations on the borders or at sea. Henry VII had his doubts
about it all, even before the wedding of 1503. On 27 June 1503 he wrote
to James IV asking the Scottish king to repudiate, or at least not to renew,
the Franco-Scottish alliance. King James replied promptly on 12 July to
the effect that although 'we and oure predecessouris has bene always
accustumyt thereto', he would not confirm the French league without
consulting Henry on the matter. This response must have been cold
comfort to the English king, who had recently lost both his wife, Queen
Elizabeth, and his elder son Arthur, and who found himself with only a
surviving son – the future Henry VIII – standing between James IV and
the English succession.

It may be added that Margaret Tudor's dowry was niggardly, less than
that which Edward IV had been prepared to allocate to his daughter

Cecilia at the time of the Anglo-Scottish alliance of 1474; and the former Spanish ambassador to Scotland, Don Pedro de Ayala, was in no doubt that peace with England was unpopular with most Scots, and had indeed only been accomplished because James IV insisted on it. Continuing Anglo-Scottish mistrust and dislike were probably mutual. According to the chronicler Edward Hall, the English guests at the Holyrood wedding privately sneered at the Scots' profuse hospitality; and Pedro de Ayala had already commented that he was the only man at the English court who could hear the word 'Scotland' pronounced without losing his temper.

By contrast, Franco-Scottish friendship grew apace in the wake of the 1502 treaty. In August 1506 James IV wrote to Louis XII of France remarking that the construction of a fleet to defend Scotland was a project of long standing which he was bent on realising. Significantly, the serious beginnings of a Scottish royal navy – as opposed to the hiring by the Crown of privately owned ships in time of crisis – are to be found towards the end of 1502, when 'John Lorans, the French wricht . . . com first for the schip bigging'. James IV was exploiting a loophole in the Treaty of Perpetual Peace to secure, first, French shipwrights, and later French timber and French money, to build a royal navy. This was King James's obsession; he spent at least £120,000 Scots on it in the course of a decade, an astonishing sum for the ruler of a small kingdom with an annual income of around £13,000 (much increased later) at the outset of the reign. He created new naval dockyards in the Forth, at Pool of Airth and Newhaven, the latter owing its existence to the creation of a single ship, the monster *Great Michael*, launched in October 1511 and for a short time the largest warship in northern Europe.

Over the years historians have fulminated against James IV for pursuing what, with benefit of hindsight, they view as a perverse diplomatic course, rejecting the formal English alliance in pursuit of an obsolete and ephemeral French understanding. His folly, it is argued, resulted in his becoming involved in an unnecessary European war in which he met his just deserts by being killed at Flodden in 1513. In R. L. Mackie's famous phrase, the king was 'a moonstruck romantic', dreaming of leading crusades against the Turk and hopelessly out of his depth in the hard world of European diplomacy.

Thus a highly successful 25-year-long reign is judged by its last day, and history, as so often, is read backwards rather than forwards. In fact, James IV's foreign diplomacy makes very good sense: like many Scottish rulers before him, he opted for the difficult course of balancing French and English alliances. Certainly he inclined towards France rather than England; for example, he lent his support to Bishop Elphinstone of Aberdeen, who in the Aberdeen Breviary (1509–10) gave Scotland a national liturgy, immortalised over seventy Scottish saints, and supplanted the English Salisbury (Sarum) use in Scotland. The new breviary was printed by a French press established by royal patent in Edinburgh in 1507, with Walter Chepman supplying the finance and Andrew Myllar, formerly of Rouen, the printing skills. And it was in Rouen that Pierre Gringoire, Louis XII's 'official' satirist and creator of pageants, published 'Les Abus du Monde', a satire dedicated to James IV, in 1510.

By contrast, the steady worsening of Anglo-Scottish relations is clearly reflected in two ambassadorial visits, English followed by French, to Scotland in 1508. The first was occasioned by Henry VII's detention in England of James IV's kinsman, James Hamilton, earl of Arran, on a technicality: Arran did not have the necessary safe-conduct. However, the real reason for the earl's arrest was that he had come directly from France, and it was feared in England that the Scots were about to renew the French alliance. The English ambassador sent north to pour oil on troubled waters was the king's almoner, Thomas Wolsey, a royal servant who was later to have a spectacular career under Henry VIII. Wolsey had to wait five days at Berwick for a safe-conduct, and could not get an early audience with James IV because the king, he was told, was busy shooting and making gunpowder. On finally being admitted to the king's presence, Wolsey was told that a renewal of the Franco-Scottish alliance was indeed imminent, and that James's council and all his subjects were daily calling upon him to renew; Andrew Forman, bishop of Moray, one of the Scottish king's most influential 'fixers', told Wolsey roundly that no-one had ever been less welcome in Scotland, for it was generally believed that he had come to argue against renewal of the French alliance. This elaborate comedy had the desired effect; Wolsey, muttering that even the wives in the market knew why he had come to Scotland, withdrew, advising Henry VII to release the earl of Arran. This was duly accomplished, and the Auld Alliance was not renewed.

Only a few weeks after Wolsey's departure, a second embassy arrived in Scotland – this time from France, and headed by Bérault Stewart and Jean Sellat, president of the Parlement of Paris. Gifts were showered on Bérault, a tournament was held in honour of the French, and James IV wrote to Louis XII asking permission to retain the Lord of Aubigny in Scotland long enough to accompany him on a pilgrimage to Whithorn, in the course of which they might discuss Bérault's commission from Louis. Though it is nowhere recorded – for the royal treasurer's accounts are missing for three years from 1508 – it must have been on this occasion that Bérault presented James IV with the collar of the Order of St Michael; for the Scottish king undoubtedly received it before the end of his life, and it was no doubt one of many inducements extended to James to encourage him to renew the Auld Alliance.

Yet the alliance was not renewed on this occasion; for this proved to be Bérault's final visit to Scotland. Falling ill in the house of his friend Sir John Forrester at Corstorphine, Bérault made his will on 8 June 1508, instructing that he should be buried in the Edinburgh Blackfriars, and his heart taken to the shrine of St Ninian at Whithorn. He died a few days later, leaving his Scottish kinsman Matthew Stewart, earl of Lennox, as his chief executor.

The great diplomat and warrior had returned permanently to the land of his ancestors. William Dunbar, who had composed a ballad in Bérault's honour, promptly had to write an elegy, directed to Louis XII and celebrating the Lord of Aubigny as a flower of chivalry. A legend in his own lifetime, Bérault would continue to be praised in later ages, even by the English. In 1629, Sir John Beaumont published a bizarre, if appropriately unionist, eulogy of the great Franco-Scot:

> A Lord of Scotland, Bernard, was their pride,
> A blossom of the Stuarts happy line,
> Which is on brittaines throne ordain'd to shine . . .
> At Bosworth Field must be the glorious stage,
> And tries those wings, which after rayse him high,
> When he beyond the snowy Alpes renown'd,
> Shall plant the French Lillies in Italian ground;
> And cause the craggy Appenine to know,
> What fruits on Caledonian mountains grow.

Bérault Stewart, Lord of Aubigny, counsellor and chamberlain of the king of France, knight of the Order of St Michael, captain of the *Garde Ecossaise*, hero of the Italian wars, great constable of Sicily and Jerusalem and French lieutenant-general within the kingdom of Naples, also played a vital role at Bosworth – as Beaumont noted – in placing the Tudor dynasty on the throne of England. But then no-one is perfect.

On 21 April 1509 Henry VII died; his most tangible legacy to his surviving son, who succeeded him as Henry VIII, was his wealth, for he died the richest monarch in Europe. Historians have differed in their assessments of the new English king. Long ago, R. L. Mackie described Henry VIII as 'the realist of eighteen who sat on the English throne'; more recently, and less flatteringly, Ranald Nicholson thought the king 'an egocentric teenager whose tantrums and petulance bespoke an inferiority complex'. More to the point, Dr Scarisbrick has reminded us that 'it is damaging historical surgery that cuts [Henry] off from his ancestry – Edward I, Edward III, Henry V – for they, surely, were his models'. In spite of a brief Anglo-French honeymoon period at the outset of Henry VIII's reign, shortly after his coronation the English king had sworn publicly that he would soon attack Louis XII of France. A war of conquest in the style of his great predecessors, making use of the 'war chest' left him by his father, was clearly Henry's intention from the outset. If Richard III had come close to drifting back into the Hundred Years' War, Henry VIII seized the opportunity to restart the war with relish.

Thus the strong likelihood, if not inevitability, of Anglo-Scottish war following a renewal of the Franco-Scottish alliance existed almost from the outset of Henry VIII's reign. It is all the more surprising, then, that historians have tended to view James IV's diplomacy during these years as inept; the Scots, we are told, were out of their depth in the morass of European politics, and King James was, to repeat Mackie's famous put-down, himself a 'moonstruck romantic'. The phrase refers to James's supposed obsession with crusades against the Turk; but the Scottish king's alleged desire to unite the princes of Europe in a great crusade rests on little more authority than the pub gossip of a discredited Venetian ambassador, together with a collective determination among historians to deny King James any intelligence. Naturally James used the language of crusading diplomacy in his letters to foreign princes; everyone did. But he paid not a penny towards a European crusading levy in 1501; when a vacancy occurred in the preceptory of Torphichen, the Scottish house of the Knights Hospitallers who would be expected to spearhead any crusade against the Turks, James IV supported as the new preceptor his ambitious and influential secretary Patrick Paniter, who was not even a member of the order and certainly no crusader. James's fleet, in which he took such pride, was not built to carry crusaders into the Mediterranean, but, as he himself remarked to Louis XII, to defend Scotland. And the gun emplacements on either side of the Queensferry narrows in the Firth of Forth, and on the island of Inchgarvie nearby, were not designed to keep out the Turks.

The truth, surely, is that James IV's 'crusade' was the kind which would have been approved of by the fourteenth-century Bishop Murray of Moray, who claimed that to fight against the English was as laudable as crusading against the infidel. Yet the Scottish king's approach to the impending conflict was both cautious and calculating. He had not renewed the French alliance in 1508, nor would he do so until March 1512; and even then he did not make war on England until the French price was right – 50,000 francs (around £22,500 Scots), the equipping and victualling of the Scottish fleet, and the service of the seven war galleys of the formidable French admiral, Gaston Prégent de Bidoux.

These terms were agreed in May 1513, a full fourteen months after James IV, after endeavouring to mediate between Louis XII and members of the 'Holy League', of which Henry VIII was a part, had renewed the Auld Alliance. But that he did so in March 1512 probably had much to do with Henry VIII's arrogant resurrection of the claim to overlordship over Scotland made in parliament two months before.

In diplomacy and war in any age, most grand designs and carefully planned campaigns either miscarry or come to grief. However, it is instructive to compare the war aims of James IV and his brother-in-law Henry VIII in 1512–13. The Scottish king sought to build a coalition to deter Henry VIII from invading the country of his ally, Louis XII of France; he hoped to involve the navy of his uncle, King Hans of Denmark, and to open another front against the English in Ireland, supported by Hugh O'Donnell of Ulster. This part of the projected alliance foundered on the death of the Danish king and the defection of the Irishman; but James IV, financially backed by the Scottish clergy and militarily by a remarkably united nobility, was still prepared to support his French ally with an 'armée de mer', carried to Normandy by the Scottish fleet, and by opening a second front himself in Northumberland, making the taking of Norham Castle – a Scottish target for fifty years – his primary objective. His breaking of the Treaty of Perpetual Peace earned him excommunication from Pope Julius II, who had created the 'Holy League' against France; and this sentence was confirmed by Julius's successor Leo X in 1513. However, the Scots probably saw papal threats as inextricably linked with English arrogance; for the individual charged to deliver the ban of excommunication against James IV was Christopher Bainbridge, Cardinal-archbishop of York, who represented a potential menace to the Scottish church. If the xenophobic Bainbridge used his influence at Rome to resurrect York's old claim to act as metropolitan over the Scottish church, then his pretensions must be resisted at all costs. Small wonder that James IV's war was popular with church and nation alike; and his war aims, to reduce the English pressure on France and to win territory and rewards for himself and his countrymen, were limited and sensible.

By contrast, Henry VIII's schemes, both in planning and execution, were wildly over-ambitious and unrealistic. Belatedly he attached himself to Pope Julius II's disreputable 'Holy League' – the pope, Venice, Ferdinand of Spain and Emperor Maximilian – because membership of the League would further his French ambitions. But the League had virtually collapsed before the war: the Venetians withdrew because they could not abide the Emperor Maximilian; worse, they made a treaty with France. Ferdinand of Spain, shifty and calculating as ever, concluded a secret one-year truce with Louis XII of France in April 1513. When the young and idealistic Henry VIII finally took the field in the summer of 1513 with his remaining ally Maximilian, the latter was quite happy to let Henry pay the costs of the war and to receive the stronghold of Thérouanne in Artois from an English king flushed with success and rapidly exhausting the vast sums bequeathed to him by his father. As to Henry's ultimate war aims in France, these seem to have been similar to those of Christopher Bainbridge, Cardinal of York, an aggressively patriotic Englishman whose hatred of the French extended in 1513 to demanding that the pope be ready to come to Rheims to crown Henry VIII as King of France. Instead, within a year the English king would have returned home without allies or money; and in 1514, neither overlord of Scotland nor King of France, he made peace with Louis XII, sealed by his former adversary's marriage to his younger sister Mary Tudor. If anyone was a 'moonstruck romantic' in 1513, it was Henry VIII, not his brother-in-law James IV.

Whatever his follies, however, the English king survived the 1513 war. Had Henry died in, or in transit to or from, France, James IV would have been his heir; but the Franco-Scottish war effort of the summer and autumn of 1513 miscarried in the case of the war at sea and foundered totally in Northumberland.

At first things went well. James IV's fleet of around thirteen ships, carrying to France an 'armée de mer' of some thousands of troops, sailed from the Forth in late July, turned north and by way of the Hebrides and the Irish Sea eventually reached Carrickfergus, the main English stronghold in Ulster. The town was attacked, though the castle remained untaken; and the Scottish fleet returned briefly to Ayr, probably to pick up recruits from those south-western families who had kinsmen in France. Thereafter, responding to anxious admonitions from Louis XII, James Hamilton, earl of Arran, James IV's cousin and commander of the Scottish fleet, sailed on to Brest. The plan thereafter appears to have been for the combined Franco-Scottish fleet, under the overall command of Louis de Rouville, to enter the Channel and to attack Henry VIII's transports, his lifeline back to England. But the bad weather which had delayed the Scottish fleet en route to France persisted, the combined fleet was scattered soon after its assembly in Normandy in September 1513, the *Great Michael* ran aground, and the enterprise was finally abandoned.

Worse – much worse – had already occurred in Northumberland. At the end of August 1513, James IV, at the head of one of the finest and best-appointed Scottish armies ever to cross the border, had laid siege to Norham Castle and taken it within a week. However, James then stayed in the field, probably to prevent the castle's immediate recapture by Thomas Howard, earl of Surrey, who had been left in England by the absent Henry VIII to guard the north against the Scots. On the afternoon of 9 September James IV, who had been outmanoeuvred by Surrey – the English earl had placed himself between King James and Scotland – fought the battle of Flodden. Using Swiss or 'Almayn' tactics, involving the swift deployment of huge phalanxes of spearmen, James advanced down Branxton Hill; but the rough terrain of Northumberland soon broke up the Scots' tight formations, and at close quarters the 22-foot spear was a hopeless weapon against the English halberd. In four hours of wind and rain, the carnage on the Scottish side was appalling – James himself was killed, together with his illegitimate son Alexander Stewart, archbishop of St Andrews, one bishop, two abbots, nine earls (out of twelve present), fourteen lords of parliament, and thousands of others. The great Scottish field army had been disastrously defeated, and a whole generation of Scottish political leaders – including the king himself – had been lost. The Stewart dynasty survived in the person of an infant, James V, born as recently as April 1512.

A Frenchman in Charge? (1513–17)

Little enough was salvaged from the disaster of Flodden. Within the next year, the best ships in James IV's fleet – the *Great Michael*, the *Margaret*, and the *James* – would have been sold off to the French. The late king's specialist in shuttle diplomacy, Andrew Forman, bishop of Moray, had gained the enormous prize of the archbishopric of Bourges, his candidacy forced on the Bourges chapter by Louis XII; though Forman made his solemn entry into the city in November 1513, he had no real power base there, and his services as diplomat and a strong supporter of the French connection were soon urgently required in Scotland. While still in France, however, Forman – together with Bérault Stewart's successor Robert – successfully petitioned Louis XII to grant Scots in France the right to dispose of their goods by will, to inherit estates, and to hold religious benefices in France, without requiring letters of naturalisation. It was a small return for a huge Scottish outlay.

Yet the aftermath of Flodden for the Scots could have been much worse. There was no English follow-up to the battle, and the infant James V was duly crowned at Stirling on 21 September, less than a fortnight after Flodden. And the result of that battle did not damage the Auld Alliance; on the contrary: although Louis XII made peace with England and married Henry VIII's sister in November 1514, the strain brought on by marriage to a Tudor proved fatal to King Louis. He died on New Year's Day 1515, to be succeeded by his son-in-law, the flamboyant 20-year-old Francis I, who would renew the Franco-Scottish alliance in little over two years.

In Scotland the old order had largely passed away. In addition to those lost at Flodden, the ancient William Elphinstone, bishop of Aberdeen, shouted down in council in 1513 because like 'a mad old man' he had argued against the war with England, just failed to achieve the primacy at St Andrews, dying in 1514 in his early eighties. Archibald Douglas, the maverick fifth earl of Angus, a *bête noire* of James III and a dissident during much of the reign of his son, died at the end of October 1513, having avoided Flodden (though his two sons were killed there). Forman returned from Bourges to claim the archbishopric of St Andrews; and James Hamilton, earl of Arran, who had sailed with the Scottish fleet, came back to Scotland in 1514 to advance his own career as a magnate very close in blood to the crown. Though there were new men in the Scottish political élite, the policies which the government would pursue were very traditional.

There was of course no immediate prospect of a lasting peace with England, nor, for that matter, any sign of the 'Flodden complex' – the supposed fear of the Scots to conduct military expeditions into England on account of what had happened to them in 1513 – much beloved of later historians. Equally it was clear that James IV's widow Margaret Tudor would not command widespread support among the Scots, even as tutrix to her infant son James V; when, in August 1514, she compounded her existing problems by marrying the young Archibald, sixth earl of Angus, a rapid solution to a growing political crisis had to be found.

It had already been mooted as early as the autumn of 1513, when the earl of Arran, still in France, received the news of Flodden. The heir presumptive to James IV was John, duke of Albany (1481–1536), the son of James III's forfeited brother Alexander. Though a Frenchman – like the Lords of Aubigny pursuing a military career in the Italian wars – and the offspring of a forfeited Scottish duke, Albany had been largely rehabilitated during James IV's last years, acting for the Scottish king in the thankless task of attempting to mediate between Pope Julius II and Louis XII of France. As early as 26 November 1513 a Scottish general council agreed that Albany should come to Scotland with men and munitions, and that the Auld Alliance should be renewed. The English marriage, and subsequent death, of Louis XII, delayed Albany's return to his father's native land; but when at last he came, in a squadron of eight ships which touched briefly at Ayr before the duke disembarked at Dumbarton on 26 May 1515, he came as Governor, second person in the realm, and a persuasive advocate of the French alliance. The

government of Scotland had been committed to the care of a Frenchman; and there followed the most important single achievement of
Albany's governorship, the Treaty of Rouen (26 August 1517). Less than
six years after James IV had formally committed himself to the French
side, and in spite – or perhaps because – of the disaster of 1513 which
had followed that choice, the Auld Alliance had been renewed.

6

Indian Summer: 1517–1560

Like earlier Franco-Scottish treaties, the Treaty of Rouen of 1517 was an offensive and defensive alliance directed against England, differing from its predecessors not so much in its terms as in the fact that both contracting parties were in France. John, duke of Albany, in Stuart's words 'the Scot who was a Frenchman', signed and sealed the treaty on behalf of the infant James V, while Charles, duke of Alençon, did the same for Francis I of France. In many respects, the treaty recalled those made two hundred years previously, Corbeil in 1326 or perhaps even Paris-Dunfermline in 1295–6; for like the latter, the Treaty of Rouen contained a matrimonial clause, albeit a rather nebulous one. Thus Francis I agreed that, if the promise of his eldest daughter – whether Louise or Charlotte is not specified – made to the king of Spain or his brother did not take place, then at a suitable age she would be married to the King of Scots; alternatively, if the Spanish marriage went ahead, and Francis I had the good fortune to have another daughter, that daughter would be married to James V.

A treaty of this kind put the Scots firmly in their place in the matrimonial stakes and diplomatic pecking order. The truth was that the European diplomatic map was changing with remarkable speed in the early sixteenth century, and that many of the certainties which had long sustained the Auld Alliance were being undermined. France's entry into the Italian wars from 1494 had certainly provided a lifetime's employment for soldiers in the service of Charles VIII, Louis XII and Francis I. However, in place of the old Franco-Burgundian and Anglo-French struggles of the fifteenth century, there arose a far more formidable enemy, the greatest power ever seen in Europe, the Emperor Charles V. In 1519 Charles, already King of Spain for three years, was elected Emperor in succession to Maximilian, thus adding to his kingdoms of Spain, Naples and Sicily (and Spain's New World wealth) the Netherlands, Germany, Flanders, Artois, Franche-Comté and Austria. French fear of encirclement led Francis I – temporarily – into alliance with Henry VIII of England, whose feeble shy at restarting the Hundred Years' War in 1512–13 was by 1520 safely behind him, if not for ever.

The mutual antagonism of the leaders of Europe's super-powers,

Charles V and Francis I, and a new Anglo-French amity, did not seem to augur well for the Franco-Scottish alliance. However, peace between England and France ran counter to hundreds of years of history, and Henry VIII's alternative was to try to build an imperial alliance with Charles V. His concern with Scotland was and remained her ability to open a 'second front' in the north if England were embroiled in war with France; and this concern was in no way diminished by Surrey's victory at Flodden. After all, the Treaty of Rouen of 1517 stipulated that should the king of England make war either on Scotland or France, the French king would give to the King of Scots a payment of 100,000 *écus* and the services of 500 mounted spearmen, 500 infantry and 200 archers. The French king's fear of encirclement by potential or real enemies was mirrored, on a smaller scale, by that of Henry VIII.

Thus English diplomacy in the north tended towards a mixture of promises and threats: that is, offers to the Scots of English marriage alliances coupled with demands that they break the French connection. However, Henry VIII unwittingly compounded his own difficulties, and gave the Scottish kingdom a status in Europe quite out of proportion to its size and importance, when in the early 1530s he rejected papal authority and declared himself Supreme Head of the English church. For a generation thereafter Scottish foreign policy had a clear, consistent direction – the pursuit of an often lucrative French alliance underpinned by an adherence to Catholicism which acquired a new importance given the existence of a heretic England. Far from being relegated to the status of a distant sideshow, therefore, in what proved to be its final years the Auld Alliance experienced an Indian summer, with the French providing three royal marriage alliances, troops to fight in Scotland, and wealth to support them, on an unprecedented scale. And the period which had opened with a Frenchman in charge of government would end with a Frenchwoman as Regent.

From Rouen (1517) to St Quentin (1536)

Unravelling the politics of the long and fractious minority of James V (1513–1528) would try the patience of a saint; thus far, saintly patience has been granted only to Ken Emond, whose scholarly thesis on the subject has yet to appear in print. However, amidst the general gloom of powerful magnates jockeying for position, changing sides frequently in order to improve their fortunes or even to acquire temporary control of government for their families, certain issues stand out clearly.

The most striking of these is the ability of John, duke of Albany, governor for nine years from his first arrival in Scotland in May 1515 until what proved to be his final departure to France nine years later, in May

1524. As the steadfast representative of the Franco-Scottish alliance, above all as the man who had negotiated the Treaty of Rouen, Albany was of course anathema to the English, who saw him as a French agent in Scotland. The Scots had a different view, best expressed in parliament at Edinburgh in February 1522. Henry VIII, who had managed to have Albany kept in France for over four years from 1517, was alarmed at his return to Scotland in November 1521, and demanded that the Scots dismiss him as Governor. The Estates' resolute response to Henry VIII is worth quoting at some length:

> We will with his [Albany's] presence take our adventure of peace or war as shall please God to send it; assuring your grace that . . . we neither may nor will, at the request of your grace, nor any other prince, consent nor suffer in any manner that our said Lord Governor depart furth of this realm during the king our sovereign lord's minority . . . And if, for this cause, we happen to be invaded, what may we do but take God to our good quarrel in defence, and do, as our progenitors and forbears have been constrained to do, for the conservation of this realm heretofore.

This reply by the Chancellor and Three Estates of Scotland goes beyond a mere refusal to dismiss Albany; indeed, the Scots were concerned to show their approval of the Governor, remarking that 'he is chosen by us all, and so lovably has exercised [his office of Governor] during all the time of his being in this realm, that no creature may reasonably lay reproach or dishonour to his charge'.

There is, perhaps, a pardonable exaggeration on the part of the Scots in suggesting that Albany had been chosen as Governor by them all. Certain powerful political players, above all the Queen Mother, Margaret Tudor, her husband Archibald, sixth earl of Angus, and James Hamilton, first earl of Arran and second in line to the throne after the Governor, had their own individual agendas, and their intrigues were fomented by Henry VIII in order to destabilise the Albany government. But the various brief alignments and realignments of powerful individuals opposed to Albany hardly merit the collective title sometimes accorded to them of an 'English party' seeking power in Scotland. There was nothing new in treasonable activities by disaffected magnates during royal minorities. In 1491 Archibald, fifth earl of Angus, had been involved in a plot to remove the 18-year-old James IV from the control of his Hepburn guardians and to become the liege man of Henry VIII of England; over a generation later, in 1526, Angus's grandson, the sixth earl, would be involved in the retention of the person of the 14-year-old James V in order to place the Angus affinity at the heart of government *and* because he was acceptable to the English as a man with whom they could do business. And there was always Margaret Tudor, moving swiftly from her 1514 marriage to Angus – 'a young witless fool' in the opinion of his uncle – to divorce and remarriage to Henry Stewart, Lord Methven; indeed, Margaret's capriciousness was so notorious that her brother Henry VIII was moved to write to her warning her about the damage to her reputation which might result from too many marriages. So she continued, politically a floating iceberg during her son's minority, but thereafter a much less significant figure until her death in 1541.

None of these individuals had a coherent or consistent policy in either domestic or foreign affairs. Albany had both. At home he proved himself an honest and firm Regent; and even during his long absence in France (1517–21) he contrived to use his influence in favour of the Scottish crown and merchants. Thus in January 1519 he managed to have the pope renew an indult whereby the Scottish crown was guaranteed the right to make nominations to important ecclesiastical benefices; and a bull of June 1520 took Scotland and its king into papal protection and confirmed Albany's authority as Governor. In May 1518, on Albany's request, Francis I of France granted a concession freeing Scottish traders from duties laid on foreign goods at the French port of entry of Dieppe.

These practical demonstrations of the worth of the Auld Alliance – and above all of having a powerful advocate abroad – help to explain its continuing popularity with the Scots. And their desire to retain Albany as Governor, so forcefully expressed by the Three Estates in 1522, may in part be a reflection of a collective desire to avoid the mayhem which occurred when he was abroad, most notably the 'Cleanse the Causeway' incident of 1520, when the Hamiltons had driven the Douglases out of Edinburgh.

The price which the Scots had to pay for Albany's good governance was to become involved in war on the borders against the English. In the late summer of 1522 an English army invaded Picardy, and Francis I required the Scots to open a second front. Albany duly mustered the host at Roslin in Midlothian, and an act was passed, recalling the Flodden campaign of 1513, freeing the heirs of those who lost their lives in the campaign from the onerous feudal payment of relief on the estates which they would inherit. The Scottish objective was Carlisle on the west march; the army was a large one, and it seems to have advanced to within five miles of Carlisle. At this point a truce was made between Albany and the English warden, Lord Dacre, and the Scots host withdrew. Much – probably too much – has been made of the Scots' reluctance to cross the border in the interests of France – though if Cardinal Wolsey's letter to Henry VIII describing the campaign is accurate, the Scottish army was already over the border when the truce was made – and the ubiquitous 'Flodden complex' has been advanced as a reason for the host's failures in 1522, and again in 1523. In 1522, however, Francis I, committed to supplying armies in Picardy, Gascony, and Italy, and prevented by an English blockade from sending ships from Breton ports, may have been telling the Scots no more than the truth when he pointed out to their ambassadors that he could not give greater help at present. Thus the Scots, in 'scaling' (disbanding) their army, may have been responding to the letter rather than the spirit of the Treaty of Rouen.

In the autumn of 1523, however, French aid was duly forthcoming in the shape of 4,000 footmen, 600 mounted troops, artillery, money and supplies. During the summer and early autumn English forces had crossed the border and burned Kelso and Jedburgh; Albany's campaign was a response to these raids, and his target was Wark Castle, just south of the River Tweed. In this case, it was bad timing rather than any 'Flodden complex' which made the campaign a failure. It began extraordinarily late in the season, with French reinforcements reaching Dumbarton only in mid-October, and the combined Franco-Scottish forces of Albany, Argyll and Lennox reaching Wark at Hallowe'en, about the same time that the earl of Surrey arrived at Belford in Northumberland, an easy day's march from Wark. Albany bombarded Wark for two days; but with Surrey in front of him and the Tweed in spate behind him, the Governor wisely withdrew on 3 November. He had done his best, personally summoning the host as soon as he arrived back in Scotland on 24 September. The season and the weather, rather than the reluctance of the Scots, were against him.

On 20 May 1524 Albany departed for France for the third time since his initial arrival in Scotland in 1515. In the event, he would not return; but it should be noted that his reason for going was not so much disillusionment with the Scots – on many subsequent occasions he would propose returning – as the illness of his wife, the duchess Anne, who died in June 1524. It is of course true that prominent Scottish magnates – Angus, Arran and Lennox among them – were glad to see the back of Albany and an end to the strong guiding hand which he had provided for the young king; and they were quick to ignore, to their own profit, the provisions which the Governor had made for the safety of James V during his absence. Ill luck dogged Albany to the end, for the French troops brought to Scotland for the 1523 campaign, attempting to return home, were shipwrecked in the Hebrides and many were drowned, a fact reported by Lord Dacre, with considerable satisfaction, to Cardinal Wolsey.

It would be a mistake, however, to equate the failure of the two autumn

campaigns of 1522 and 1523 with any lasting change in attitude towards
the Auld Alliance on the part of the Scots. Certainly there was a
temporary break in the mid- and late 1520s, occasioned as much as
anything else by Francis I's capture by the Imperialists at the battle of
Pavia in 1525, and the subsequent conclusion of Anglo-French treaties in
April 1527. It is also true that some Scottish merchants were concerned to
keep open profitable English markets for Scottish wool and fish by
avoiding war with England. And Anglo-Scottish union had a persuasive
advocate in John Mair (Major), whose *History of Greater Britain* dates from
1521. However, these straws in the wind had been blown away by the end
of the decade; and it should be noted that John Mair's dark inferences
about Albany's supposed ambitions as heir presumptive to the young
king hardly qualify the writer as an impartial observer of the politics of
his times.

In time, it would be Albany's able tutelage of the king which would
bear fruit; if Bishop Lesley is to be believed, the Governor spent his last
Sunday in Scotland at Stirling with the 12-year-old James V, talking to
him at length about his duties and responsibilities. When James took
charge of affairs in 1528, it would be to Albany that he would turn for
advice and assistance in the negotiation of foreign marriages;
unsurprisingly the duke continued to advance the claims of potential
French brides, and if the Franco-Scottish alliance had faltered in the
1520s, it prospered mightily thereafter.

Yet though Albany's matrimonial negotiations were valued by James V,
it was the absent duke rather than the ever-present Governor whom the
king cherished. James had no more desire than the English to see Albany
back in Scotland; the former Governor would be an embarrassment to
an adult king. Whether Albany himself wished to return is another
matter. Certainly the English, in the late 1520s, had an almost paranoid
fear of the duke's return, and spread a story that Albany was hiring ships
to sail to Scotland early in 1528, assisted by Robert Stewart, Lord of
Aubigny. Nothing of the sort happened. Albany stayed in France, a
diplomat and soldier, conducting a voluminous correspondence with
James V and other Scots, dying at his castle of Mirefleur in the Auvergne
on 2 June 1536. In terms of the furtherance of the Auld Alliance, the
duke's importance equals that of his fellow Franco-Scot, Bérault Stewart
of Aubigny. But Albany's crucial role as Governor for James V gives him
a quite unique status among French 'ecossois'. That status also made him
a target, in his own day and later, for scandal perpetrated by his enemies,
with English diplomats well to the fore in efforts to blacken his name.
However, rumours of a sexual liaison between Albany and Margaret
Tudor may be discounted; and later tales that the Governor, when in a

rage, used to throw his hat into the fire, if true, simply reflect the problems of a man charged with the unenviable task of governing Scotland in the post-Flodden era.

Albany's young charge, James V, rapidly showed himself an able pupil. Having endured four years of government by groups of magnates, the king escaped from Edinburgh to Stirling Castle at the end of May 1528. He was sixteen; he was backed by a magnate coalition including eight prominent earls; and he was determined to free himself from control by the Angus Douglases, who had ruled since June 1526 on the strength of their possession of the person of the king. This dangerous game had certainly brought the family short-term gains: Angus himself became Chancellor, his uncle Archibald was made Treasurer, and his brother George Master of the Royal Household. If the English had regarded Albany as a French agent, it can at least as accurately be argued that Chancellor Angus was an English agent, encouraging James V to abandon the French and put his trust in 'his good uncle of England.' James appears to have simulated compliance with the pro-English faction for a time, but he was well aware of the fact that a majority of the Scottish nobility and clergy favoured the French alliance. Even James Hamilton, earl of Arran, who argued for an English treaty, was clearly moved by the fact that, with Albany excluded from Scotland, he was one step nearer to becoming James V's heir presumptive. From an English standpoint, however, there was no doubt that Angus was 'better than five earls of Arran'; the only English concern was Margaret Tudor, who loathed her former husband and was likely to join any coalition that would bring him down.

The English were right to be concerned, for it was to Queen Margaret's castle of Stirling that James V escaped between 27 and 30 May 1528, returning to Edinburgh in strength on 6 July. Angus had prudently withdrawn from the city four days previously; within a week the king had summoned him for treason, and he was duly forfeited in parliament the following September. At the age of sixteen, earlier than any of his Stewart predecessors, James V had taken control of his kingdom.

For the adult James the immediate problem, having forfeited Angus, was how to get rid of the earl. A botched royal siege of Angus's great East Lothian stronghold of Tantallon in the late autumn of 1528 did not solve the problem, for the earl simply retired to Coldingham, and subsequently to the north of England, and for a few years the possibility of his return with English assistance concentrated King James's mind and influenced his policies. Following the king's coup of May 1528, a greater subtlety on the part of English diplomats might have better served their cause. Instead they seem to have gone out of their way to alienate James V. In the autumn of 1528, the earl of Northumberland saw no hope of redress of breaches of the truce on the borders 'unless the earl of Angus be put in authority again'; and in January of the following year Thomas Magnus, the English ambassador, meeting James in Edinburgh, warned him in no uncertain terms about the dangers of 'young counsel', telling him that 'the fall and destruction of King James the Third, his grandfather' had been caused by that king's being 'totally advised, ruled and governed by a light and young council'.

This was not only threatening but also quite inaccurate. If it was designed to woo James back into the English fold, it failed signally. In the early 1530s, Henry VIII moved to the rejection of papal authority and the assumption of the title of 'Supreme Head' of the English church; and a conciliatory, rather than threatening, approach to a staunchly Catholic Scotland would have been appropriate. For the young James V found himself with the ability to deal to his profit with the major European powers and with the papacy. The Emperor Charles V, who was the nephew of Katharine of Aragon, Henry VIII's discarded wife, was alienated from England, and was keen to have an ally against the spread of Lutheranism in the Empire and elsewhere. He was prepared to pay for James V's support with projected marriage alliances, favourable commercial treaties, gifts of cannon and ammunition, and the Order of the Golden Fleece, conferred on the Scottish king in May 1532. Francis I of France, though still loosely bound by the Anglo-French treaty of 1527, was sufficiently concerned about a possible alliance between James V and Charles V as to offer sweeteners to the Scottish king – the Order of St Michael (in 1536) and a series of marriage proposals, though Francis continued to prevaricate over Scottish requests for the hand of his daughter Madeleine for James V, excusing her on grounds of her youth and frailty.

As for Pope Clement VII, he faced in James V a young man with a very old head on his shoulders. James might impress Clement by promising 'to banish the foul Lutheran sect' from Scotland, but there was a price to be paid for his orthodoxy. With Henry VIII leading England into heresy in 1532, King James's influence with the pope increased; he used it to confirm royal privileges over the church, to screw money out of his own clergy, and to have Clement VII acquiesce in the appointment of four of his bastard infant sons to major Scottish benefices. It was all polite blackmail, driven perhaps by material rather than spiritual considerations; but it was extremely effective in augmenting Scottish crown revenues.

Thus when Henry VIII came to negotiate seriously with James V, he was dealing with a Scottish king who had acquired firm control of church and state in a remarkably short time. In 1530, still fearing an English attempt to re-impose Angus on Scotland, James had taken the precaution of warding most of the border lords; there was no backlash, apart from the young and foolish Patrick, third earl of Bothwell, who in December 1531 offered to assist Henry VIII in an invasion of Scotland. The earl was punished by warding (temporary custody) followed by exile. By February 1535, therefore, when Henry VIII conferred the Order of the Garter on James V, James had no need to respond to his uncle's blandishments. He was well aware that Henry hoped to prevent him from contracting a French or Imperial marriage; but really Henry had little to offer by way of alternative. His marriage to Anne Boleyn in 1533 raised the possibility of male heirs and would affect James V's place in the English succession; and Henry was not willing to respond to James's request for the hand of his daughter Mary. Later Henry recommended to his nephew that James should follow his lead and dissolve the monasteries; but James was already milking the Church financially to such an extent that the idea, even had he wished to pursue it, would have brought him immense problems and little, if any, additional wealth. In effect, by the mid-1530s, the English diplomatic cupboard was bare; and with the breakdown of the Anglo-French alliance and Henry VIII's subsequent pursuit of an understanding with the Emperor from 1536 – a diplomatic revolution, as Gordon Donaldson calls it – the effective renewal of the Franco-Scottish alliance was only a matter of time.

On 1 September 1536 James V set sail from Kirkcaldy in a fleet of six ships headed by the *Mary Willoughby*, taking with him trusted members of his household including David Beaton, abbot of Arbroath, the Privy Seal, and an escort of 500 men. Probably as a matter of prudence, the king also had with him the young James Hamilton, second earl of Arran, his heir presumptive since Albany's death at the beginning of June. For the first time in over two hundred years a Scottish king was voluntarily leaving his kingdom – not as a refugee, but to have a nine-month holiday in France at the French king's expense and to contract a prestigious French marriage. It says a great deal for James's – justified – confidence in his strength and authority in Scotland that he could appoint six vice-regents to rule in his absence, and was in no hurry to return.

The marriage proposed was to Mary of Bourbon, daughter of the duke of Vêndome. The negotiations had been entrusted to the duke of Albany, in what proved to be his last public act on behalf of his nephew; and the marriage contract had been drawn up in March 1536, at the same time as James V was duping Henry VIII by agreeing to a meeting with the English king in the autumn. In the autumn, however, King James was already in France, landing at Dieppe on 10 September and heading due east to the duke of Vêndome's court at St Quentin in Picardy, to inspect the prospective bride. Reports that Mary of Bourbon was physically less than attractive are perhaps confirmed by the fact that the Scottish king, on seeing her portrait, demanded a pension of 20,000 *livres* on top of the dowry of 100,000 crowns.

James V's trip to France marked the end – or almost the end – of a tortuous period of matrimonial negotiations which stretched back to 1516 and involved the consideration of no less than seventeen brides. Four were Danish, two were proposed by the Emperor, one was Scottish, James's mistress Margaret Erskine, one Italian, Albany's niece Catharine de Medici, and one English, Henry VIII's daughter Mary; but no less than eight were French, a clear indication, in spite of the greatly changed Europe in which it was functioning, of the durability of the Auld Alliance.

Two Weddings and a Funeral (1537–42)

A later commentator remarked that 'there was nothing but merriness, banqueting and great cheer' at St Quentin. But there was no wedding. James V inspected Mary of Bourbon (whether he did so in disguise or not is a moot point), and returned to Rouen, the Scottish headquarters in France during the visit. James was in pursuit of a richer prize than even the duke of Vêndome's daughter, the bride promised to him before her birth as part of the Treaty of Rouen of 1517. By 15 October 1536, French sources were already suggesting that James V would be marrying Madeleine, Francis' daughter. The details were presumably arranged during a tour of the Loire valley – Moulins, Amboise, Châtelherault, and Blois – in October and November. On 26 November a new marriage contract was drawn up, and on New Year's Day 1537, James V married Madeleine of France in the cathedral of Nôtre Dame in Paris.

The Scottish king was in no hurry to return home. February 1537 found the royal couple at Chantilly and Compiègne, where James received marks of papal favour – a ceremonial sword and hat – together with an admonition to support France against heretic England. James V, enjoying himself drinking Bordeaux wine and spending 1100 crowns on a diamond for Madeleine's 'spousing' ring, probably needed no such admonition. At Rouen on 3 April, shortly before his 25th birthday, James issued his Act of Revocation, allowing him to revoke all grants of land and offices which had been made during his minority, and even those made 'by evil or false suggestion' since his assumption of power in 1528. The fact that James could do this in France, where he had already spent close on eight months, without fear of repercussions at home, is a clear indication of his mastery within his own kingdom; and he was now the son-in-law of the King of France.

But not for long. Francis I had probably meant it when he repeatedly excused his daughter from the Scottish match on account of her frailty. Already in March 1537, she had been ill at Rouen. She left Le Havre with her husband on 10 May, arriving at Leith nine days later. But on 7 July, aged only 17, Madeleine died at Holyrood Palace. The premature death of 'the flower of France and comfort of Scotland' was duly lamented in a long poem by Sir David Lindsay of the Mount, who saw Madeleine as 'the confirmatioun of the weill keipit ancient alyance maid betuix Scotland and the realme of France'. Lindsay's 'Deploratioun' contains not only formal praise of Madeleine, but lengthy lamentations over what might have been, the Renaissance pageantry surrounding the queen's formal entry into Edinburgh, for which Lindsay as a royal herald would have had a major role in planning. He was, however, to be compensated for his disappointment in less than a year.

For James V wasted little time in plunging back into the European marriage market, on this occasion with a much clearer focus than ever before. During his French holiday he had met Mary, duchess of Longueville, daughter of Claud of Guise-Lorraine, duke of Aumale. Mary of Guise, as she is popularly known, was widowed about a month before James V; her obvious attractions included Catholic orthodoxy, maturity, her birth into one of the great houses of France, and enormous wealth. The Scottish king would have no second trip to France; negotiations were conducted by David Beaton, soon to become archbishop of St Andrews, whose forceful diplomacy won him the small bishopric of Mirepoix in the south of France, and – eventually – a Cardinal's hat in December 1538. A ruthlessly ambitious career cleric, Beaton may be regarded, a generation on, as a more successful version of Andrew Forman.

Beaton's success lay partly in negotiating the Mary of Guise marriage in the face of strong competition from James V's uncle Henry VIII, who was once more a widower following the death of his third wife Jane Seymour. The marriage contract was drawn up in January 1538. A proxy marriage took place in May, and Mary of Guise sailed for Scotland early the following month, landing at Balcomie, near Crail in Fife, on 10 June. Sir David Lindsay had his chance at last, arranging the festivities for the queen's entry into St Andrews on Whit Sunday, and taking part in the more formal celebrations for her entry into Edinburgh the following month. On 22 February 1540, already six months pregnant, Mary of Guise was crowned at Holyrood. James V, who must have been more comfortable than his wife, used the occasion to wear the newly remodelled and enriched Scottish imperial crown.

The king was certainly comfortable financially as the result of his two French marriages. Together the dowries for Madeleine and Mary of Guise amounted to £168,750 Scots, dwarfing James IV's paltry £35,000 for Margaret Tudor in 1503–5. And the Stewart dynasty appeared secure through the prompt births, in 1540 and 1541, of two legitimate sons, James and Arthur, to offset the king's illegitimate brood by no less than six mistresses.

In some ways, the years 1537–42 marked the zenith of the Auld Alliance. James V's 'imperial' pretensions are demonstrated not only in the remodelled Scottish crown, but also on his superb gold coinage, the 'bonnet piece' of 1539, and on the contemporary portrait of the King and Mary of Guise (see Plate 13). Above all, King James's determination to show that he was a ruler of European significance found expression in architecture. To some extent, he was following the example set by John, duke of Albany, who had used French workmen to add to Holyrood Palace and Edinburgh Castle. But James V's most remarkable creations – a Renaissance palace at Stirling and a remodelled and extended palace at Falkland in Fife – were probably inspired by his tour of the Loire valley with Francis I in the late autumn of 1536. The Falkland ranges have been compared with Francis I's château of Villers-Cotterets, started in 1533, while the portrait roundels in Falkland's north range bear comparison with many French buildings, including the Hôtel d'Alluye in Blois, which James would certainly have seen. At Falkland, and probably also at Stirling, the Scottish king employed French masons, including Nicholas Roy and Mogin Martin. The accounts of the royal Master of Works survive for this period, and show an expenditure on royal buildings of at least £41,000; Mary of Guise, suitably impressed, declared Linlithgow the finest palace which she had seen.

Thus the French alliance provided James V with European prestige, money, and legitimate male heirs. Its principal disadvantage was that it provoked an increasingly frustrated Henry VIII into bitter enmity. Fears of encirclement by a hostile Empire and France, backed by Scotland, led him to put increasing pressure on the Scots. He proposed a meeting with James V at York in September 1541, and made the long journey north; but James did not appear, probably because of his council's fears that he would be kidnapped by Henry VIII. This would have created a very dangerous situation, because in the spring of 1541 James had suffered the double blow of the loss of both his sons, James and Arthur, and in September had no surviving heir. The Anglo-Scottish war of 1542, however, only followed after a further eleven months of tortuous negotiations. The danger to Henry VIII from a Franco-Imperial alliance had abated somewhat by 1541, as the two great powers had once again turned against each other and both were looking for England's aid. Thus the immediate cause of war between England and Scotland in the autumn of 1542 was Henry VIII's failure to obtain an assurance from James V that he would not support Francis I in the event of an English attack on France. In some ways, it was 1513 all over again.

The results of the autumn war were mixed. In August the earl of Huntly, Scottish lieutenant in the temporary absence of James V's half-brother Moray, who was sick, won a victory over an English invading force under Sir Robert Bowes at Hadden Rig in the east march. A further English army, led by the duke of Norfolk, crossed the border, burned Kelso Abbey, and would have been opposed by the Scottish host under James V himself, who called for a muster of part of the army at Lauder in October; but Norfolk fell ill and disbanded his army at Berwick at the end of the month. James had moved to Peebles by November; he was not present when, in a sideshow on the River Esk on 24 November – subsequently described as Solway Moss – a Scottish raiding party under Lord Maxwell was out-manoeuvred by Sir Thomas Wharton, the English warden-depute, and, caught between a bog and a river, 'lighted at the water's side and fought valiantly' (according to a contemporary English account), subsequently surrendering as an alternative to drowning in the Esk.

By 28 November 1542, James V was back in Edinburgh, giving orders for the further defence of the west march. In early December entries in the Treasurer's accounts indicate royal preparations for a renewal of the war in the spring. On 8 December, at Linlithgow Palace, Mary of Guise bore the king a daughter, Mary. However, six days later, at Falkland Palace, James V died, possibly of cholera. He had been ill many times during the personal rule – in 1533, 1534, in Paris in 1536, and in 1540 – of complaints variously described as fevers or the pox. He was thirty years of age.

With the single exception of the recent scholarly biography of the king by Jamie Cameron, James V has not been treated kindly by historians; and a myth has grown up about his character and policies which is the more durable for having started within a generation of his death. A combination of benefit of hindsight – the Protestant Reformation of 1560 – and wishful thinking on the part of contemporary English diplomats created a picture of James V as a 'priest's king', a man out of step with his nobility – indeed conducting something akin to a reign of terror against them in his last years – who stubbornly adhered to the French and papist alliance and was very properly abandoned by his own subjects in time of war. Plunged into melancholy at the end – the birth of a daughter being the last straw – he muttered about the imminent end of the dynasty, turned his face to the wall, and expired. This myth of James V found its most persuasive modern advocate in Gordon Donaldson, who remarked with something approaching Old Testament severity that 'however far the views of sixteenth-century narrators and modern psychologists might go to explain James V's character, they do little to lessen the revulsion with which he must be regarded'.

It would be inappropriate to replace Donaldson's moralising with propaganda on behalf of James V. Unlike his popular father, he was not generous in his patronage to his supporters; and he could be ruthless in pursuit of those guilty of treason, as the execution of the Master of Forbes and the burning of Lady Glamis in 1537 clearly showed. But though on occasions he employed what Jenny Wormald has aptly termed 'sharp practice' against some of his nobility, he was no more guilty in this respect than the popular James IV; and it is significant that he was widely supported throughout the 1542 war. Even Lord Maxwell's raid, which ended in failure at Solway Moss, was an example of a Scottish force crossing the border, seemingly unaware of the 'Flodden complex' with which they were supposedly afflicted.

Equally unconvincing is the portrayal of James V as a 'priest's king'. It is of course true that he spent much of the reign screwing money out of the First Estate, and that the clergy contributed hugely towards the cost of the 1542 war. But there was really nothing new in this; James IV, furthering his policy of 'liturgical nationalism', had raised huge sums from the clergy for a popular war in 1513. The difference between 1513 and 1542, it is argued, is the advent of the European Reformation and the spread of Lutheranism amongst James V's subjects. This is difficult to quantify. Certainly parliament had passed an act as early as 1525 – a mere eight years after Luther's protest – forbidding the importation of Lutheran books into Scotland. But the spread of heresy does not seem to have constituted a major problem for James V; in the thirty years after 1528 there were only twenty-one executions for Protestant heresy. In the 1570s the Protestant laird Robert Lindsay of Pitscottie made much of the appointment of the king's familiar, Sir James Hamilton of Finnart, as a judge to try heretics; Finnart, he claimed, promised James V that he would give heretics 'hott ersis for his pleasour and the kirkis'. Given the numbers involved, Finnart can have had very little job satisfaction.

In the post-Reformation era, James V's crimes were to have been an orthodox Catholic and the father of Mary Queen of Scots. The first of these attributes made him a consistent, though not uncritical, supporter of the Auld Alliance; but it did not involve him in the compilation of a 'black list' of heretics – 360 of them, including the earl of Arran and most of the major magnates – which was most likely a fabrication, possibly by Arran himself, early in the next reign. As to the latter, the birth of a daughter provided wonderful copy for Protestant chroniclers, including John Knox, a heretical priest turned reformer, who combined a sure instinct for self-preservation with a remarkable talent for creative writing. On his deathbed, according to Knox, the king had thoughts only of the fate of his favourite Oliver Sinclair of Pitcairn, at Solway Moss; after that defeat, sneered the reformer, James had visited a whore; and appropriately his last words were 'All is lost'. Pitscottie, by contrast, recounts James's most famous – and inaccurate – deathbed prophecy: 'It came with a lass, it will pass with a lass', referring to the Stewart dynasty's descent from Marjorie Bruce and likely extinction with Mary Queen of Scots. It was left to the staunchly Catholic bishop John Lesley to supply James V's most convincing last words: 'Scotland suld be afflicted with the Inglismen shortlie, and sourlie'.

James V died much too early; but he died a rich man, leaving around £26,000 in his treasure chests at Edinburgh Castle. And he died a committed supporter of the Auld Alliance. In the 1540s, this was not a perverse diplomatic stance. As Jamie Cameron reminds us, 'Henry VIII was the maverick monarch in 1542; James, like Charles V and Francis I, represented the prevalent orthodoxy'. Thus his premature death struck a tremendous blow to his dynasty and his kingdom. Early in January 1543, after James V's body had been brought from Fife across the Queensferry to its final resting place in Holyrood Abbey, and following an elaborate funeral devised by Sir David Lindsay of the Mount, there must have been many who had grave fears for the future.

'Extreme Necessity':
the End of the Auld Alliance (1543–1560)

In what proved to be the final two decades of its formal existence, the Franco-Scottish alliance was strained to its limits and beyond by a bewilderingly rapid sequence of political, military, dynastic, and religious changes in those countries most directly affected by its terms. The Scots had lost their king; certainly they had an able and well-connected Queen Dowager in Mary of Guise, but she was still finding her way in the morass of Scottish politics. James Hamilton, earl of Arran, the heir presumptive to the infant Mary, was an inept and inconstant Governor whose only loyalty was to the Hamilton interest; Cardinal David Beaton, archbishop of St Andrews, was a ruthless and committed supporter of the orthodox status quo; and at the centre of this political witches' brew was the life of a frail child whose marriage was nevertheless a matter of vital diplomatic concern in the first year of her existence.

Scotland's ally France, of little or no value to her in 1542, found herself faced with a bellicose Henry VIII and an Emperor anxious to renew the war. Fears of encirclement led to a renewed French interest in the old ally, and this proved to be an extremely expensive investment. The death of

Francis I at the end of March 1547, two months after his rival Henry VIII, brought Henry II to the French throne, and commitment to Scotland increased hugely, mainly through the influence of Mary of Guise's brothers – Francis, Duke of Guise, and Charles, Cardinal of Lorraine – upon the new French king. The wars initiated by Charles VIII when he had invaded Italy in 1494, and which had continued intermittently ever since, were brought to an end by the peace of Cateau-Cambrésis (March–April 1559); and as part of the peace, Henry II's elder daughter Elizabeth was to marry Philip of Spain. At the beginning of July 1559, the wedding celebrations proved fatal to the French king; taking part in a joust with Montgomery, captain of the *Garde Ecossaise*, Henry II was pierced in the eye by a lance splinter and mortally wounded, dying on 10 July.

Scotland's enemy, the England of Henry VIII, was likewise afflicted with swift and bewildering changes. Henry died in 1547, to be succeeded by his three offspring in turn – the sickly Edward VI (1547–53), under whom Protestantism flourished; Mary (1553–8), a zealous Catholic, married to Philip II of Spain; and Elizabeth (1558–1603), who sought a *via media* and whose early years were fraught with religious and dynastic difficulties. Thus as regards Anglo-Scottish relations between 1543 and 1560, the death of Henry VIII in 1547 was an important turning point. It removed from the scene an aggressive ruler whose view of Scotland, at the beginning and end of his reign, had been that the northern kingdom was a client, or even vassal, state which must be coerced into submission; significantly the issue of overlordship was raised in both 1512 and 1542. Henry's death and the gradual dilution of his more bellicose policies, coupled with an inevitable weakness at the heart of an English government which lurched from support of radical Protestantism to Catholic orthodoxy and part of the way back again, provided obvious opportunities for England's enemies. France was one of the winners; Calais, the last English stronghold across the Channel, was lost to Francis, duke of Guise – Mary of Guise's brother – on 7 January 1558.

A Scotland united and strongly led would certainly have been able to take advantage of many of these changes. But the death of James V was rapidly followed by political chaos: a coup removed Cardinal Beaton, the head of the pro-French and papal party, and replaced him with the earl of Arran, who was acknowledged as Governor in March 1543. Arran had the support, for what it was worth, of the 'assured lords': Scottish prisoners of Solway Moss who, in order to secure their release, agreed to further English interests in Scotland. In practical terms, what this amounted to was a recommendation, speedily adopted, by the most distinguished of the Solway Moss lords, Robert Lord Maxwell, that the scriptures should be issued in the vernacular.

The March parliament of 1543 was however responsible for authoris-
ing a step which went much too far for many Scots – the opening of
negotiations with Henry VIII for the betrothal of the infant Queen Mary
to the English king's son and heir Edward. Within a month Cardinal
Beaton, who had been placed in ward, was free and had joined together
with John Hamilton, abbot of Paisley, Arran's half-brother and the future
archbishop of St Andrews, to reverse the Governor's policy. Arran was
reminded by the Scottish clergy that his legitimacy, and therefore his
claim to the throne, depended upon ecclesiastical authority; that authority had annulled his father's first marriage, and could, if it chose, set aside
his legitimacy. At the same time Matthew Stewart, fourth earl of Lennox,
was brought over from France; as heir presumptive if Arran were
declared illegitimate, Lennox in Scotland would surely help to concentrate the Governor's mind.

Thus the summer of 1543 saw a remarkable *volte-face* in Scottish politics
which set the Franco-Scottish alliance on its final course. Arran, having
negotiated the Treaties of Greenwich (Anglo-Scottish alliance and marriage agreements, 1 July 1543), dithered and then ratified them towards the
end of August, repudiated them almost immediately, renounced his policy
of ecclesiastical reform and came to an understanding with Beaton (who,
significantly, required the delivery of Arran's son as a hostage for the
Governor's good faith). By the end of a chaotic year, a Scottish parliament,
meeting in December 1543, had denounced the Greenwich treaties,
reaffirmed the laws against heresy, and cited Henry VIII's violation of the
peace through the arrest of Scottish merchants and the seizure of their
goods as a reason for abandoning the entire English package. Meanwhile
Cardinal Beaton, who had transferred both the infant queen and her
mother from Linlithgow to the relative safety of Stirling during the
summer, was able to organise the coronation of Queen Mary, now nine
months old, in the Chapel Royal of Stirling Castle on 9 September 1543.
Thirty years to the day after the battle of Flodden, another Scottish
government looked to repudiate an English alliance in favour of an
accommodation with Scotland's longstanding but often fickle ally.

Henry VIII's predictable reaction was one of fury; and from May 1544
to the end of his life and beyond he sought to terrorise the Scots into
accepting the repudiated English marriage; these 'Rough Wooings',
recently graphically described by Marcus Merriman, were conducted by
Edward Seymour, earl of Hertford, and consisted of English invasions in
1544, 1545, and 1547. The destruction caused, though not as frightful as
suggested in Hertford's instructions before he set out, resulted in a
devastated south-east, with the great border abbeys – Melrose, Jedburgh,
Dryburgh and Kelso – and the more vulnerable abbeys of Newbattle

and Holyrood all burned, together with the burghs of Haddington, Edinburgh, Leith, Craigmillar, Musselburgh, and Dunbar; in Fife Kinghorn, St Monans, Pittenweem, and Burntisland were all attacked. At the end of the fourteenth century Richard II had torched the border abbeys on the grounds that the Scots, as supporters of the anti-Pope during the Great Schism, were heretics and schismatics; now, 160 years later, the lieutenant of Henry VIII, former Defender of the Faith and now himself a heretic and schismatic, did the same thing. *Plus ça change . . .*

The challenge presented by the 'Rough Wooings' revealed hopeless splits amongst the Scots themselves. Some of this can be explained by the spread of Protestantism – first Lutheranism, then Calvinism – in some areas of the country, though its extent and its influence on Scottish politics have always been a source of controversy among historians. In some rural areas – Ayrshire, Angus and the Mearns, Fife and parts of the Lothians – reforming opinions are apparent from an early stage, supported by local members of the nobility but in no sense forming a national movement; in the burghs Protestantism was weaker still. As Michael Lynch has pointed out, as late as Easter 1561, eight months after the Reformation parliament had abolished the mass, only 1200 – that is one in six adults out of Edinburgh's population of 12,500 – went to John Knox's new Protestant communion. But numbers alone do not make a revolution; what mattered was the attitude of the leaders of society – magnates, lairds, and burgh councils – to reforming opinions, for these were the groups who had the power to promote change.

When considering an age in which the Most Christian King of France could make an alliance with the infidel Turkish Sultan against his co-religionist, the Emperor Charles V – as Francis I did in 1536 – it is perhaps dangerous to be too dogmatic about the extent to which the leaders of European society were moved primarily by religious considerations. In the case of the higher nobility in Scotland, politics – local and national – and dynastic considerations often seemed to dictate which side individuals favoured in the pre-Reformation decades. Thus Arran's dynastic rival, Matthew, earl of Lennox, invariably sided with opponents of the Governor; Angus, the bane of James V's existence, was understandably an 'assured lord', loyal to Henry VIII, in the early 1540s; but he changed sides in 1545, winning a victory over the English at Ancrum Moor, a few miles north of Jedburgh, in February of that year. Arran himself, taking advantage of the unpopularity of Cardinal Beaton and the French interest, proposed that Queen Mary should remain in Scotland and be married to his son. Thus as the '40s advanced there emerged powerful advocates of every conceivable shade of political opinion in Scotland, right across the spectrum from those who were prepared to take Henry VIII's money to others who were totally committed to the French alliance; those who blamed Henry VIII for the 'Rough Wooings', others who held Cardinal Beaton responsible for them; those who were attracted by Protestantism, and by extension, by amity with England, others who favoured Catholic reform, and some, like Beaton, who advocated, and sought to promote, the extirpation of heresy. The Scottish kingdom, lacking a king or even a capable regent, had not been so weak and divided since the 1290s.

On 29 May 1546, a few Fife lairds – opponents of the Cardinal, pro-English and pro-Reformation in outlook – broke into St Andrews Castle and assassinated Beaton; they then retained possession of the castle, called for English help, and – quaintly named the 'Castilians' – withstood an inept siege by Governor Arran – whose son was a hostage in the castle – for more than a year. However, in July 1547, a French fleet and expeditionary force invested St Andrews Castle; it fell at the end of the month, and the Castilians were either imprisoned in France or sent to the galleys.

This temporary success was followed by an appalling reverse only six weeks later. Edward Seymour, earl of Hertford, Lord Protector of England since Henry VIII's death the previous January, shattered a huge Scottish army assembled by Arran at Pinkie, near Musselburgh, on 10 September 1547. Divisions amongst the Scottish leadership may have been as much responsible for the defeat as anything else: Arran had little in common with Angus, and the Scottish clergy saw themselves as conducting yet another crusade against heretics and schismatics. The Scottish losses were enormous; worse, unlike the aftermath of Flodden, Pinkie was followed by a widespread English garrisoning of strongpoints in the south-east and east, with their main centre at Haddington and troops posted as far north as Broughty, near Dundee. And many Scots, especially in the east, began as a matter of urgency to look to peace with England as essential, outweighing any possible loyalty to an ancient alliance whose principal supporters could not defend the country, or, for that matter, capture St Andrews Castle without French help.

Therein lay the problem for any Scottish government acting in Queen Mary's name. The choice lay between English or French domination; for the new king of France, Henry II, was prepared to intervene on the side of his old allies only on his own terms. After Pinkie, it is unsurprising that the Scots accepted these with little negotiation. Queen Mary, then in her sixth year, had been sent for safety to the priory of Inchmahome, on an island in the Lake of Menteith, during the Pinkie campaign. In January 1548 Arran, who was so unpopular that he did not dare to set foot on the streets of Edinburgh, agreed that, in return for a French dukedom for himself, he would secure Scottish parliamentary consent for Queen

Mary's marriage to the dauphin Francis, and would arrange for the infant queen to be conveyed to France. Arran, putting the Hamilton interest first as ever, also acquired the marriage of the elder daughter of the duke of Montpensier for his son and heir, and an agreement that he would not be pursued for financial claims arising out of his period as Governor; he had had the advantage of the use of James V's sizeable monetary legacy for a few years, and may have misappropriated some of it to feather the Hamilton nest. In February 1549 Arran secured his own prestigious bolt-hole, the dukedom of Châtelherault.

Arran's machinations provided the background to the last formal renewal of the Auld Alliance. Unquestionably, Henry II of France regarded Scotland simply as a pawn – though an important one – in his wars with England, and initially believed that the Scots could hold on against what Gordon Donaldson colourfully describes as England's 'action for breach of promise'; but Pinkie and its aftermath changed all that, and French fears of an Anglo-Scottish union based on the marriage of Mary to Edward VI produced a sensational French financial and military commitment – at least £1,000,000 Scots and 6,000 troops – to the defence of Scotland. In his demand for a huge *aide* to finance the war, Henry II spoke of Scotland's 'extreme necessity' and urged the maintenance of an alliance which stretched back for centuries to 'le Roy Charlemaigne'. His view of Scotland, however, cogently expressed in September 1550, was not one which would have found favour with many Scots, whatever their political or religious affiliations. Commenting on his recent success in the war, Henry II remarked: 'I have brought peace to Scotland which I hold and possess with the same order and obedience that I have in France'.

The first French forces in Scotland arrived at Leith, and a joint Franco-Scottish army immediately laid siege to Haddington. On 7 July 1548, in the nunnery outside the town, the formal acceptance by the Scots of their queen's marriage to the dauphin Francis was enshrined in the Treaty of Haddington. Thereafter south-east Scotland became a cockpit for an Anglo-French war in which the English were not dislodged from Haddington by Franco-Scottish assaults, but rather by news of events on the continent, where the English garrison was expelled from Boulogne.

The 'Rough Wooing' was over; and already Mary Queen of Scots had reached the comparative safety of France. After lying off Dumbarton for a week at the beginning of August 1548, waiting for a fair wind, the young queen sailed for Brittany in the ship of Nicolas Durand, lord of Villegaignon, arriving at Roscoff by 18 August. Thereafter she was escorted overland at an easy pace, reaching St Denis in the middle of October. Her life for the next decade was spent at the French court, a travelling circus which moved regularly among the royal palaces of St-Germain, Fontainebleau, Blois and Chambord. Educated together with members of Henry II's family, Mary was reunited with her mother only once, when Mary of Guise visited France in 1550–51; but Guise influence was constantly present in the shape of Mary's grandmother Antoinette, and her uncles, the Duke and Cardinal of Guise. On 24 April 1558 the last great ceremony of the Auld Alliance took place in front of the cathedral of Notre Dame in Paris: Mary, Queen of Scots, aged fifteen, was married to the fourteen-year-old dauphin Francis. Twenty-one years before, Mary's father had married the daughter of the King of France on the same spot; but James V had been an adult sovereign in full control of his realm. Mary was a minor in the pocket of the Guises.

Her absence from Scotland during the 1550s left her mother, Mary of Guise, as the principal political player, more than a match for the earl of Arran, who was finally removed from the governorship, and Mary of Guise appointed Regent, in the parliament of April 1554. The Queen Mother played her political cards skilfully, displaying toleration towards the Reformers, buying support through liberal distribution of pensions and, where appropriate, the Order of St Michael; and she had the good fortune to take control when, in England, the radical Protestantism of Edward VI had been succeeded by the firm Catholic orthodoxy of Mary Tudor.

Yet Mary of Guise may have been swimming against the tide. Already in 1552, with France and the Empire once again at war, the Scots had refused to resume hostilities on behalf of their ally, or to send troops to serve in the French army. So much for Henry II's boast that he had brought Scotland to order and obedience. And there is no doubt that the Frenchmen on whom the Queen Mother relied for counsel – De Roubay, the Vice-Chancellor, Villemore, the Comptroller, and perhaps above all D'Oysel, the resident French ambassador – were disliked by more than those whose political positions they usurped.

In the end, it was events outwith Scotland which broke the alliance. On 17 November 1558, Mary Tudor died and the English succession went to her sister Elizabeth, whose administration moved cautiously towards a Protestant stance. The death of Henry II of France the following July made his sickly son king of France as Francis II; and Mary, Queen of Scots, his wife, became Queen of France, and, on the basis that Elizabeth was illegitimate (a view taken by many English Catholics), Francis II and Mary assumed the titles and arms of sovereigns of England. The new English queen, fearing that the French – freed from war in Europe by the Treaty of Cateau-Cambrésis – would use Scotland as a base to launch an attack on England, was prepared to give some cautious support to the Scottish Reformers. Aware that Mary, as queen of France, was unlikely ever to return to Scotland, Elizabeth sought her deposition there; but who could possibly succeed Mary? Her half-brother, Lord James Stewart, James V's eldest surviving bastard, could perhaps be the power behind the throne, but he could never sit on it. The alternative, hardly a popular one, was Arran in his new role as Châtelherault, and temporarily reconciled to Protestantism.

Scottish civil war had broken out between Mary of Guise and the Protestant 'Lords of the Congregation' in 1559; the Queen Mother, who was well served by professional French soldiers, would probably have won the day if there had been no outside interference; but English troops entered Scotland in March 1560, and an English fleet had already entered the Firth of Forth to blockade the principal French stronghold of Leith. Once again an Anglo-French struggle was being fought out in south-east Scotland. Its outcome, however, was decided when Mary of Guise, who had steadfastly refused to negotiate on any terms but the insurgents' return to their allegiance, died of dropsy in Edinburgh Castle on 11 June 1560.

At a stroke Guise influence was removed from Scotland; English and French commissioners moved to Edinburgh and concluded the Treaty of Edinburgh on 6 July. English and French troops were to withdraw from Scotland; it was suggested that Mary Queen of Scots, absent in France, should give up use of the English arms and thus recognise Elizabeth's title as Queen of England; and the selection of a Scottish council was to be entrusted jointly to a parliament and to Mary herself. That parliament, meeting in August 1560, abolished the Mass and adopted a reformed Confession of Faith, but did nothing to inhibit the jurisdiction of the leading Catholic clergy within their benefices.

Neither the Treaty of Edinburgh nor the statutes of the 'Reformation' parliament would be ratified by Francis II and Mary Queen of Scots. The Scots had carried through a dubious political and religious revolution which left them in a kind of limbo, at odds with their sovereign yet having no alternative to Mary but Châtelherault, and no clear feature save as an English client state. But any Scottish search for security in England suddenly became irrelevant on 5 December 1560, when Francis II, Mary's adolescent husband, died of an ear infection in spite of frantic Guise threats against his physicians and public prayers for his recovery. Guise influence at the French court collapsed in December 1560, just as it had failed in Scotland six months earlier with the death of Mary of Guise. And the Auld Alliance, arguably long obsolete in the changed European world of the mid-sixteenth century and sustained only by a French commitment to the domination of Scotland, was at an end.

A Path not Taken

The Franco-Scottish alliance had been born out of the Scottish kingdom's need for a powerful ally to offset the huge menace represented by Edward I of England in 1295–6. It was sustained in the fourteenth and fifteenth centuries by France's continuing need for military assistance against the same enemy. The Wars of Independence and the Hundred Years' War alike held together what at first sight might appear unlikely allies, to the mutual profit of both. It could indeed be argued that, in the 1330s and 1420s, that mutual profit extended to the saving of both kingdoms from external domination.

Thereafter, from the mid-fifteenth to the mid-sixteenth centuries, the nature of the alliance changed. Scots had settled in France in considerable numbers, and the substantial influence of their leaders with the French crown was an important by-product of the Hundred Years' War. But the spate of marriages of fifteenth-century Stewart princesses in France, Austria, Brittany, and Flanders, with the French king acting as marriage broker with his allies abroad, had little long-term effect on Scottish diplomacy or the Scottish kingdom's perceived importance on the Continent.

The likelihood that the Auld Alliance would settle down into a comfortable but distant diplomatic understanding had however been removed by the re-emergence, towards the end of the fifteenth century, of a bellicose England under Richard III, and then by Henry VIII's unrealistic quest for military glory and the crown of France in 1512–13. If the Scots had suffered most during these passages of arms, most obviously by losing the unnecessary battle of Flodden, they were the gainers in the 1530s, when their geographical position to the north of a heretic England made their king, James V, a highly desirable ally in Europe and provided him with lucrative French marriages.

However, the old medieval certainties had already gone, and the existence of the colossal empire of Charles V inevitably put both France and England – respectively Scotland's ally and enemy – on their guard; put in simple terms, France's principal enemy was no longer England, and the Auld Alliance became something of a sideshow as a result. The exception came in the late 1540s, with Henry II of France's huge investment in Scotland; but like Henry VIII of England before him, he regarded the Scottish kingdom as little more than a province, to be dominated through the happy combination of a royal marriage and the deployment of large numbers of troops and huge sums of money.

Arguably, things might have been very different. James V died at 30, when he might have been expected to live for many years, with Mary of Guise giving birth to royal Stewarts to guarantee an easy succession. Instead, the Scots had to face a predatory England and to endure the duplicity and ineptitude of James Hamilton, earl of Arran, who must surely rank as the kingdom's worst-ever Governor. The consequences of Arran's many political U-turns could have been even worse than they were; but he was perhaps fortunate to die a French duke rather than be stoned to death by an Edinburgh mob.

Unpredictable events – the death of Edward VI and accession of Mary Tudor in 1553, the death of Mary Tudor and accession of Elizabeth in 1558, the deaths of Henry II of France in 1559, and of Mary of Guise and Francis II in 1560 – came thick and fast. Yet neither the Scots nor the French can have imagined that the alliance would not be revived after 1560. The French had after all invested very heavily in Scotland in the recent past; and after December 1560 Mary, Queen of Scots and Dowager Queen of France, was the sole ruler of Scotland. Her return to her native land, and further close intercourse with France, were to be expected.

In the event, when Mary returned to Scotland in August 1561 she had already reached an accommodation with Lord James Stewart, her half-brother, when he had visited her in France in the spring. Mary tried to play the role of a *politique* monarch, rather in the manner of her formidable mother-in-law, Catherine de Medici, in France: that is, she endeavoured to rise above religious faction by permitting a wide degree of toleration and by taking counsel from Catholic and Protestant alike. When she failed – only at the very end, in the spring of 1567 – it was her personal judgment rather than her political sagacity which was tempo- rarily – and fatally – at fault.

France, like Scotland, faced severe religious and dynastic problems in the later sixteenth century, and no further alliance would have been productive. The wars of religion, that violent struggle between Catholic and Protestant (Huguenot) which afflicted France intermittently be- tween 1562 and 1598, also witnessed the end of the Valois dynasty – Catherine de Medici's incompetent and highly unpleasant sons, Charles IX (1560–74) and Henry III (1574–89) – and the triumph of the *politiques* in the form of Henry of Navarre (Henry IV, 1589–1610), the founder of the Bourbon dynasty. But by that time, Mary Queen of Scots was dead and her son James VI well embarked on the only diplomatic course which made any sense for himself, the succession to Elizabeth of England.

Thus the French alliance of the 1550s ultimately proved to be a path not taken by the Scots; the price was too high, amounting at its worst – that is, if Mary should die without heirs – to the surrender of the Kingdom of Scotland, as a gift, into the hands of the King of France. Beyond the factor of French territorial ambition, however, lay the Stewart preoccupation with the English succession, a concept which had originated in the marriage of James IV to Margaret Tudor in August 1503. Both James IV and James V had actively pursued their rights as the Tudor line alternately faltered and then briefly recovered; and by the 1560s, with only one life between Queen Mary and the English succession, the topic had understandably become obsessional on both sides of the border.

So the Auld Alliance was laid to rest, surviving in the persons of the expatriate Scottish families in the Touraine, Berry, Anjou, Poitou, and the Auvergne, and in the collective memory of the two countries' shared past. The alliance ended, perhaps, not with a bang but a whimper. But if it had been possible for the Scots of 1560 to look forward even 150 years, they might well have regarded the centuries of the Auld Alliance as a lost golden age. For what lay ahead for Scotland was no Brave New World, but rather a continuing nightmare of cul-de-sac diplomacy, absentee monarchy, rebellion, revolution, civil war, bloody religious struggles, comprehensive military defeat, and – eventually – absorption within the English state. *Sic transit gloria.*

FURTHER READING

The list which follows is selective rather than comprehensive. Works cited are in English, Latin with English translation, French, and German.

General and Reference

Barrow, G. W. S., *Kingship and Unity: Scotland 1000–1306* (London, 1981)

Dickinson, W. C., Donaldson, G., Milne, I. A. (eds.), *A Source Book of Scottish History*, vol. i: From the Earliest Times to 1424 (Edinburgh, 1952); vol. ii: 1424–1567 (Edinburgh, 1953)

Donaldson, G., *Scotland: James V–James VII* [1513–1689] (Edinburgh, 1967)

Donaldson, G., *La Vieille Alliance: Histoire de L'Amitié Franco-Ecossaise* (Adaptation française par Ginette Dalleré et Michel Duchein): Association Franco-Ecossaise (Edinburgh, 1995)

Donaldson, G., *Scottish Kings* (Edinburgh, 1967)

Duchein, M., *Histoire de l'Ecosse* (Paris, 1998)

Duncan, A. A. M., *Scotland: The Making of the Kingdom* [to 1286] (Edinburgh, 1975)

Francisque-Michel, *Les Ecossais en France, Les Français en Ecosse* (2 vols.) (London, 1862)

Grant, A., *Independence and Nationhood: Scotland, 1306–1469* (London, 1984)

Hume Brown, P. (ed.), *Early Travellers in Scotland* (Edinburgh, 1978)

Laidlaw, J. (ed.), *The Auld Alliance: France and Scotland over 700 Years* (Edinburgh, 1999)

Lynch, M., *Scotland: A New History* (London, 1991)

Mackay, Angus, and Ditchburn, D. (eds.), *Atlas of Medieval Europe* (London, 1997)

McNeill, P. G. B., and MacQueen, H. L. (eds.), *Atlas of Scottish History to 1707* (Edinburgh, 1996)

Macquarrie, Alan, *Scotland and the Crusades, 1095–1560* (Edinburgh, 1985)

Nicholson, R., *Scotland: The Later Middle Ages* [1286–1513] (Edinburgh, 1974)

Paul, J. B. (ed.), *The Scots Peerage*, 9 vols. (Edinburgh, 1904–14)

Watt, D. E. R., *A Biographical Dictionary of Scottish Graduates to AD 1410* (Oxford, 1977)

Webster, Bruce, *Medieval Scotland: The Making of an Identity* (London, 1997)

Wormald, J., *Court, Kirk and Community: Scotland, 1470–1625* (London, 1981)

Introduction: 'The Oldest Alliance in the World'

The Auld Alliance of France and Scotland (Exhibition catalogue, Edinburgh, 1996. Text: Michel Duchein, trans. Joanna Goodrick)

Autrand, Françoise, *'Aux Origines de l'Europe moderne: l'alliance France-Ecosse au XIVe siècle'*, in J. Laidlaw (ed.), *The Auld Alliance* (Edinburgh, 1999), 33–46

Bower, Walter, *Scotichronicon* [in Latin and English], vol. 8, ed. D. E. R. Watt (Aberdeen, 1987)

Prebble, John, *The Lion in the North* (London, 1971) (included for the author's comments on the Auld Alliance on p. 190)

Chapter One: Uncertain Beginnings: 1295–1326

Barbour, John, *The Bruce*, ed. with translation and notes by A.A.M. Duncan (Edinburgh, 1997) (much the best edition of Barbour's epic poem of 1375)

Barrow, G. W. S., *Robert Bruce* (3rd edn., Edinburgh, 1988)

Bower, Walter, *Scotichronicon* [in Latin and English], vol. 6, ed. N. F. Shead, W. B. Stevenson and D. E. R. Watt (Edinburgh, 1991) (covers the period 1286–1319)

Duchein, M., 'Le Traité franco-écossais de 1295 dans son contexte international', in J. Laidlaw (ed.), *The Auld Alliance* (Edinburgh, 1999), 23–32

Duncan, A. A. M., 'The Community of the Realm of Scotland and Robert Bruce', *Scottish Historical Review* xlv (1966), 184–201

Duncan, A. A. M., *The Nation of Scots and the Declaration of Arbroath* (Historical Association Pamphlet, 1970)

Duncan, A. A. M., 'The War of the Scots, 1306–1323', *Transactions of the Royal Historical Society*, 6th series, ii (1992), 125–151

Macdougall, N., 'L'Ecosse à la fin du XIIIe siècle: un royaume menacé', in J. Laidlaw (ed.), *The Auld Alliance* (Edinburgh, 1999), 9–22

McNamee, Colm, *The Wars of the Bruces: Scotland, England and Ireland, 1306–1328* (East Linton, 1997)

Maxwell, H. (ed. and trans.), *The Chronicle of Lanercost* (Glasgow, 1913)

Maxwell, H. (ed. and trans.), *Scalacronica, by Sir Thomas Grey of Heton, Knight* (Glasgow, 1907)

Penman, M., " 'A fell coniuracioun agayn Robert the douchty king': the Soules conspiracy of 1318–1320", *Innes Review* xlx (i) (Spring, 1999), 25–57

Prestwich, M., *The Three Edwards: War and State in England, 1272–1377* (London, 1980)

Prestwich, M., *Edward I* (London, 1988)

Reid, N., 'The Kingless Kingdom: The Scottish Guardianships of 1286–1306', *Scottish Historical Review* lxi (1982), 105–129

Reid, N., 'Crown and Community under Robert I', in A. Grant and K.J. Stringer (eds.), *Medieval Scotland: Crown, Lordship and Community* (Edinburgh, 1993), 203–222

Rothwell, H. (ed.), *The Chronicle of Walter of Guisborough* (Camden 3rd series, lxxxix, 1957)

Stones, E. L. G. (ed.), *Anglo-Scottish Relations, 1174–1328: Some Selected Documents* (London, 1965)

Stones, E. L. G., and Simpson, G. G. (eds.), *Edward I and the Throne of Scotland, 1290–1296*, 2 vols. (Oxford, 1978)

Strayer, J. R., *The Reign of Philip the Fair* (Princeton, 1980)

Young, A., *Robert the Bruce's Rivals: The Comyns, 1212–1314* (East Linton, 1997)

Watson, F., *Under the Hammer: Edward I and Scotland* (East Linton, 1998)

Chapter Two: Two Theatres of War: The Fourteenth Century

Boardman, S., *The Early Stewart Kings: Robert II and Robert III* (East Linton, 1996)

Boardman, S., "Chronicle Propaganda in Fourteenth Century Scotland: Robert the Steward, John of Fordun and the 'Anonymous Chronicle' ", *Scottish Historical Review* lxxvi (1997), 23–43

Bower, Walter, *Scotichronicon* (in Latin and English), vol. 7, ed. A. B. Scott and D. E. R. Watt (Edinburgh, 1996) (covers the period 1320–1390)

Brereton, G. (ed. and trans.), *Jean Froissart's Chronicles* (London, 1968)

Brown, M., *The Black Douglases: War and Lordship in Late Medieval Scotland, 1300–1455* (East Linton, 1998)

Campbell, J., 'England, Scotland and the Hundred Years War in the Fourteenth Century', in *Europe in the Late Middle Ages*, ed. J. R. Hale, J. R. L. Highfield and B. Smalley (London, 1965)

Contamine, P., 'Froissart and Scotland', in G. G. Simpson (ed.), *Scotland and the Low Countries, 1124–1994* (East Linton, 1996), 43–58

Duncan, A. A. M., " 'Honi soit qui mal y pense': David II and Edward III, 1346–52", *Scottish Historical Review* lxvii (1988), 113–141

Goodman, A., 'A Letter from an Earl of Douglas to a King of Castile', *Scottish Historical Review* lxix (i) (April 1985), 68–75

Nicholson, R., *Edward III and the Scots* (Oxford, 1965)

Nicholson, R., 'David II, the Historians and the Chroniclers', *Scottish Historical Review* xlv (1966), 59–78

Penman, M., *David II* (East Linton: forthcoming)

Perroy, E., *The Hundred Years War* (London, 1951)

Skene, W. (ed.), *John of Fordun's Chronicle of the Scottish Nation*, 2 vols. (Edinburgh, 1872: Facsimile reprint, 1993)

Webster, B., 'Scotland without a King', in A. Grant and K. Stringer (eds.), *Medieval Scotland: Crown, Lordship and Community* (Edinburgh, 1993), 228–238

Webster, B., 'David II and the Government of Fourteenth Century Scotland', *Transactions of the Royal Historical Society*, 5th series, xvi (1966), 115–130

Chapter Three: 'La Grande Armée Ecossaise': 1419–1429

Balfour-Melville, E. W. M., *James I, King of Scots* (London, 1936)

Beaucourt, G. du Fresne de, *Histoire de Charles VII*, 6 vols. (Paris, 1881–91)

Bower, Walter, *Scotichronicon* (in Latin and English), vol. 8, ed. D. E. R. Watt (Aberdeen, 1987) (covers the period 1390–1437)

Brakelond, Jocelin of, *Chronicle of the Abbey of Bury St Edmunds*, ed. and trans. D. Greenway and J. Sayers (Oxford, 1989)

Brown, M., *James I* (2nd edn., East Linton, 2000)

Chevalier, B., 'Les Ecossais dans l'armée de Charles VII jusqu'à la bataille de Verneuil', in *Jeanne d'Arc: une époque, un rayonnement* (Paris, 1982), 85–94

Chevalier, B., 'Les Alliés écossais au service du roi de France au XVe siècle', in J. Laidlaw (ed.), *The Auld Alliance* (Edinburgh, 1999), 47–57

Ditcham, B., 'The Employment of Foreign Mercenary Troops in the French Royal Armies, 1415–70' (unpublished Ph.D. thesis, University of Edinburgh, 1978)

Ditcham, B., " 'Mutton Guzzlers and Wine Bags': Foreign Soldiers and Native Reactions in Fifteenth Century France", in C. T. Allmand, *Power, Culture and Religion in France* (Woodbridge, 1989), 1–13

Harriss, G. (ed.), *Henry V: The Practice of Kingship* (Oxford, 1985)

Skene, F. (ed.), *Liber Pluscardensis* (The Book of Pluscarden), 2 vols. (Edinburgh, 1877–80)

Stevenson, J. (ed.), *Letters and Papers illustrative of the Wars of the English in France during the reign of Henry the Sixth*, Rolls Series, 2 vols. (London, 1861–64)

Vale, M., *Charles VII* (London, 1974)

Vaughan, R., *John the Fearless* (London, 1966)

Vaughan, R., *Philip the Good* (London, 1970)

Wolffe, Bertram, *Henry VI* (London, 1981)

Chapter Four: Diplomacy and the Scottish Diaspora: The Mid-Fifteenth Century

Barbé, L., *Margaret of Scotland and the Dauphin Louis* (London, 1917)

Bawcutt, P., and Henisch, B., 'Scots Abroad in the Fifteenth Century: The Princesses Margaret, Isabella and Eleanor', in E. Ewan and M. M. Meikle (eds.), *Women in Scotland, c.1100–c.1750* (East Linton, 1999), 45–55

Baxter, J. H., 'The Marriage of James II', *Scottish Historical Review* xxv (1928), 69–72

Brown, J. (ed.), *Scottish Society in the Fifteenth Century* (London, 1977)

Chevalier, B., *Tours: Ville Royale, 1356–1520* (Paris, 1975)

Contamine, P., *Guerre, Etat et Société à la fin du Moyen Age: études sur les armées des rois de France, 1337–1494* (Paris, 1972)

Ditchburn, D., 'The Place of Gueldres in Scottish Foreign Policy, c.1449–c.1542', in G.G. Simpson (ed.), *Scotland and the Low Countries, 1124–1994* (East Linton, 1996), 59–75

Downie, Fiona, " 'La voie quelle menace tenir': Annabella Stewart, Scotland, and the European Marriage Market, 1444–56", *Scottish Historical Review* lxxviii (2), (October, 1999), 170–191

Dunlop, A. I., *The Life and Times of James Kennedy, Bishop of St Andrews* (Edinburgh, 1950)

Harthan, John, *Books of Hours and their Owners* (London, 1982) (for Isabella, duchess of Brittany's book)

Köfler, M., and Caramelle, S., *Die beiden Frauen des Erzherzogs Sigismund von Österreich* (Innsbruck, 1982)

Loches: *Société des Amis du Pays Lochois: Fête ses Cinquante Ans* (Loches, December, 1997) (contains short articles on Scottish families in the area of Loches, in Touraine, and at Poitiers)

Macdougall, N., *James III: A Political Study* (Edinburgh, 1982)

McGladdery, C., *James II* (Edinburgh, 1990)

Ribault, Jean-Yves, 'Les Souvenirs Ecossais en Berry', *Bulletin d'information du département du Cher*, Nos. 101–106 (Bourges, 1973–74)

Ross, Charles, *Edward IV* (London, 1974)

Soyer, J., 'Donation par Charles VII à Jean Stuart des Terres de Concressault et d'Aubigny-sur-Nère, *Memoires de la Société historique du Cher* (Bourges, 1899)

Vaesen, J., and others (eds.), *Lettres de Louis XI, roi de France*, 11 vols. (Paris, 1883–1909)

Vaughan, R., *Charles the Bold* (London, 1973)

Chapter Five: Renewal: 1484–1517

Baumgartner, Frederic, *Louis XII* (London, 1996)

Burns, J. H., 'John Ireland and 'The Meroure of Wyssdome', *Innes Review* vi (1955), 77–98

Chrimes, S. B., *Henry VII* (London, 1972)

Comminges, Élie de (ed.), *Traité sur L'Art de la Guerre, de Bérault Stuart, Seigneur d'Aubigny* (The Hague, 1976)

Contamine, P., 'The War Literature of the Late Middle Ages: the Treatises of Robert de Balsac and Bérault Stuart, Lord of Aubigny', in Philippe Contamine, *La France au XIVe et XVe siècles: Hommes, mentalités, guerre et paix* (London, 1981)

Contamine, P., 'Entre France et Ecosse: Bérault Stuart, Seigneur d'Aubigny (vers 1452–1508), chef de guerre, diplomate, ecrivain militaire', in J. Laidlaw (ed.), *The Auld Alliance* (Edinburgh, 1999), 59–76

Grant, A., 'Richard III and Scotland', in A. J. Pollard (ed.), *The North of England in the Age of Richard III* (Stroud, 1996), 115–148

Herkless, J., and Hannay, R. K., *The Archbishops of St Andrews*, 4 vols. (Edinburgh, 1907–1910) (vol. i for biography of William Scheves; vol. ii for biography of Andrew Forman)

Macdougall, N., *James IV* (East Linton, 1997)

Macdougall, N., " 'The Greattest Scheip that ewer saillit in Ingland or France': James IV's 'Great Michael' ", in N. Macdougall (ed.), *Scotland and War, AD 79–1918* (Edinburgh, 1991), 36–60

Macdougall, S., with Macdougall, N., 'Les Liaisons Dangereuses: Jacques IV d'Ecosse, Louis XII de France, et l'Angleterre, 1498–1513', in J. Laidlaw (ed.), *The Auld Alliance* (Edinburgh, 1999), 77–88

Mackie, R. L. (ed.), *The Letters of James the Fourth, 1505–1513* (Scottish History Society, Edinburgh, 1953)

Mackie, R. L., *King James IV of Scotland: A Brief Survey of his Life and Times* (Edinburgh, 1958)

McRoberts, Rev. David, 'The Scottish Church and Nationalism in the Fifteenth Century', *Innes Review* xix (i), (1968), 3–14

Ross, C., *Richard III* (London, 1981)

Scarisbrick, J. J., *Henry VIII* (London, 1968)

Scofield, C. L., *The Life and Reign of Edward the Fourth*, 2 vols. (London, 1923)

Spont, A., *Letters and Papers relating to the War with France, 1512–1513* (Navy Records Society, 1897)

Stuart, A., *Genealogical History of the Stewarts from the Earliest Period of their Authentic History to the Present Times* (London, 1798)

Tanner, R., *The Late-Medieval Scottish Parliament: Politics and the Three Estates, 1424–1488* (East Linton, 2001)

Toulier, B., *Aubigny-sur-Nère: La Cité des Stuarts* (Orléans, 1994)

Wood, M. (ed.), *Flodden Papers, 1507–1517* (Scottish History Society, Edinburgh, 1933)

Chapter Six: Indian Summer: 1517–1560

Bapst, E., *Les mariages de Jacques V* (Paris, 1889)

Bingham, C., *James V, King of Scots* (London, 1971)

Caldwell, D., *The Battle of Pinkie*, in N. Macdougall (ed.), *Scotland and War, AD 79–1918* (Edinburgh, 1991)

Cameron, J., *James V: The Personal Rule, 1528–1542* (East Linton, 1998)

Dickinson, W. (ed.), *John Knox's History of the Reformation in Scotland*, 2 vols. (Edinburgh, 1949), vol. i

Donaldson, G., *Mary Queen of Scots* (London, 1974)

Donaldson, G., *All the Queen's Men: Power and Politics in Mary Stewart's Scotland* (London, 1983)

Duchein, M., *Marie Stuart: la femme et le mythe* (Paris, 1987)

Dunbar, J., *Scottish Royal Palaces: The Architecture of the Royal Residences during the Late Medieval and Early Renaissance Period* (East Linton, 1999)

Edington, C., *Court and Culture in Renaissance Scotland: Sir David Lindsay of the Mount, 1486–1555* (East Linton, 1995)

Emond, W. K., 'The minority of King James V, 1513–1528' (unpublished Ph.D. thesis, St Andrews University, 1988)

Fawcett, Richard, *Scottish Architecture from the Accession of the Stewarts to the Reformation: 1371–1560* (Edinburgh, 1994)

Hadley Williams, J. (ed.), *Stewart Style, 1513–1542: Essays on the Court of James V* (East Linton, 1996)

Hannay, R. K., and Hay, D. (eds.), *The Letters of James V* (Edinburgh, 1954)

Knecht, R., *Francis I* (Cambridge, 1982)

Lesley, J., *The History of Scotland from the Death of King James I in the Year 1436 to the Year 1561* (Bannantyne Club, 1830)

Lynch, M. (ed.), *Mary Stewart: Queen in Three Kingdoms* (Oxford, 1988)

Major (Mair), John, *A History of Greater Britain* (Scottish History Society, Edinburgh, 1892)

Marshall, R. K., *Mary of Guise* (London, 1977)

Merriman, M., *The Rough Wooings: Mary Queen of Scots, 1542–1551* (East Linton, 2000)

Pitscottie, Robert Lindsay of, *The Historie and Cronicles of Scotland*, 3 vols. (Scottish Text Society, 1899–1911), vol. i

Sanderson, M., *Cardinal of Scotland: David Beaton, c.1494–1546* (Edinburgh, 1986)

Stuart, M.W., *The Scot who was a Frenchman: being the Life of John Stewart, Duke of Albany, in Scotland, France and Italy* (London, 1940)

Thomas, A., *'Princelie Majestie': The Court of James V of Scotland, 1528–1542* (East Linton, 2001)

INDEX

Abercorn castle, siege of (1455), 86
Abernethy, Hugh de, 12
Achaius, mythical Scottish king, 4
Agincourt, battle of (1415), 58
Albany, Alexander Stewart, duke of (d. 1485), 88, 91, 97–98, 119
    French marriage of, 98
    and Treaty of Fotheringhay (1482), 100
    and likely collusion with Scots magnates, 100–101
    in crisis of 1482–1483, 101–102
    forfeiture of (1483), 103
    and defeat at Lochmaben (1484), 104
    arrested and imprisoned in Edinburgh castle (1485), 106
    death of, 106
Albany, John Stewart, duke of, Governor (d. 1536):
    career reviewed, 119–120
    and Treaty of Rouen (1517), 121
    career as Governor (1515–1524), 122–126, 132
    and campaigns of 1522–1523, 124–125
    final departure to France (1524), 125
    subsequent diplomatic career, 126, 129
    death of, 126
Albany, Murdoch Stewart, duke of, Governor (d. 1425), 58, 60, 71, 75
Albany, Robert Stewart, duke of, Governor (d. 1420), 56, 59–60, 71
Alençon, Charles, duke of, 121
Alençon, Jean, duke of, 72–73, 76
Alexander III, king of Scots (1249–1286), 9, 10, 11, 13
Alexander III, pope, 53
Ancrum Moor, battle of (1545), 138
Anglo-Scottish Treaties:
    1328 (Edinburgh-Northampton), 28–29
    1474, 90
    1502 (Treaty of Perpetual Peace), 110, 111
    1543 (Greenwich), 137
Angus, Archibald Douglas, fifth earl of (d. 1513), 119, 123
Angus, Archibald Douglas, sixth earl of, 119, 128–129, 138
    political role in minority of James V, 123–124, 127
    forfeited (1528), 127
    wins battle of Ancrum Moor (1545), 138
Annabella, daughter of James I, 84, 85
Anne of Beaujeu, Regent for Charles VIII of France, 103, 105

Arbroath, Declaration of (1320), 26
'Army of Scotland', the, 91–92, 96
Arran, James Hamilton, first earl of, 113, 117, 119, 123, 125
Arran, James Hamilton, second earl of, Governor, 129, 134, 135, 136, 137, 138,
    139, 141, 142, 144
    becomes duke of Châtelherault, 140
Arras, treaty of (1435), 81
Artois, Robert, count of, 34
'Assured lords', 136, 138
Atholl, Walter Stewart, earl of (d. 1437), 82
Aubigny-sur-Nère (Berry), 5, 66, 71
Audrehen, Arnoul d', 39
Auld Alliance, the:
    definition and perceptions of, 3–7
    shift in emphasis in 1450s, 86–87
    Treaties:
    1295–1296 (Paris-Dunfermline), 9, 18–20, 24, 121
    1326 (Corbeil), 26–27, 32–33, 46, 121
    1359 (abortive Paris), 45–46
    1371 (Vincennes), 46, 48
    1391, 48
    1428 (Perth-Chinon), 75–76, 79
    1448–1449 (Tours-Edinburgh), 83
    1484, 103–104
    1492, 108
    1512, 115–116
    1517 (Rouen), 120, 121–122, 130
    1548 (Haddington), 140
    overall assessment of, 143–145
Ayala, Pedro de, Spanish ambassador, 112

Bainbridge, Christopher, Cardinal-archbishop of York, 116, 117
Balliol, Edward, 15, 18–19, 27, 43–44
    wins battle of Dupplin, 31
    crowned at Scone (1332), 31
    as vassal king of Scots, 31–32, 35
    and resignation of the kingdom, 44
Balliol, John, king of Scots (1292–1296), 9, 11, 14, 15, 31
    reign of, 15–22
    deposition of, 22
    as prisoner in England, 23–24
    released (1299), 24
    news of death of (1314), 26
Bannockburn, battle of (1314), 26, 106, 109
Baudricourt, Robert de, captain of Vaucouleurs, 76
Baugé, battle of (1421), 3, 65–66, 79

Beaton, David, abbot of Arbroath, archbishop of St Andrews:
    Cardinal, 129, 131, 135, 136, 137, 139
Beaugency (Loire), near-confrontation at (1421), 67
Bedford, John, duke of, English lieutenant in France (d. 1435), 70, 73, 74
Bek, Anthony, bishop of Durham, 14, 23–24
Benedict XIII, anti-pope, 58, 60
Berwick, burgh and castle of:
    siege and sack of (1296), 20, 21, 22
    Scottish recovery of (1461), 87
    loss of (1482), 101
    James III seeks recovery of, 106
Berwick, treaty of (1357), 42
Birgham, treaty of (1290), 14, 16
Bisset, Master Baldred, 24
Black Rood of St Margaret, 22, 41
Boniface VIII, pope, 24, 25
Borselen, Wolfaert van, of Veere, 84
Bosworth, battle of (1485), 105, 114
Bower, Walter, chronicler, 3, 40–41, 49, 60, 65, 69, 73, 79, 91
Boyd, Sir Thomas, of Kilmarnock, 96
Brakelond, Jocelin of, chronicler, 53
Brascha, Erasmus, Milanese ambassador (1491), 108
Brétigny, treaty of (1360), 45
Bruce, Sir Alexander, of Earlshall, 105
Bruce, Robert, lord of Annandale ('the Competitor', d. 1295), 11, 14, 15, 19, 26
Bruce, Robert, lord of Annandale (d. 1304), 21, 22–23
Bruce, Robert, earl of Carrick, king of Scots (1306–1329), see Robert I, king of Scots
Brueil, Audart de, 55
Brussels, treaty of (1449), 86
Buchan, John Stewart, earl of (d. 1424), 3, 60, 71, 72, 75
    and victory at Baugé (1421), 65–66
    created Constable of France, 66
    killed at Verneuil (1424), 73
Buironfosse (Flanders), military confrontation at (1339), 39
Buittle, castle of (Galloway), 12, 44
Burgundy, Charles the Bold, duke of (d. 1477), 88
Burgundy, John the Fearless, duke of (d. 1419), 58, 59, 62, 63
Burgundy, Philip the Good, duke of (d. 1467), 74, 81, 84, 85–86, 88
'Burnt Candlemas', the (1356), 44

Calais, siege of (1346), 40
Cambray, Guillaume de, archbishop of Bourges, 95
Cantiers, Guillaume de, 55
Carmichael, John, bishop of Orléans, 77
Carrickfergus, Scottish raid on (1513), 117

Cassel, battle of (1328), 34
Castile, kingdom of:
    civil war in (1360s), 48, 55
    and sea battle with English off La Rochelle (1372), 48
    and alliance with Douglas (1379), 55
    and naval assistance to dauphin Charles, 59, 60–62
    and mediation between France and Burgundy (1458), 87
Cateau-Cambrésis, peace of (1559), 136, 141
Catherine of Valois, sister of Charles VII, 62, 64
Celestine V, pope, 18
Charlemagne, 4, 140
Charles IV, king of France (1322–1328), 27
Charles V, king of France (1364–1380):
    as Regent, 45–46
    renews war with England (1369), 46–48
Charles VI ('The Mad'), king of France (1380–1422), 55, 58, 59, 62–63, 64, 67
Charles VII, king of France (1422–1461), 5, 6, 108
    as dauphin (from 1417), 56, 59
    and 'kingdom of Bourges', 59, 62
    and Scottish reinforcements, 63–64
    and campaigns of 1420–1421, 66–67
    as king (from 1422), 69
    and problems of 1423, 70
    recruits more Scots (1423–1424), 71–72
    and post-Verneuil diplomacy, 74–76
    and Joan of Arc, 76–77
    and Treaty of Perth-Chinon (1428), 75–76
    and 'army of Scotland' (1430s), 92
    and treaty of Arras (1435), 81
    and Ordonnance of 1445, 92–93
    as Scottish marriage broker (1440s), 84–86
    and Franco-Scottish relations (1450s), 86–87
    death of, 87–88
Charles VIII, king of France (1483–1498), 103, 104, 108, 109
Charles V, Emperor (d. 1558), 121–122, 128, 135, 138
Charlotte of Savoy, second wife of Louis XI, 81
Chartier, Alain, ambassador (1428), 75
Chepman, Walter, printer, 113
Clarence, George, duke of (d. 1478), 91
Clarence, Thomas, duke of (d. 1421), 3
    killed at Baugé, 65–66
'Cleanse the Causeway' (1520), 124
Clement V, pope, 25
Clement VI, pope, 43
Clement VII, anti-pope (Robert of Geneva), 50
Clement VII, pope, 128

Comyn, Alexander, earl of Buchan, 11, 12
Comyn, John, earl of Buchan, 21
Comyn, John, lord of Badenoch, 11, 12
Comyn, John, lord of Badenoch (son of above), killed by Bruce (1306), 25
Concressault (Berry), 66, 71
Conty, Étienne de, 7, 51
Courtrai, battle of (1302), 24–25
Crambeth, Matthew of, bishop of Dunkeld, 18
Cravant, battle of (1423), 70, 72
Crécy, battle of, 40
Crichton, William lord (d. 1454), 83, 85–86
Culblean, battle of (1335), 36, 40

Daltoun, Thomas, bishop of Galloway, 16
Darnley, Alan Stewart (Stuart) of, 91
    killed in Scotland (1438), 96
Darnley, Sir John Stewart (Stuart) of (d. 1429), 63, 65–66
    at Issoudun, 70
    captured at Cravant, 70, 96
    ransomed and rewarded, 71, 96
    ambassador to Scotland (1428), 75–76
    death of, 77
David II, king of Scots (1329–1371), 6, 30
    coronation (1331), 31
    in France (1334–1341), 33–34, 54
    and return to Scotland, 38
    and Robert the Steward, 38–39
    and 'first reign' (1341–1346), 39–41
    and Neville's Cross campaign (1346), 40–41
    as Edward III's prisoner (1346–1357), 41–42
    and 'second reign' (1357–1371), 42–46, 79–80
    death of, 46
Douglas, Adam, cousin of the Tyneman, 72
Douglas, Sir Archibald, guardian (d. 1333), 32
Douglas, Archibald 'the Grim', third earl of Douglas (d. 1400), 44, 46, 55
Douglas, Archibald 'the Tyneman', fourth earl of Douglas (d. 1424), 58, 59, 60, 71
    career reviewed, 69–70
    receives dukedom of Touraine, 72
    killed at Verneuil (1424), 73
Douglas, Archibald, earl of Wigtown (fifth earl of Douglas from 1424), 63, 65–66, 71
    made count of Longueville, 66
Douglas, Hugh, earl of Ormond (d. 1455), 83
Douglas, Sir James (d. 1330), 28, 31
Douglas, Sir James, second son of the Tyneman (d. 1424), 71, 73
Douglas, James, ninth earl of Douglas (d. 1491), 104
Douglas, William, first earl of Douglas, 40, 44, 49, 55

Douglas, William, eighth earl of Douglas (d. 1452), 83, 86
Douglas, William, 'Knight of Liddesdale', 40
Dunbar, battle of (1296), 21
    castle, siege of (1338), 38
Dunbar, William, poet, 107, 111, 114
Dupplin, battle of (1332), 31

Edinburgh, treaty of (1560), 142
Edward I, king of England (1272–1307), 9, 10
    and the Scots post-1286, 12–13
    and the Great Cause, 14–15
    and king John Balliol, 16–23
    and Philip the Fair, 17
    and Scottish wars of 1296, 20–23
    and France (1299–1303), 24
    in Scotland (1301–2, 1303–4), 24–25
    and ordinance for the government of Scotland (1305), 25
    death of (1307), 26
Edward II, king of England (1307–1327), 13, 14, 26, 27
Edward III, king of England (1327–1377), 6, 27, 31, 46, 55
    and claim to French throne, 28, 33–35
    and war in Scotland (1333–1338), 32, 35–38
    and Gascony, 33–35
    and battle of Crécy, 40
    and treaty of Brétigny (1360), 45
    death of, 48–49
Edward IV, king of England (1461–1483), 87
    and Scottish treaty of 1474, 90
    and invasion of France (1475), 90
    and war with Scotland (1480–1482), 99–102
    death of, 102
Edward V, king of England (1483), 102–103
Edward VI, king of England (1547–1553), 136, 137, 140
Edward, the 'Black Prince', 44, 48, 56
Eleanor, daughter of James I, 84–85
Elizabeth, queen of England (1558–1603), 136, 141–142
Elphinstone, William, bishop of Aberdeen (d. 1514), 112–113, 119
Eric II, king of Norway, 16, 18, 19
Evreux, county of, 71, 75, 96

Falkirk, battle of (1298), 23
Falkland, palace of, 5, 132, 133
Fife, Duncan, earl of (guardian 1286–1289), 11, 12
Flodden, battle of (1513), 58, 112, 118
'Flodden complex', 119, 125, 134
Fogo, John, abbot of Melrose, 79

Fordun, John of, chronicler, 40
Forman, Andrew, bishop of Moray, archbishop of Bourges, 54, 95, 113, 118
    becomes archbishop of St Andrews (1514), 119
Foulis, William, archdeacon of St Andrews, ambassador, 84
'Foul Raid', the (1417), 60
Francis I, king of France (1515–1547), 118–119, 121–122, 124, 125, 132–133, 135–
    136, 138
Francis II, king of France (1559–1560), 141, 142
Fraser, William, bishop of St Andrews, 11, 12, 14, 18
Froissart, Jean, chronicler, 41, 49–50

Garancières, Eugene de, 39, 44
Garde Ecossaise, 63, 91, 93, 94, 95, 96, 98, 136
Gaunt, John of, duke of Lancaster, 50, 56
Gloucester, Richard, duke of, *see* Richard III, king of England
Graham, Sir Robert, conspirator (d. 1437), 82
Great Cause, the (1291–1292), 14–15
Great Michael, warship of James IV, 112, 117, 118
Great Schism, the (1378–1417), 50
Gringoire, Pierre, satirist, 113
Gueldres, Arnold, duke of, 85–86, 88
Guesclin, Bertrand du, 48, 55
Guise, Francis, duke of, 136, 141, 142

Hadden Rig, battle of (1542), 133
Halidon Hill, battle of (1333), 32, 77
Hamilton, Sir James, of Finnart, 134
Hamilton, John, abbot of Paisley, later archbishop of St Andrews, 137
Hans, king of Denmark (d. 1513), 116
Henry II, king of France (1547–1559), 136, 139, 141
Henry IV, king of England (1399–1413), 56, 58
Henry V, king of England (1413–1422)
    and conquest of Normandy, 58–59
    and treaty of Troyes (1420), 62–63
    and French campaigns (1420–1421), 64, 67
    and final campaigns of 1422, 67–69
    death, 67–69
Henry VI, king of England (1422–1461), 71, 79
    mental instability of, 86
    as refugee in Scotland, 87
    brief restoration (1470–1471) and death, 89
Henry VII (Tudor), king of England (1485–1509) 103, 104
    wins battle of Bosworth, 105
    and James III, 106–107
    and James IV, 110–112
    and detention of earl of Arran, 113
    death of, 114

Henry VIII, king of England (1509–1547)
    character, 114–115
    claims overlordship of Scotland, 116
    unrealistic diplomatic schemes, 116–117
    and Scottish diplomacy post-Flodden, 122
    and break with Rome, 122, 128
    demands Albany's dismissal (1522), 123
    and adult James V, 128–129
    and Scottish war of 1542, 132–133
    and treaties of Greenwich, 137
    and 'Rough Wooings', 137–138
    death of, 136
Herrings, battle of the (1429), *see* Rouvray
Hertford, Edward Seymour, earl of, 137, 139
'Holy League' the (1511), 116–117
Humbleton (Homildon), battle of (1402), 55, 58, 77
Hundred Years' War, the (1337–1453), 6, 105
    causes of, 28, 33–35
    importance of in sustaining Auld Alliance, 54–55, 143
    end of, 78, 87

Ireland, John, ambassador, 98–99, 103–104
    royal confessor, 107
Isabeau of Bavaria, queen of Charles VI of France, 59
Isabella, daughter of Philip the Fair, queen of Edward II, 27, 28, 30
Isabella, second daughter of James I, 84, 85

James I, king of Scots (1406–1437), 6, 56, 58
    as Henry V's prisoner, 60, 64, 67
    released and returns to Scotland, 71
    removes Albany Stewarts (1425), 74–75
    and treaty of Perth-Chinon (1428), 75–76
    and diplomacy in the 1430s, 79–80
    and siege of Roxburgh (1436), 81–82
    assassination of (1437), 82
James II, king of Scots (1437–1460), 6
    career reviewed, 82–83
    and foreign marriage diplomacy, 83–86
    and marriage to Mary of Gueldres (1449), 86
    death of (1460), 87
James III, king of Scots (1460–1488), 81, 128
    and foreign policy pre-1474, 88–90
    and collapse of English alliance, 91
    and war of 1480–1482, 99–102
    and Lauder Bridge crisis (1482), 101
    and English truce of 1484, 104

James III, king of Scots (1460–1488) *continued*
    and English marriage proposals (1486–1487), 105–106
    killed at Sauchieburn (1488), 106–107
James IV, king of Scots (1488–1513)
    wins battle of Sauchieburn (1488), 106–107
    abortive French marriage proposals for (1491), 108
    early career reviewed, 109–110
    and Henry VII (1496–1502), 110–111
    marries Margaret Tudor (1503), 111
    builds royal navy with French aid, 112
    foreign diplomacy (1502–1513), 112–118
    sends fleet to France (1513), 117
    takes Norham castle (1513), 117–118
    killed at Flodden (1513), 118
James V, king of Scots (1513–1542), 5, 118, 119
    minority of, 122–127
    takes control of government (1528), 127
    and religious policy, 128
    and marriages, 129–132
    and Act of Revocation, 130
    and birth of legitimate sons, 132
    and 'imperial' view of kingship, 131, 132
    and building programmes, 132
    and death of sons, 132
    and war of 1542, 132–133
    death of, 133
    estimates of character and policies, 133–135
Jargeau, battle of (1429), 77
Jeanne, niece of Philip the Fair, 19
Joan, first wife of David II, 28, 32, 38
Joan of Arc, 76–77, 91
Joan Beaufort, queen of James I, 71, 79, 82
Joanna, daughter of James I, 84–85
John II, king of France (1350–1364), 43–46
Julius II, pope, 116

Keith, Sir Robert, 39, 41
Kennedy, Sir Hugh, 65, 80
Kirkpatrick, Humphrey, abbot of St Denis, 54
Knox, John, reformer, 134–135, 138
Lauder Bridge crisis (1482), 101
La Verrerie (Oizon, Berry), château of, 5, 109
Leith, siege of (1560), 142
Lennox, Matthew Stewart, fourth earl of, 137, 138
Leo X, pope, 116
Lesley, John, bishop of Ross, 126, 135

Lindsay, Sir David, of the Mount, 131, 135
Linlithgow, palace of, 132, 133
Llywelyn, Madog ap, 17
Lochindorb, siege of (1336), 36–38
Lochmaben, battle of (1484), 104
Logie (Drummond), Margaret, second wife of David II, 42
Louis XI, king of France (1461–1483)
    as dauphin, 6, 76, 87, 97
    marriage to Princess Margaret (1436), 80–81
    as king, 88
    and Treaty of Picquigny (1475), 90
    and Alexander, duke of Albany, 98
    death of (1483), 103
Louis XII, king of France (1498–1515), 92, 95, 106, 108, 112, 113, 115, 116, 117
    and grant to Scots in France (1513), 118
    death of, 118–119
Lutheranism, 128, 134, 138

Macduff appeal case, 16–17
MacRuari, Ranald, 40
Madeleine, daughter of Francis I of France, first wife of James V, 6, 128, 130, 131
Magnus, Thomas, English ambassador, 128
Mair (Major), John, 126
'Mammet', the, 60
Mar, Alexander Stewart, earl of (d. 1435), 59, 63
Mar, Donald, earl of (d. 1332), 31
Mar, John Stewart, earl of (d. 1480), 99
March, Agnes Randolph, countess of ('Black Agnes'), 38
Margaret, 'Maid of Norway', granddaughter of Alexander III, 9–10, 14
Margaret, eldest daughter of James I, 6, 76
    married to dauphin Louis (1436), 80–81
    death of (1445), 81, 84–85
Margaret of Anjou, queen of Henry VI, 87
Margaret, younger sister of James III, 90–91
Margaret Tudor, wife of James IV, 110–111
    marries Archibald, sixth earl of Angus (1514), 119
    political role in minority of James V, 123–124, 126, 127
Martin V, pope, 3, 66
Mary, third daughter of James I, 84
Mary of Bourbon, proposed bride for James V, 129–130
Mary of Gueldres, queen of James II (d. 1463), 85–86, 87, 88
Mary of Guise-Lorraine (d. 1560), 6
    as queen of James V, 131, 132, 133
    as queen dowager, 141
    as Regent, 141–142
    death of, 142

Mary, Queen of Scots (1542–1567), 6, 133, 134, 135
   coronation of (1543), 137
   sent to France (1548), 140
   marries dauphin (1558), 141
   as queen in Scotland, 144
Mary Tudor, sister of Henry VIII, 117, 118
Mary Tudor, queen of England (1553–1558), 136, 141
Mazun, John, wine merchant, 16
Melun, siege of (1420), 64
Mercer, John, seaman, 55
Millet, Master Pierre, ambassador, 103–104
Mirefleur (Auvergne), 126
Montreuil, Anglo-French peace of (1299), 24
Monypenny, Alexander, ambassador, 89
Monypenny, Sir William, lord of Concressault, ambassador, 84, 85, 88, 94, 95, 107
Monypenny, William, abbot of Saint-Satur, 95
Moray, Andrew (resistance leader, 1297), 23
Moray, Sir Andrew, guardian (d. 1338), 36–38
Moray, John Randolph, earl of, 33, 35, 40, 41
Moray, Thomas Randolph, earl of (d. 1332), 31
Mortimer, Roger, 28, 30
Mure, Elizabeth, first wife of Robert II, 43
Murray, David, bishop of Moray, 54, 115
Murray, John, ambassador, 89
Myllar, Andrew, printer, 113

Neville's Cross, battle of (1346), 40–41, 77
Nicholas IV, pope, 13

O'Donnell, Hugh of Ulster, 116
Ogilvy, Patrick, 'sheriff of Angus', 91
Oliphant, Sir William, defender of Stirling (1304), 25, 36
Orléans, Louis, duke of (d. 1407), 58, 62
Orléans, siege of (1428–1429), 76–77, 91
Otterburn, battle of (1388), 55

Paniter, Patrick, royal secretary, 115
Paris, Anglo-French treaty of (1303), 25
Patay, battle of (1429), 77
Pavia, battle of (1525), 126
Philip IV 'the Fair', king of France (1285–1314), 9, 10, 17
   and the Scottish and Norwegian treaties of 1295, 18–19
   and war with England (1295), 20
   and the Scots (1298–1303), 24–25
   and Robert I, 26
   death of, 27

Philip VI (Valois), king of France (1328–1350), 6, 28, 39
    and the Bruce cause, 32–33, 54
    and Gascony, 33–35
    and war against the English, 40
    death of, 43
Picquigny, treaty of (1475), 90
Pinkie, battle of (1547), 139, 140
Pitscottie, Robert Lindsay of, chronicler, 86, 134, 135
Poitiers, battle of (1356), 44, 55

Ramsay, Alexander, of Dalhousie, 40
'Reformation' parliament (1560), 142
Regnault de Chartres, archbishop of Rheims, ambassador (1428), 75–76
Richard II, king of England (1377–1399), 49, 50, 58, 138
    deposition of, 56
Richard III, king of England (1483–1485):
    as duke of Gloucester:
        campaign of 1482, 100–101
        border palatinate (1483), 102
        seizes throne (1483), 102–103
    as king:
        negotiates Scottish truce at Nottingham, 104–105
        killed at Bosworth (1485), 105
Richemont, Arthur de, 71–72, 74, 76
Robert I, king of Scots (1306–1329), 16, 19, 23
    and killing of John Comyn (1306), 25
    and reign, 25–30
    and Philip the Fair, 26
    and propaganda, 26
    and treaty of Corbeil (1326), 26–27
    and treaty of Edinburgh-Northampton (1328), 28–30
    sword of, 80–81
Robert II (Stewart), king of Scots (1371–1390)
    as Steward before 1371, 32, 35, 40
        and return of David II (1341), 38–39
        as lieutenant, 42–43
        and negotiations for new Franco-Scottish alliance (1359), 45–46
    as king:
    renews Auld Alliance, 46
    and Charles V of France, 48
    and Scottish magnates, 48–49
    and bad press from Froissart, 49–50
Robert III, king of Scots (1390–1406), 49, 56
    renews Auld Alliance (1391), 48
Ross, William, earl of, 40
Rothesay, David, duke of (d. 1402), 56

'Rough Wooings', the (1544–1547), 137–138
Rouvray, battle of (1429), 77
Roxburgh, sieges of:
    (1436), 82
    (1460), 87

St Andrews castle, siege of (1546–1547), 139
St Michael, Order of, 104, 113–114, 128
Saintonge, French county of:
    in 1428 negotiations, 76
    claimed by James II (1458), 87
    claimed by James III (1473), 89
    Monypenny made seneschal of (1474), 89, 95
St Quentin (Picardy), 129–130
Salisbury, treaty of (1289), 13
Salisbury, William Montagu, earl of, 38
Samson, abbot of Bury St Edmonds, 53–54
Sark, battle of (1448), 83
Sauchieburn, battle of (1488), 81, 106–107
Scheves, William, archbishop of St Andrews, 99
Scone:
    stone of ('The Stone of Destiny'), 22
    coronation of James IV at (1488), 109
Scottish settlers in France (fifteenth century), 91–96
Sellat, Jean, president of the Parlement of Paris, 113
Seton, Thomas, Scottish commander in France (1420s), 63
Sforza, Giangaleazzo, duke of Milan, 90, 108
Sforza, Ludovico, duke of Milan, 109
Sigismund, archduke of Austria, 85, 99
Solway Moss, battle of (1542), 133, 134, 135, 136
Soules, Sir John de, guardian, 18, 25
'Soules Conspiracy', the (1320), 26
Steward, James the (guardian, 1286), 11, 12
Steward, Robert the, see Robert II, king of Scots (1371–1390)
Steward, Walter the (d. 1332), 31
Stewart (Stuart), Bérault, of Aubigny (d. 1508), 93, 95, 96, 118
    and John Ireland, 98
    and Franco-Scottish treaty of 1484, 103–104
    at Bosworth (1485), 105
    and Scottish embassy of 1491, 107–108
    and career in Italian wars, 109
    ambassador to Scotland (1508), 113
    death of (1508), 114
Stewart, Henry, lord Methven, 124
Stewart, James, 'bastard of Scotland', 92, 94
Stewart, Lord James, later earl of Moray, 142, 144

Stewart (Stuart), John, of Aubigny, 96
Stewart (Stuart), Robert, of Aubigny, 118, 126
Stewart, Robert, of Ralston, 65
Stewart, Sir Walter, son of duke Murdoch of Albany, 71
Stirling Bridge, battle of (1297), 21, 23
Stirling castle, James V's palace within, 132
Strathbogie, David of, earl of Atholl (d. 1335), 32, 35, 36
Stronkalter, the wood of, 36–38
Surrey, John de Warenne, earl of, 21
Surrey, Thomas Howard, earl of, 117–118
Swinton, Sir John, 55

Thibouville, Germain de, astrologer, 66, 72
Towton, battle of (1461), 88
Trastamara, Henry of, king of Castile, 48, 55
Turnberry bond (1286), 12

Umfraville, Sir Ingram de, 18
Urban VI, pope, 50

Verneuil, battle of (1424), 73
    effects of, in Scotland, 74–75
Vernon, Laurence, 66, 94
Vienne, Jean de, Admiral of France, 49–50

Wallace, Sir William (guardian, 1297–1298), 23, 25
Warbeck, Perkin, Yorkist pretender, 110
Wark, siege of (1523), 125
'Wars of the Roses', 86
Whitelaw, Archibald, ambassador and orator, 104–105
Wishart, Robert, bishop of Glasgow, 11, 12
Wolsey, Thomas:
    almoner of Henry VII, 113
    Cardinal, 124
Wyntoun, Andrew, chronicler, 49

Yolande of Dreux, second wife of Alexander III, 10, 11, 12
York, Richard, duke of (d. 1460), 86

Zouche, William la, archbishop of York, 41